Innovate or Perish

INNOVATE OR PERISH

Managing the Enduring Technology Company in the Global Market

EDWARD KAHN

John Wiley & Sons. Inc.

This book is printed on acid-free paper. ∞

Published by John Wiley & Sons, Inc., Hoboken, New Jersey.

Published simultaneously in Canada.

For general information on our other products and services, or technical support, please contact our Customer Care Department within the United States at 800-762-2974, outside the United States at 317-572-3993 or fax 317-572-4002.

Wiley also publishes its books in a variety of electronic formats. Some content that appears in print may not be available in electronic books.

For more information about Wiley products, visit our Web site at http://www.wiley.com.

Library of Congress Cataloging-in-Publication Data:

Innovate or perish : managing and enduring technology company in the global market / [edited by] Edward Kahn.

p. cm.

Includes index.

ISBN-13: 978-0-471-77930-8 (cloth)

ISBN-10: 0-471-77930-X (cloth)

1. Intellectual capital—Management. 2. Intellectual property—Management. 3. Technological innovations—Management. I. Kahn, Edward (Edward A.)

HD53.I557 2007

658.4'038—dc22

2006030756

Printed in the United States of America

10 9 8 7 6 5 4 3 2 1

ACKNOWLEDGMENTS

Face it. If you have been blessed with good fortune, it's impossible to say "thank you" enough. And you are bound to miss some fine people, for which I apologize in advance.

Having had the good fortune to ride the remarkable wave of interest in intellectual property and technology transfer over the last 20 years, I can personally attest that it's better to be lucky than good.

It was my good fortune to start EKMS, Inc., at just the right time, in 1986, and three institutions contributed to this turn of events.

Institution number one is the United States Constitution and its brilliant patent system, which was established by some of the most ingenious inventors of their day, the nation's founding fathers. How about a technology transfer business that opens for business shortly after the passage of the Bayh-Dole Act and the establishment of the CAFC, the so-called patent court? That's timing. But it was pure luck. Here's hoping that the patent system and the U.S. Constitution survive and continue to make great ideas bloom.

Institution number two? The New York City public schools. Public schools do not get good press these days, and there, I was once again very lucky. Thank you to the incredible public schools of my youth, and to my alma maters Bronx Science and City College of New York for giving me just enough intellectual ammunition to be dangerous.

The third institution to thank is the Licensing Executives Society (LES). Because of LES's openness to newcomers and its commitment to free-flowing knowledge, I had a chance to learn from sage experts. Their wisdom contributed greatly to the lessons and philosophies assembled in *Innovate or Perish*. Particular thanks go to LES leaders and teachers, Jay Simon, Woody Friedlander, Mark Peterson, Sarah Cabot, Emmett Murtha, and the late Dave Braunstein and Ed Shalloway. There are many, many more who lent a hand—too numerous to name—and a disproportionate number are Canadian. You know who you are. Eh?

Paradoxically, an out-of-the-box theorist needs a box even more than the linear thinker. For almost 20 years I did my nonlinear thinking about how intellectual property could be put together in better ways for better use within the four walls of EKMS, later UTEK-EKMS, after the acquisition by UTEK Corporation.

Thanks to some daring pioneers, who transformed my theories of patent mining and strategy into working reality, EKMS was able to encourage, in its small way, the societal realization of the hidden value trapped in raw IP. I'm very grateful to my merry band of geniuses, my PhDs whom I lovingly and admiringly called DDEs—"Doctors of Dangerous Eclecticism." When they weren't chemical engineers, they were physicists or chemists, computer scientists or electrical engineers. The exact natures on their degrees never stopped them from seeing the valuable connections—across technologies and across scientific and industrial boundaries.

Thank you, in particular, Dr.'s David Lewis, Jim Spanswick, Alan Craig, Eric Fossel, and Eric Dowling!

But I never would have started EKMS without the backing, both moral and financial, of my wonderful angel investors. A special thanks to the two who jumped in first, the late Nelson Wasserman and Dr. Walter Golub. All I can say is "Thanks" and "What were you thinking???"

These otherwise sane investors were rounded up by Richard Narva, who calls himself a "recovering attorney." Thanks for being who you are. And thanks for acting as the patriarch who begot two generations of the EKMS advisory board: Henryk Szjenwald, Bruce Sunstein, Nathan Lewinger, Paul Serotkin, Sandy LeDuc, Sheldon Apsell, and Elliot Quint, and my most skeptical yet steadfast partner, Ruth Bauman. (More about her later . . .)

Thanking the suppliers and customers—especially the innovators (thanks again, Emmett!)—and the competitors (who made us better!) would require a very long list indeed, so I must say thanks, collectively, to one and all.

And now I turn to my crewmates on the ride. As founder and sole President, I was indeed blessed with incredibly bright and dedicated team members.

Without Heidi Bleau, EKMS's marketing director supreme, this book would not have been possible. Special thanks also go to Nan Bauroth of North Carolina, who helped me by taming the "Edspeak" in these pages.

In the turbulent and formative period of the history of EKMS, I was very fortunate to have the help of Lynne Johnson, an extraordinary general manager. Without her, the best of me would never have emerged—on many levels, not just entrepreneurial.

And then there's Tova Greenberg, EKMS's executive vice president, who demonstrates that there are no limits to human endurance! She put up with me for almost 18 years and we still call each other colleague and friend. All this while shaping the EKMS's IP practice and helping to steer the company through many rough seas.

Before turning to my family, I'd like to humbly thank my esteemed collaborators on *Innovate or Perish*. I am honored that you were willing to share your great teachings and experiences in this book.

Thanks to my family must start with my partner in the institution of marriage, Ruth Bauman.

With nerves of steel, my wife Ruth Bauman put up with me through over 20 years, in which the business went from an idea to a start-up, and then became a fledgling enterprise that consumed sweat and blood, grew, evolved, and finally closed out with the company's sale and transition to new management. If she had just been a confidante, friend, wife, and mother, she would have earned medals galore. But Ruth risked being an active cofounder, an advisory board member, fellow thinker and arguer, designer and brand builder, and marketing and communications guru. Ruth, thank you. You are truly my best friend.

To my brother Jeff and sister Shirley: Thank you for listening so patiently and advising me wisely in copious phone calls.

To my beloved sons, Daniel and Alex: Thanks for still being willing to ski with me! And thanks for not letting the sound of my entrepreneurial wheels make you crazy.

Last but certainly not least, I want to send loving thanks to my late father, Willy Kahn, and to my mother, Frances Kahn.

Without their love, loyalty, persistence, courage, adaptability, and positive attitudes, they never would have found the strength to escape prewar Europe for a new country and emerge from the shadows of the Shoah and their grievous losses to give life to a new family.

Those strengths and unconditional love—the latter so often tested—were the fuel that made a great life possible. Thanks, Mom and Dad.

Summer 2006
Cambridge, Massachusetts

CONTENTS

PART 3 INNOVATION 123

ABOUT THE EDITOR

EDWARD KAHN FOUNDED EKMS, Inc., in 1986, helping to initiate the explosion of interest in intellectual property (IP) exploitation. While at the helm of EKMS from 1986 to 2004, and then after the company's sale to UTEK Corporation (listed on AMEX:UTK) from 2004 to 2005, Ed crafted novel approaches to IP portfolio management, pioneering the practice that came to be known as patent mining.

He led client engagements for dozens of *Fortune* 500 companies, including IBM, Boeing, DuPont, Pitney Bowes, United Technologies, International Paper, Pharmacia, and Dow Chemical. EKMS also served notable small and venture-funded companies including J2 Global and Exos.

Ed's main areas of expertise are technology assessment and deal making. Under his leadership, EKMS (which became UTEK-EKMS, Inc. and is now UTEK Intellectual Capital Consulting) was known for its remarkably broad outlook. It represented technologies and clients in telecommunications, diagnostics, biotechnology, semiconductors, and in the automotive and aerospace sectors. This eclectic, expansive worldview guaranteed that creative connections would be found for projects aimed at repurposing technology portfolios, developing new strategies, and spinning off company technology.

For many years, EKMS was active in the Association of University Technology Managers (AUTM). In its early years, the company carried out licensing and analysis programs for two dozen teaching hospitals and universities, including Harvard, Massachusetts General Hospital, Rutgers, Northwestern, and the University of Chicago.

Ed is frequently asked to comment on intellectual property topics in the business and trade press and at conferences around the world.

He has spoken and written extensively on licensing, patent litigation, and IP strategy, and has been quoted in *Forbes*, the *Wall Street Journal*, and the *Boston Globe*. Published works include those by John Wiley & Sons and *Euromoney*. He has been a frequent speaker, moderator, and panelist for the Licensing Executives Society, as well as the Boston Patent Lawyers' Association and the MIT Enterprise Forum.

Prior to founding EKMS, Ed was employed in the marketing of semiconductor packaging, small business advocacy organizations, and economic development.

Educated at the City College of the City University of New York, Ed lives in Cambridge, Massachusetts, with his wife and two children.

ABOUT THE AUTHORS

Frank Chambers

Frank Chambers is President and owner of F. Chambers & Associates, Inc., a firm specializing in business and technology solutions in the fiber-optics industry. Previously he has been a Director of Technology Innovation at Eaton's Innovation Center and Vice President of Research and Development for GN Nettest. During his career he has been involved in a wide range of technologies and business fields. His emphasis has been on the generation of new technology and applications. Most recently, as a Director at Eaton, he focused on the front end of the innovation process.

Frank holds a BS in physics from St. John's University and an MA and PhD in physics from Princeton University.

Abha Divine

Abha Divine launched and currently serves as President and CEO of AT&T Knowledge Ventures, the IP management and marketing unit of the AT&T family of companies. In this role, she is responsible for generating revenue and other strategic value from the broad set of patent, trademark, software, and "know-how" assets developed throughout the corporation through commercialization and portfolio development.

Abha has managed and directed a variety of efforts aimed at introducing new capabilities to market via new business ventures and enhancement of existing product portfolios to accommodate changing technology and market environments. Prior to her current role, she was Vice President of National Data Services for SBC, providing a family of regional and long-haul data networking services to business clients. She has also served as SBC's Vice President for Corporate Strategy, where she led the development of comprehensive, integrated strategies for data/IP services, broadband communications, hosting, e-commerce, wireless communications, and long distance. In this role, she launched SBC's hosting and business e-service offerings in 2000 and established the company's current broadband strategy and approach. Previously at SBC, she provided technical direction for new product and service development and deployment in her positions at SBC Technology Resources.

Abha earned her MBA from the University of Texas at Austin and an MSEE degree from the Massachusetts Institute of Technology, where she completed her research at the Media Lab.

Wayne Jaeschke

Wayne Jaeschke is an attorney with Connolly, Bove, Lodge & Hutz, LLP, and practices in the Intellectual Property Group. His practice is related to the enforcement of patents and trade secrets, strategies for building and exploiting IP portfolios, patent prosecution, due diligence, licensing, and other IP matters. His specialities include patenting and enforcing patents on complex technologies, nanotechnology, and process engineering.

Wayne graduated with a BS in chemical engineering from Cornell University and holds a JD from Fordham University School of Law. His bar admissions include USPTO New York, U.S. Supreme Court, and U.S. Court of Appeals Federal Circuit.

Karl Jorda

Karl Jorda is the David Rines Professor of Intellectual Property Law as well as Director of the Germeshausen Center for the Law of Innovation and Entrepreneurship at Franklin Pierce Law Center. He is also Adjunct Professor at the Fletcher School of Law and Diplomacy, Tufts University. At these institutions he teaches primarily IP licensing, IP management, and international IP law.

Before joining Franklin Pierce in 1989, he was Chief IP Counsel for 26 years at Ciba-Geigy Corporation (now Novartis).

Karl was President of the Pacific Intellectual Property Association (PIPA) and the New York Intellectual Property Law Association and served on the boards of directors of the American Intellectual Property Law Association, ABA-IPL Section; International Trademark Association; Intellectual Property Organization; Association of Corporate Patent Counsel; and International Association for the Protection of Intellectual Property–American Group.

Karl is the recipient of the 1989 PIPA Medal for "outstanding contributions to international cooperation in the intellectual property field," the 1996 Jefferson Medal of the New Jersey Intellectual Property Law Association for "extraordinary contributions to the U.S. intellectual property law system," and the 1998 Distinguished Alumni Award of the University of Great Falls.

He is a frequent speaker in IP programs in foreign countries under the auspices of the World Intellectual Property Association, United States Agency for International Development, and the United States Information Agency and has served as a consultant to the Indonesian and Bulgarian IP offices.

In 1999, the U.S. Arms Control and Disarmament Agency appointed him as the U.S. representative to the Commission on the Settlement of Disputes Relating to Confidentiality of the Organization for the Prohibition of Chemical Weapons, located in The Hague, Holland.

Karl received his undergraduate degree from the University of Great Falls and an MA and a JD from Notre Dame University. He is admitted to the bars of Illinois, Indiana, and New York, as well as to practice before the U.S. Supreme Court, the Court of Appeals for Federal Circuit, and the U.S. Patent and Trademark Office.

Edward Kahn

Edward Kahn founded EKMS, Inc. in 1986, helping to initiate the explosion of interest in IP exploitation. While at the helm of EKMS from 1986 to 2004, and then after the company's acquisition by UTEK Corporation (UTK:AMEX) from 2004 to 2005, he crafted novel approaches to IP portfolio management, pioneering the practice that came to be known as patent mining.

He led client engagements for dozens of *Fortune* 500 companies, including IBM, Boeing, DuPont, Pitney Bowes, United Technologies, International Paper, Pharmacia, and Dow Chemical. EKMS also served notable small and venture-funded companies including J2 Global and Exos.

Ed's main areas of expertise are technology assessment and deal making. Under his leadership, EKMS (which subsequently became UTEK-EKMS and now UTEK Intellectual Capital Consulting) was known for its remarkably broad outlook. It represented technologies and clients in telecommunications, diagnostics, biotechnology, semiconductors, and the automotive and aerospace sectors. This eclectic, expansive worldview guaranteed that creative connections would be found for projects aimed at repurposing technology portfolios, developing new strategies, and spinning off company technology.

For many years, EKMS was active in the Association of University Technology Managers. In its early years, the company carried out licensing and analysis programs for two dozen teaching hospitals and universities, including Harvard, Massachusetts General Hospital, Rutgers, Northwestern, and the University of Chicago.

Ed is frequently asked to comment on intellectual property topics in the business and trade press and at conferences around the world. He has spoken and written extensively on licensing, patent litigation, and IP strategy, and been quoted in *Forbes*, the *Wall Street Journal*, and the *Boston Globe*. Published works include those by John Wiley & Sons and *Euromoney*. He has been a frequent speaker, moderator, and panelist for the Licensing Executives Society, as well as the Boston Patent Lawyers' Association and the MIT Enterprise Forum.

Prior to founding EKMS, Ed was employed in the marketing of semiconductor packaging, small business advocacy organizations, and economic development. Educated at the City College of the City University of New York, Ed lives in Cambridge, Massachusetts, with his wife and two children.

Michael Kayat

Michael Kayat has extensive business development experience in a wide range of industries. He is currently President of UTEK Intellectual Capital Consulting, part of UTEK Corporation. UTEK is a specialty finance company focused on technology transfer. He and his team support global clients who are adopting open innovation, with IP strategy, analysis and business development utilizing state-of-the-art IP analysis tools and a large pool of diverse industry and technology experts. He previously served as Vice President, Business Development at UTEK-EKMS, Inc. while Ed Kahn was President.

Mike has been a guest speaker on IP strategy and innovation, and has been quoted in a number of wide-ranging publications. He has also written several articles on IP strategy and analysis. Earlier in his eclectic career, he was a physicist focused on space research before embarking on an executive career in management consulting, sales, and marketing in high technology.

Mike graduated with a BSc in physics from Bristol University in the United Kingdom and holds a PhD in physics from the University of Leicester, together with an MBA from Pepperdine University. He is a member of several professional societies including the Intellectual Property Owners Association and Licensing Executives Society.

Ronald Lindsay

Ronald Lindsay has worked in the biopharmaceutical industry for more than 20 years, leading discovery and preclinical research efforts primarily in neuroscience but also in genomics and cancer. Following postdoctoral work at the Friedrich Miescher Institute in Basel, Switzerland, Ron was a staff member at the National Institute for Medical Research, Mill Hill, London, prior to moving to industry as head of cell biology at the Sandoz Institute, for Medical Research, University College, London. During postdoctoral and subsequent studies, Ron was a codiscoverer of the neurotrophin family of nerve growth factors, a class of proteins that are crucial in shaping neural development and the maintenance of function of the adult nervous system. He has authored over 150 scientific articles in neural development and neurodegenerative diseases and was cited by the Institute for Scientific Information as one of the most highly cited neuroscientists of the 1990s.

Ron entered the biotechnology industry as a founding program director of Regeneron Pharmaceuticals, Inc., New York, and has subsequently held senior executive positions at Regeneron (1988–1998), Millenium Pharmaceuticals, Inc. (1998–2001), and Diadexus, Inc. (2000–2004). Currently, Ron is a nonexecutive director of several biotechnology companies in both the United States (Sequenom, Inc., Arqule, Inc., HistoRx, Inc.) and France (N3D) and runs a biotechnology consulting enterprise. He is also senior advisor to the German-U.S. venture group TVM Capital GmbH and is chairman of the scientific advisory board of Serono SA, Geneva, Europe's largest biotechnology company. He is also a member of the Globalscot network.

Ron holds a BSc in chemistry from the University of Glasgow, Scotland, and a PhD in biochemistry from the University of Calgary, Alberta, Canada.

Vincent Magnotta

Vincent Magnotta is Manager, Corporate Technology Transfer at Air Products and Chemicals, Inc., where he manages external global technology partnerships and in-licensing. Technology partnerships developed include academia, corporations, and technical institutes. Vincent is also experienced in technology valuation and technology donation.

Vincent's entire career has been with Air Products in R&D, product management, commercial development, and technology management. He developed five licensed process technologies, four of which are commercially applied in over 30 installations worldwide. His technical expertise is in advanced materials, electronic materials, and forest products process technology. He has 21 U.S. patents, and has published 72 journal articles and national conference presentations. His 30 years of industrial experience have been split almost evenly between research and technology management/technology transfer.

Some of his key awards include the American Institute of Chemical Engineers' (AIChE) National Chemical Engineering Practice Award (1998), Chemical Engineering's Kirkpatrick Award (1995–1997), AIChE fellow (2000), and AIChE National Forest Products Division Award (2000).

Vincent graduated with a BS in chemical engineering from Pennsylvania State University in 1974, an MS in chemical engineering from the University of Delaware in 1976, and an MBA from Lehigh University in 1988 (emphasis in technology management).

Damon Matteo

Damon Matteo joined PARC in 2003 as the Vice President of Intellectual Capital Management. He leads all of PARC's IP operations, including IP creation, IP legal, and external licensing relationships. Specializing in leading-edge technology, Damon has over 15 years' direct experience developing and implementing intellectual capital management strategies. He brings to PARC extensive experience in the full-spectrum management of corporate intellectual capital assets, from optimizing their creation and capture to extracting value from them through vehicles such as licensing and spinouts.

Prior to taking his current role, Damon led Hewlett-Packard's world-class licensing organization, directing intellectual property licensing for the entire corporation. He worked previously with PARC as the Xerox Licensing Manager in charge of IP licensing for PARC, Xerox's European research centers, and intellectual capital aspects of Xerox's spinout and M&A activities. Before joining Xerox, Damon served as president of Savanteque, Inc., a technology management consulting firm specializing in intellectual capital management. His international experience includes several years of living in Europe and in Japan, where he directed technology licensing and strategic alliances for several of the country's largest computer manufacturers. In addition to his private sector work, Damon has led licensing efforts for Lawrence Livermore National Laboratory and the University of California.

Dennis McCullough

Dennis McCullough has extensive experience in commercial development of new technologies and formation of major technology alliances. During his career he has held positions responsible for IP management, licensing, strategic business development, strategic planning, alliance formation, and acquisitions. He also has managed major technology alliances.

Dennis earned a BS degree in chemical engineering from the University of Houston and master's and doctorate degrees in chemical engineering from Texas A&M University. He has been associated with ABB Lummus Global, Bechtel, Litwin, and Eastman Chemical. Dennis is a member of the AIChE, the Licensing Executives Society International, and the Association of Strategic Alliance Professionals. He also is a registered professional engineer in Texas and a registered U.S. patent agent.

John Tao

John Tao is Corporate Director of Technology Partnerships for Air Products and Chemicals, Inc., an $8 billion company headquartered in Allentown, Pennsylvania, that produces and supplies high-quality industrial gases and specialty chemicals for customers in the manufacturing, process, and service industries. He is responsible for worldwide external technology development, intellectual asset management, licensing and technology transfer with outside organizations, and government contracts.

During more than 30 years with Air Products, John has been involved in engineering management, R&D management, commercial development, venture management, and planning and business development. He has a BS and a PhD in chemical engineering from Carnegie-Mellon University, and an MS in chemical engineering from the University of Delaware.

John is a director of the Commercial Development Association, member of the advisory board of yet2.com, member of the Licensing Executive Society, past chair of the University Research Committee, Science and Technology Committee, the External Technology Directors Network and the Network Leadership Council, and current chair of the New Business Development Network of the Industrial Research Institute (IRI), past voting representative and member of the governing board of the Council of Chemical Research, and a fellow of the American Institute of Chemical Engineers. He was the chairman of Chemical

Industry Environmental Technology Projects, a board member of the Penn State Research Foundation, and the chairman of the management committee of the Air Products/Imperial College Strategic Alliance, the Air Products Alliance with Georgia Tech, and the Air Products/Penn State Research Alliance. He served as a member of the visiting committee of the Department of Chemical and Petroleum Engineering at the University of Pittsburgh, served on the advisory council for the chemical engineering department of the University of Pennsylvania, and is active in Lehigh Valley United Way and the Business-Education Partnership.

Bruce Vojak

Bruce Vojak is Associate Dean for External Affairs in the College of Engineering, and Adjunct Professor of General Engineering and of Electrical and Computer Engineering, at the University of Illinois at Urbana-Champaign. Previously, he held various technical and management positions at MIT Lincoln Laboratory, Amoco, and Motorola.

Throughout his career he has focused on developing disruptive electronic and photonic technologies at the material, component, and subsystem levels of the value chain. Prior to joining the University of Illinois in 1999, he was director of advanced technology for Motorola's frequency generation products business.

He holds BS, MS, and PhD degrees in electrical engineering from the University of Illinois at Urbana-Champaign and an MBA from the University of Chicago.

Edmund Walsh

Ed Walsh is an attorney at Wolf, Greenfield & Sacks, PC, and is a member of the Electrical and Computer Technologies Practice Group as well as the IP Transactions Group. He has over 14 years' experience serving as in-house counsel for technology companies. Most recently, Ed served as Chief Intellectual Property Counsel for Teradyne, a position he held for ten years.

Electrical and computer-related clients benefit from his experience in IP strategy development and execution, including patent prosecution, clearances and counseling, IP portfolio management, litigation, licensing, consulting agreements, and joint development agreements. His areas of technical expertise include semiconductor processing and high-speed circuit design, software, networks and network management, connectors and interconnection technology, and many types of test equipment. Previous positions held by Ed include that of Division IP Counsel for Textron Specialty Materials and Patent Attorney for Raytheon. Prior to entering law school, he worked as an electrical engineer, developing operating system software and analyzing communications systems.

Ed's academic credentials include experience as both an Adjunct Professor and Lecturer in Electrical Engineering at Boston University, where he taught classes in circuit theory and dynamic systems theory. He was a Fellow of the National Science Foundation and has also been a faculty member for both the Massachusetts Continuing Legal Education IP program and Suffolk University Law School's Advanced Legal Studies program. Recently, Ed taught a Suffolk Advanced Legal Studies course entitled "Maximizing Business Value From IP." Ed is a member of the Massachusetts Bar and is admitted to practice before the USPTO.

Teri Willey

At the time of this writing, Teri's professional focus is equity-based deal structure in commercializing university-based bioscience. She is a member of the board of directors of Rubicon Genomics, Inc., PanCel Corporation, and NephRx Corporation, and a business development adviser to Endocyte, Inc. Additionally, Teri serves on the board of governors for the Bioscience Research and Commercialization Center, the Southwest Michigan Innovation Center, Spring Mill Ventures, and the Michigan Venture Capital Association. She is a Notre Dame Business School Adjunct Professor.

Teri is currently Managing Partner and cofounder of ARCH Development Partners, LLC. Prior to the start of ARCH, she was most recently Vice President of Start-Ups at ARCH Development Corporation, a subsidiary of the University of Chicago, which commercialized technology from the University and Argonne National Laboratory, and she performed similar work in positions at Northwestern University and Purdue University. Teri is a past President of the Association of University Technology Managers (AUTM), one of Chicago's "Women in Black" for leadership in new venture support, and the recipient of the Indiana governor's "Sagamore of the Wabash" award.

In August 2006, Teri will begin an engagement as the Chief Executive of Cambridge Enterprise at Cambridge University in England. Cambridge Enterprise provides faculty consulting and intellectual property and new venture creation assistance to university faculty and students.

Cartsen Wittrup

Carsten Wittrup is Global Technology and Commercialization Director for the BOC Group, the second largest company worldwide in the field of industrial gas supply, generation, applications technology, and services.

He is responsible for technical and commercial development and holds a broader responsibility for licensing and sourcing of solutions and technologies, with a focus on strategic alliances and acquisitions. More recently, he is focused on new innovation processes, emphasizing people communication and idea generation within large corporations.

He joined the BOC Global Team in 2001, building on more than 15 years of international experience in business development, R&D, and sales director roles in related industries in Latin America and Europe.

Carsten holds an MS degree from the Technical University of Denmark and is an active member of the Licensing Executive Society International and the Association of University Technology Managers. He has recently given several speeches on the topic of value through innovation, the latest at the Food Technology Summit in Amsterdam, November 2003, and the Biscuit, Cake, Chocolate and Confectionery Association's technology seminar in London, April 2003.

PREFACE

HENRY CHESBROUGH

NOT LONG AGO, the life of most patents was a quiet life. Individuals and companies filed for patents, which after a two- to three-year process were issued to them by the patent office. These patents were held by their owners until their expiration, which used to be 17 years after issuance, and now is 20 years after filing. Most of these patents, in turn, were never used. They were held in reserve, in case of a litigation episode, or, in other cases, they were forgotten as the business went in a different direction.

The management of patents was also not very exciting. The chief counsel of a firm, or the outside patent counsel of a smaller firm, worked to keep the firm out of trouble. Firms wanted freedom of action to practice their technologies, and didn't wish to infringe on anyone else or let anyone else stop them from their practice. As long as nothing went wrong, patent managers were happy. They typically reported to the Chief Financial Officer and were evaluated on how well they stayed within their budget.

The life of patents is getting more exciting these days. The Tenth Federal Circuit Court was created to adjudicate patent disputes, and this demonstrably strengthened the value of patents for their owners.[1] Soon after, the U.S. Patent and Trademark Office (USPTO) started charging renewal fees for patents, at 3.5 years, 7 years, and 11.5 years after issuance. Some patents became very valuable, while many more were understood to be worth very little. Companies realized that patents needed to pay their own way, if these renewal payments were to be made. And if a particular patent wasn't worth renewing, maybe it would be worth more to someone else. Rather than simply abandon the patent, why not try to sell it instead? Others donated nonstrategic patents to a university or

[1]Jaffe, Adam B., and Lerner, Josh. *Innovation and Its Discontents: How Our Broken Patent System Is Endangering Innovation and Progress, and What to Do About It* (Princeton, NJ: Princeton University Press, 2004).

nonprofit that might benefit from the patent, a practice that flourished in the late 1990s until the IRS tightened the rules on patent valuation.

New entrants into the patent market figure to make patents' lives still more exciting in the near future. There are now well-capitalized firms, such as Ocean Tomo in Chicago, that will lend money to firms with attractive patent portfolios, and let those firms use their patents as collateral for loans. There are other well-capitalized firms, like ThinkFire, that will work with a company to license its patents, and take a percentage of the royalties as their fee. Still other firms with money, like Intellectual Ventures, will offer to buy your nonstrategic patents from you. They will aggregate these patents and create bundles of patents for licensing to other companies. And companies like UTEK have developed highly effective processes for placing university technologies into small and medium-sized technology firms that need an injection of new technology to grow their business.

These changes and new players figure to make the management of patents (as well as other forms of intellectual property) more challenging and more strategic. It is no longer sufficient to manage patents so as to keep the firm out of trouble. It is now necessary to engage with others in the active license, exchange, and transactions of patents for a variety of strategic objectives. Freedom to practice is only one such objective. Generating revenues from intellectual property (IP) is a second important objective. Enabling new standards and building partnerships with other companies that support your standards and your architectures is a third critical objective.

To offer a very brief example of this last kind of objective, consider IBM Corporation. IBM has led the world in the number of patents received from the USPTO for the past nine years. IBM generates hundreds of millions of dollars each year in licensing its robust patent portfolio. More recently, though, IBM has chosen to give away some 500 of its software patents to a foundation in the open source software area. IBM is not avoiding the renewal payments for these patents, because its gift included the commitment for IBM to continue paying these fees. Instead, IBM is trying to encourage third-party companies to build on the technologies associated with these patents, secure in the knowledge that no one will come after them for patent infringement. In a word, IBM is building an intellectual commons by donating these patents. And IBM has positioned itself to benefit from the work of this community, based on these technologies.

As I have written elsewhere,[2] industrial innovation processes are becoming more open. Useful ideas are widespread around the world. Companies need to

---

[2]Chesbrough, Henry. *Open Innovation: The New Imperative for Creating and Profiting from Technology* (Boston: Harvard Business School Press, 2003).

utilize others' ideas in their business and let their ideas be utilized in others' businesses.

IP management is going to have to change to keep pace with this evolution in industrial innovation processes. Companies cannot bring in external ideas without having appropriate legal protections in place. Companies will not enable internal ideas to flow outside without legal rights to profit from a portion of those technologies (unless, of course, they choose to give them away).

This may sound daunting to experienced patent professionals and their management. These changes require a new mind-set, new processes, and new issues to be managed. Making these changes will take time and money, and will involve a degree of risk that many patent managers will find uncomfortable.

This book can help ease that discomfort and can point the way toward more effective ways to realize the potential of patents and other IP for the firm. In so doing, IP managers and corporate executives can help unleash the innovative potential of their company's ideas, and enhance their company's ability to leverage the useful ideas of others in the company's own business processes.

Your life, and the life of your IP, is about to get more exciting. This book will offer you a guide to what is in store. These writers have been there, managing IP in this new environment, providing legal advice to companies confronting this new environment, or creating a new business to create value in this new environment.

PART 1

PRINCIPLES OF GLOBAL LEADERSHIP IN THE ENDURING TECHNOLOGY COMPANY

1

The Polymath CEO: Enlightened Leadership for the Enduring Technology Company

By Edward Kahn

The Global Picture from a Lofty Perch

Credit the thin atmosphere. As I dangled on a ski lift climbing above up to 11,000 feet above sea level last winter, an insight into an economic truth I had learned on a ski lift years before suddenly came to mind.

The initial lift trip took place in the late 1980s. Ascending the snowy slopes of Sunday River, Maine, I listened intently as my lift partner, a Jewish émigré from Poland who had worked many years in America as an electrical engineer for Japanese-owned NEC, spoke reassuringly into my half-frozen ears about the fearful specter of that Asian country's phoenix rising in the East.

"Sure, Ed, everyone is convinced that this is the end of American industrial dominance," he said, shaking his head in disbelief. "Everyone is writing best-selling books about how we are all going speak Japanese and eat sushi. Rockefeller Center is being sold to the Japanese. Well, not to worry. We are cowboys. They can't invent anything. They're not allowed to think. They have to be in agreement with everyone. They will never be able to outthink us in America."

The man was a prophet in his own (adopted) country. Just two years later, the Japanese industrial "apocalypse" had vanished. Poof, and the Rising Sun was yesterday's hysteria.

Twenty years later, again on a ski lift, I remembered that engineer's prophetic view of Asian cultural stumbling blocks as I thought about the current debate raging over globalization's impact on our country's supremacy in innovation.

Once more, corporate America is in a cold sweat over the apparition of a flat world, as Thomas Friedman has so articulately envisioned. But how much of this earth-shattering scenario is for real?

Clyde Prestowitz, a former Reagan trade official, makes a plausible case for a tectonic shift of economic power in *Three Billion New Capitalists: The Great Shift of Wealth and Power to the East.*[1] But his prediction is like "déjà vu all over again," considering that in 1990 he also authored *Trading Places: How America Allowed Japan to Take the Lead.*[2] That being said, the times truly are changing. Although America has been synonymous with innovation since our founding, in the past few years disturbing signs have emerged that our dominance in scientific and technological brainpower may be on the verge of a precipitous decline.

Witness the meteoric rise of India's star. Five hundred fifty-five million young people under the age of 25 are now vying for coveted jobs outsourced from America. Dubbed "Zippies" by the Indian magazine *Outlook* for the "zip" in their optimistic stride, this horde of high-tech college grads represent cheap labor by our standards, but their salaries often approach nine times that of the average Indian.

The rush to get in on the American outsourcing gold mine has spawned a bumper crop of engineers in India—200,000 in 2004 alone, compared to a mere 70,000 in the United States. Meantime, China dwarfs India's output, graduating 500,000 engineers that same year.

Intel's recent experience may be a harbinger of things to come. Chief executive officer (CEO) Craig Barrett reported that his company's 2004 annual science competition attracted 50,000 American high school student entries. In China, that same competition sparked *6 million* student entries.

Asia is sending students by the jet load to America for the best education our tax money can buy. In 2005, the National Academy of Science reported that students from China, India, and the former Soviet Union accounted for almost half of all U.S. doctorates awarded in engineering and science in 2004.

Microsoft's Bill Gates has seen the future of intellectual capital and it is not the United States. According to *Barron's*, his software behemoth anticipates hir-

---

[1]Prestowitz, Clyde. *Three Billion New Capitalists: The Great Shift of Wealth and Power to the East* (Boulder, CO: Basic Books, 2005).

[2]Prestowitz, Clyde. *Trading Places: How America Allowed Japan to Take the Lead* (North Clarendon, VT: Tuttle Publishing, 1990).

ing 3,000 more engineers in India, with the firm's employment growth there exceeding that of its U.S. operations.

As Friedman observes, "The potential speed and scale of this outsourcing phenomenon makes its potential impact enormous and unpredictable." At the same time, he notes that we should be fine "as long as America maintains its ability to do cutting edge innovation."

The optimum word here is *maintains*. Our aptitude for retaining our prized innovative status is in jeopardy not only because of a shortage of engineers, but also a lack of investment in research and development (R&D). Ever since the tech bubble burst and the economy contracted, stakeholders and Wall Street analysts have pushed corporations for beefy bottom lines, causing many companies to shrink their internal R&D.

For years, American blue chips including Microsoft, Boeing, United Technologies, Electronic Data Systems, and Guidant have lobbied Congress for better R&D tax credits, arguing that most industrialized nations offer far more generous write-offs for investing in new technologies.

And where the capital goes, so go the jobs. Look how Ireland's tax structure lured tech and biotech companies, or Puerto Rico's incentives drew big pharmaceutical companies. Forrester Research estimates that in the next 15 years 3.3 million U.S. jobs and $136 billion in U.S. wages will move offshore.

For every flat-world doomsdayer, though, there is a naysayer. Conservative commentator David Brooks, for one, argues that far from some weary aging superpower, America still accounts for 40% of R&D spending in the world, and its workers remain the most productive and hardworking.

According to Brooks, a RAND Corporation report disputes studies claiming we have a science and engineering gap. Furthermore, under the Bush administration, funding for federal science research has doubled to $137 billion, and 60 members of Congress want to double the R&D tax credit and open a Defense Advanced Research Projects Agency (DARPA)-style lab in the Department of Energy, dedicating $9 billion to scientific research and education.[3]

Perhaps the most critical variable in the innovation equation that doomsdayers overlook is America's huge but largely invisible intangible economy. As *BusinessWeek* notes, statistics issued by the Bureau of Economic Analysis (BEA) in Washington do not reflect our metamorphosis into a knowledge-based economy.

The BEA can track only tangibles. They have no way to capture data on the billions corporations are now spending on innovation, research, product design,

[3]Brooks, David. "The Nation of the Future," *New York Times*, February 2, 2006.

brand-building, employee training and other intangible assets vital to competing in a global economy. Amazing as it seems, groundbreaking innovations such as inhaled insulin and the iPod aren't even counted in their numbers.

BusinessWeek calculates that since 2000, the top ten corporations that report R&D investment increased their expenditures by 42%, yet most of that outlay doesn't show up in BEA statistics.

As someone who has spent the last 20 years riding the crest of a rising wave of concern over intellectual property (IP) rights, I come down on the side of those who argue that our country is far from losing its leadership position in ingenuity.

My advice is that before you panic over India, and more so over China, remember that NEC engineer's comments. Certain unique cultural strains exist, such as the Chinese autocracy, which is basically a free market economy inside a vicious totalitarian government. In my view, that is probably a bigger barrier to innovation than anything we face. Sooner or later, the Chinese will undergo their own tensions over distribution of wealth.

Nonetheless, the dramatic changes inherent in a global economy, coupled with the rise in outsourcing and impact of the Internet and convergence in communications, have already caused a re-revolution in the way American business designs and builds new products and services.

One thing is certain: Companies that refuse to adapt to this protean IP environment will perish. Those that conform to a dynamic marketplace model for innovation will succeed. The key to surviving and thriving is for CEOs to view the management of innovation and intellectual property in a radically different light.

What's at Stake

Perhaps the best way for me to illuminate what is at stake is to share another apocalyptic anecdote from yet another chance encounter (score one for quantum physics). In this case, while on a hotel bus heading to a Licensing Executive Society (LES) meeting, I found myself seated next to the Chief Patent Counsel for one of the Big Three automakers (who must remain nameless).

In a patriotic and poignant moment, he asserted that while America's dearth of science, math, and engineering education was of great concern, what worried him far more was the ultimate fate of our beloved country.

"After Pearl Harbor, we were able to ramp up manufacturing to defeat the global axis powers," he observed. "But if we dismantle all our manufacturing in this country below some critical tipping point, what will we do when we need synthetic rubber for tank treads—order it from the Chinese in the middle of a war?"

His remark elevates the issue of where and how we innovate into a third dimension. Those who dismiss the loss of our manufacturing base because we are becoming a high-tech service—or the more sexy "innovation"—economy should think again. There are certain platitudes too mission critical to a nation state to be left to mere platitudes.

This third dimension of the innovation game bears reflection as CEOs transition into a new age of competition on a playing field that will be anything but level, and no longer confined within the boundaries of our own country.

From my perspective, the intricate complexity of variables in the coming century will require what I call the polymath CEO. These men and women will have to master an original—and for many, foreign core competency—managing intellectual property and innovation across a worldwide spectrum. They must be executive savants, learned in the acquisition and bundling of preexisting technologies and inventions and using them in ever more creative ways.

To compete in this nascent creativity economy, CEOs will have to adopt a revolutionary, polymath management style, excelling in cross-disciplinary thinking that leads to a new creative plane.

Reading this, you may think the only CEO who could fit this bill would be a Leonardo da Vinci, Thomas Edison, Henry Ford, and Bill Gates all rolled into one, with the added diplomatic finesse of a Henry Kissinger. But we all know people with that amalgam of visionary genius and inventive mind come along one at a time, and once in a blue moon, if that.

Instead, polymath CEOs will have to recognize that to succeed in this new creativity economy, they must possess a panoramic view outside their own corporate field of vision.

This new breed of CEOs will shed old notions and prejudices against partnering to embrace "anything invented anywhere"—as a former Japanese colleague cleverly termed it in the late 1980s—devising a more productive corporate process. Such a process could repurpose technology invented for one market segment to turn a profit in its own niche. The current trend in America is to cut central operating costs and keep divisions autonomous. To leverage innovative capacity, however, the flow of R&D across divisions cannot be hampered by organizational rigidity. True, General Electric may run better that way, but what happens if a plastic tubing breakthrough in the water pollution unit never passes through to the solar energy people? Companies can pay a big price for a lavish wedding to the decentralized model.

Breaking down silos will be imperative to compete. That includes barriers to external partnerships. As Henry Chesbrough sagely advised, "Not all of the smart people in the world work for us."

Procter & Gamble is so committed to breaking down silos that it has reorganized its innovative platform around collaborative models within and without the company. The *Wall Street Journal* reports that in addition to 7,400 R&D staff scattered around 21 research centers in nine countries, P&G aims to originate half of its new products from global sources like InnoCentive, a body of 88,000 scientists and technologists available at the click of a mouse.

Restructuring Financial Incentives

Another fundamental change inherent in cross-disciplinary IP management is the adoption of incentives that aid in breaking down silos. As Karl Jorda asserts in Chapter 3, delineating the fusion model of IP management, "Innovation is everyone's job."

Ron Sansone, former Vice President of Strategic Innovation at Pitney Bowes, conducted an analysis showing that the number of inventors on a patent directly correlated to the significance of a patent. In that sense, the individual inventor was found to be the ultimate silo.

Since conditions for strategic IP management require different mental styles, companies must tailor different work incentives for everyone all the way down the research, development, and engineering (RD&E) "production line." That includes any employee with a potentially profitable creative spark.

The incentive matrix of an enduring tech company may someday require royalty sharing between inventors and engineers, cross-divisional collaboration to leverage existing technology, and design of new technology or products with other companies' technology.

As evidence of this, an intriguing analysis of new product innovations by Donald Lehman, Jacob Goldenberg, and David Mazursky revealed that the highest success-to-failure rate (13/1) was an idea that took advantage of a random event. By random, they meant a "Eureka" moment in which inventors stumbled on something they were not looking for but immediately recognized its significance. The next highest rate of success (7/1) took place in solution spotting, when inventors discovered a new use for an existing technology.

This study underscores the value in breaking down silos to leverage cross-disciplinary thinking, to nurture collaboration within and without. But it also raises the issue of how a company can stimulate serendipity.

Certainly, one of the major impediments today to effective IP management is patent policies that serve as disincentives, for example, awarding $1,000 for a patent application, even if there is more than one inventor. If there are four inventors, companies must bite the bullet to prevent their filing narrow individual patents or, worse, keeping their work to themselves. Even if $4,000 is invested, the return on investment (ROI) will come.

Inadequate compensation policies like these are a prime driver for the rise of the engineer-entrepreneur. Engineers and technologists don't stay with the same company for 40 years like they used to at General Electric or Dow. They go where they are loved, monetarily speaking, which in many cases means their own start-up. Now a company has to pay far more for the same ideas that same engineer might have generated internally if properly rewarded.

Restructuring incentive policies to leverage IP also requires devising longer-term, more sublime incentives for board members and corporate officers, for example, implementing a board policy that rewards a CEO for long-term payout instead of the current Wall Street mania for short-term profits. Boards and major stakeholders of enduring tech companies will have to buy into the concept of a longer-term upside if CEOs are to manage IP spectacularly.

IP and Business Strategy Must Be Congruent

To borrow a popular phrase, "It's the corporate culture, stupid." The internal milieu of a company can determine its innovative spirit, encouraging or depressing idea generation. The CEO of the enduring tech company, therefore, will nurture a totality of employee traits, characteristics, and attitudes directed toward the same strategic goal.

Instilling a coherent innovation culture requires that you examine whether all the projects percolating in your IP portfolio are congruent with your core business strategy. This may sound obvious, but many CEOs today either assume their IP portfolio and long-term strategy operate in sync or haven't stopped to analyze the fit. Management tends to assess the value of IP projects individually instead of in the aggregate as it relates to the long-term interest of their business.

Abraham Maslow, the prominent American psychologist, developed the famous "Hierarchy of Needs" (see Exhibit 1.1), which presents a range of human physical and psychological needs. As humans grow and gain life experience, their position on the pyramid moves upward, with very few ever reaching self-actualization, or their full potential. Just as with Maslow's famous version of the human order of intangible desires, corporate leaders possess their own hierarchy of essential drives, referred to as the "IP Management Hierarchy of Needs" (see Exhibit 1.2).

At the base of this IP Management Hierarchy lie defensive needs, which, if satisfied, progress into cost control, and then upward to a profit center motive.

EXHIBIT 1.1 Maslow's Hierarchy of Needs

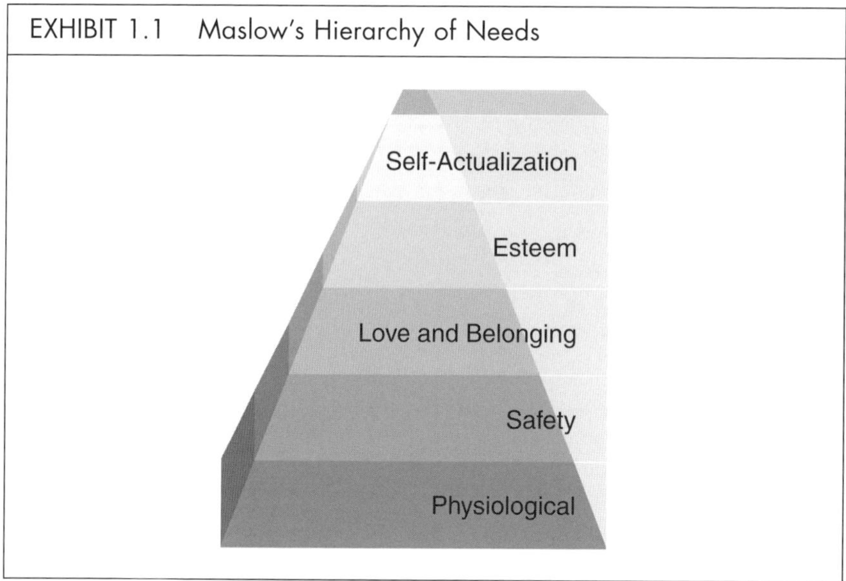

Once management fulfills this level of need, it proceeds to the next stage: integration. All too often, however, CEOs get mired in this level of the hierarchy, and as a consequence, never reach the apex of the pyramid—visionary—where most strive to reside.

Tech companies, in particular, are prone to getting bogged down at the integration stage because of management's penchant for developing a haphazard portfolio of IP projects. Many of these undertakings offer only short-term profit potential, or exemplify technology for technology's sake—ideas that bear no relation to the company's core business strategy.

In *Connecting the Dots: Aligning Projects with Objectives in Unpredictable Times*,[4] Cathleen Benko and Warren McFarlan document how many large companies have fallen prey to a scattershot approach to projects and technology-related investments.

Their mantra is "alignment." Too many projects end up in competition with each other, overlap, or work at cross-purposes, which wastes scarce resources. One study by Gartner Inc. showed that an astounding 90% of information technology (IT) companies have no defined IP portfolio management strategy, a void

[4]Benko, Cathleen, and McFarlan, F. Warren. *Connecting the Dots: Aligning Projects with Objectives in Unpredictable Times* (Boston: Harvard Business School Press, 2003).

EXHIBIT 1.2 IP Management Hierarchy of Needs

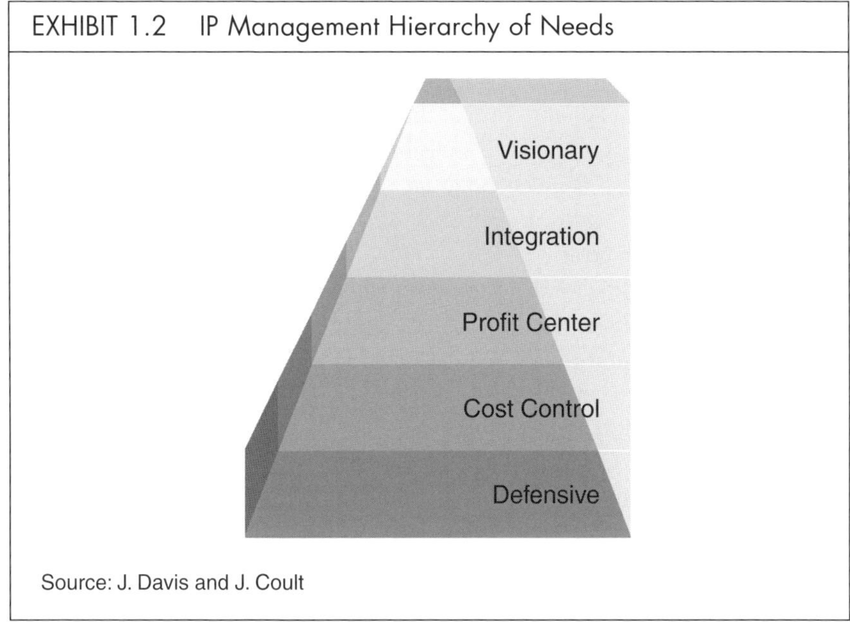

Source: J. Davis and J. Coult

that in five years led to $1 trillion of underperforming assets in the United States alone.

"Your project portfolio is your organization's future—the truest measure of organizational intent," the authors note. They suggest a grid on which a company can plot its projects and business objectives. By connecting the dots, management can clearly see if their portfolio and goals cluster or overlap as a measure of alignment.

In an age in which maximizing ROI is imperative, CEOs must ensure that everyone involved in the innovative process is operating on the same wavelength. The metaphor Benko and McFarlan employ is that of "frontier living," in which a group of pioneers work in unison toward surviving in a new territory rich in resources but subject to unpredictable technological, political, and economic forces.

"Frontiers are uncharted territories," the authors assert. "They require new mind-sets, creativity, and—most important—the ability to envision how the business can exploit the changes that are under way."

In their opinion, the confluence of linked technology advancements is fueling the dynamic business world. "The defining characteristics of this shifting landscape include increased organizational transparency, faster and faster data flows, reduced transactional friction, and the further blurring of the traditional roles of competitors, partners, suppliers and customers."

As my favorite Greek philosopher, Heraclites, presciently advised, "If you don't expect the unexpected, you will not find it." Polymath CEOs will thrive in a frontier environment by fostering a corporate culture that champions the power of intellectual capital to propel them into the future.

You might call this quality the "invisible touch." In *Invisible Advantage: How Intangibles Are Driving Business Performance*,[5] Jonathan Low and Pam Cohen Kalafut document how innovation muscle and intellectual capital impart a competitive edge in value creation.

They found that the financial success of a corporation correlates directly to a dozen different intangibles: leadership, strategy execution, communication and transparency, brand equity, reputation, alliances and networks, technology and processes, human capital, workplace organization and culture, innovation, intellectual capital, and adaptability. According to Low and Kalafut, ". . . these don't show on a balance sheet or an income statement, yet they are manageable and usually quantifiable drivers of corporate-value creation." As evidence, they cite companies like Dell and McDonald's, which learned quickly and quietly to capitalize on innovation before their competition caught on.

Low and Kalafut also maintain that anticipating change is no longer the sole province of the R&D department, but must involve services, business models, organizational structures, internal processes, profit zones, alliances, marketing, and strategy. Later in this chapter, we will see this view about business models echoed by Clayton Christensen and others. (Most well-run companies have at least removed IP decisions from the sole province of legal, or even just legal and R&D.)

"In fact, a hallmark of the Intangibles Economy is that product innovation is no longer sufficient to stay in the competitive race," say Low and Kalafut. "Rather, companies must innovate across a variety of fronts. The Intangibles Economy encourages, thrives on, and in fact requires companies to be innovative along many dimensions."

To do this, though, requires a management attitude adjustment toward cost control. They quote strategy consultant Gary Hamel's pithy assessment: "In devoting themselves entirely to the pursuit of efficiency, top management inadvertently drives out the 'waste' and 'extravagance' that is the very fuel of innovation. As top management strives for ever greater efficiency, it must learn to tolerate 'stupid' ideas and 'failed' experiments."

Indeed, innovation is now everyone's job. In this new corporate setting, CEOs must inspire idea generation from the bottom up. Later in this chapter,

---

[5]Low, Jonathan, and Kalafut, Pam Cohen. *Invisible Advantage: How Intangibles Are Driving Business Performance* (Boulder, CO: Perseus Books Group, 2002).

a few of the best practices adopted by companies in the forefront of this cultural revolution will be discussed.

Disintermediation of RD&E

Dell, Amazon, and exchange-traded funds (ETFs) exemplify the supersonic pace at which disintermediation is taking place in the marketplace today. In effect, disintermediation is cutting out the middleman in classical supply chains, which can result in dramatically lower costs to service the customer.

When I use the term *disintermediation* in the context of RD&E, I am referring to the new paradigm elucidated by Henry Chesbrough in his now classic opus, *Open Innovation: The New Imperative for Creating and Profiting from Technology*.[6]

A leading light of the open innovation business model, Chesbrough explains how companies can develop *disruptive technology*—a term coined by Clayton Christensen—to supersede entrenched competitors. By disruptive technology, Chesbrough means a technological advancement that is such a leap for mankind that it alters the way we live and interact. The automobile, telephone, and now cell phone are prime examples of new technology that revolutionized civilization and, within a short time, rendered their forerunners obsolete.

Chesbrough points to the Xerox Palo Alto Research Center (PARC) as a prime example of a company that developed promising disruptive technologies, but failed to capitalize on them because of a closed innovation model. Seeing opportunity elsewhere, some of their best and brightest departed to create successful start-ups like Adobe and 3Com.

Since the open innovation model began to evolve in the 1990s, the recognition by CEOs of the danger that disruptive technologies pose to their ability to compete and even survive has driven some to radically reengineer their innovation business model.

The open innovation model comprises how something gets designed and made, and how many different elements reside outside a division or physical plant. What Chesbrough dubs the "virtuous circle" is no longer unbroken. "Open innovation combines internal and external ideas into architectures and systems whose requirements are defined by a business model."

As he sees it, in an era when the only constant is change, "The knowledge that a company uncovers in its research cannot be restricted to its internal

[6]Chesbrough, Henry William. *Open Innovation: The New Imperative for Creating and Profiting from Technology* (Boston: Harvard Business School Press, 2003).

pathways to market. Similarly, its internal pathways to market cannot necessarily be restricted to using the company's internal knowledge. This perspective suggests some very different organizing principles for research and innovation."

Under an open innovation model, companies will no longer employ 500 R&D scientists and 200 employees in the new-product development department. RD&E will be more virtual, utilizing outsourcing when and where it works to their advantage.

Under this scenario you might buy your research in India and your development in Taiwan, with the final assembly performed in the United States. This is where the polymath CEO's skills are put to the test. You must evaluate every variable in the value creation equation. While you might prefer to do your research in Brazil for cost reasons, you can't because there is no regulation of employee theft. So you do your research in India because they have good laws on that. (Warning: this is hypothetical; consult your IP attorney!)

This simple example makes crystal clear why the polymath CEO must know—or assemble a crackerjack team of people who know—law, science, and the best source of good engineers for the type of product or service under consideration. To use a biotech metaphor, you have to become a master at recombinant DNA.

Once you adopt an open IP mind-set, though, the world becomes your innovation oyster, with many seedbeds capable of producing pearls of great price—and potential profit.

In a later section of this book, John Tao, Corporate Director of Technology Partnerships at Air Products and Chemicals, Inc., and Vince Magnotta, Technology Transfer Manager of Technology Partnerships at Air Products, offer a macro view of how they model use of universities as a source of innovation. Then, in a later chapter, Teri Willey, a former Managing Partner of ARCH Development Partners, describes how university spinouts and corporate joint purposes can come together even in what were previously considered geographically infertile environments.

With the disintermediation of RD&E, your intellectual property may not come from inside your door, your division, your company, or even your industry. Your R&D scientists may not be born in this country; they may also come from a wholly different discipline.

How much harder is the life of the global high-tech CEO? Previously, the question was relatively simple: Will the country I am exporting to enforce IP protective rights on my product sold there? Now, as stated earlier, that analysis has to be done versus research, development, manufacture, and sale, region by region.

Imagine a small entity that needs funding from your 1,000-employee midsized public company and wants to do the development in India. It turns out that they are close to those brainy Indian professors and there's a whole generation of migrated back Anglo-Indian engineers who can do the design. It might be a more seamless process to do it there—if it can be protected.

Then again, you might choose to go the iPod route, employing young American R&D techies and paying them high U.S. rates because no cost is too high for getting market share.

Here's yet another option: Say one vital part of your new product is the "secret sauce," so you decide to let that get added only in a place where you can control it physically, legally, and with the full force of IP laws established. You may decide to do 98% of it overseas; the last 2% may be the variable you can truly keep secret. So you ship it to Silicon Valley and do it there. Or you may add the secret sauce in Silicon Valley in an irreversible way, then ship it back to India where the final assembly is done because it's still worth it for the two ocean trips—one for protection and one for the assembly.

In light of the complexity of issues involved today, I'm not certain I want to be a polymath CEO—I'm not that smart. Seriously, though, be advised there is no perfect model of RD&E out there. If anything, models are deadly. If you read this book and try to find one ideal model for your situation, your days of leading an enduring tech company won't last long. The model that fits your scenario may not be the one that guides you in a different situation tomorrow.

Varied Paths of Innovation

Polymath CEOs must begin by looking at the spectrum of various business models before they can get down to practical implementation within their company.

In contemplating the paths of innovation that "diverge in the woods," a CEO has to decide where to place the company's focus, a task that to most appears daunting. Clayton Christensen, a Harvard Business School professor and leading light of the innovation movement, says that for many CEOs innovation resembles the proverbial "black box," which is a mistaken notion.

In *The Innovator's Solution: Creating and Sustaining Successful Growth*,[7] Christensen and coauthor Michael Raynor dissect the enigma wherein brilliant ideas seem to spontaneously arise out of nowhere. They insist that creating new growth businesses is predictable once you study the process by which innovation transpires.

[7]Christensen, Clayton M., and Raynor, Michael E. *The Innovator's Solution: Creating and Sustaining Successful Growth* (Boston: Harvard Business School Press, 2003).

"The quest for predictability in an endeavor as complex as innovation is not quixotic. What brings predictability to any field is a body of well-researched *theory*—contingent statements of what causes what and why." The goal, they say, is for managers who need to grow new businesses with predictable success to become disruptors instead of disruptees and kill the well-run established competitors.

In their opinion, top management has three jobs: "The first is a near-term assignment. To personally stand astride the interface between disruptive growth businesses and the mainstream businesses to determine through judgment which of the corporation's resources and processes should be imposed on the new business and which should not."

The second is longer-term, shepherding the creation of a process the authors term a *disruptive growth engine* that reliably churns out successful growth businesses. The third is the perpetual role of sensing when circumstances are changing and teaching others how to read these tea leaves.

We seem to be back to that recombinant da Vinci, Edison, Ford, and Gates persona. Since geniuses like that are in short supply, however, the solution for most CEOs is a transformation in management mind-set.

As Christensen has noted, leadership attributes that propel a large corporation with a profitable core business do not translate to a marketplace driven by the growth imperative. In an age of disruptive technology, the best management practices that ensured a company's success can prove to be its Achilles' heel, abruptly bringing about its downfall.

Instead, CEOs must engage their imagination, relying more heavily on their creative right brain. Much as the Renaissance flowered under original thinkers, the creativity economy will reward executives who possess intellectual vigor and a belief in endless possibilities—and inspire those same qualities down the line.

According to Daniel Pink, author of *A Whole New Mind: Why Right-Brainers Will Rule the Future*,[8] unlike employees of yesterday who were technology competent and left-brain dominant, the employee of the future must have a well-developed right-brain talent that reflects the attributes of an artist (i.e., creativity, inventiveness, empathy, and meaning), as well as those of an inventor—one who has the ability to see new combinations and relationships that lead to breakthrough thinking and innovation.

Ingenuity by top management will be even more critical to sustain growth. CEOs will have to develop mastery of innovation intelligence gathering. This

[8]Pink, Daniel. *A Whole New Mind: Why Right-Brainers Will Rule the Future* (New York: Riverhead Books, 2006).

synthesized approach includes inspiring; acquiring; in-licensing; out-licensing; spin-offs; enforcement; and cross-company, cross-industry, and cross-border partnering.

"Commoditization of technology offers a wealth of new opportunities as innovators around the world tinker with cheap, ubiquitous information technology commodities," declares Hal Varian, a professor of business, economics, and information management at the University of California at Berkeley and regular contributor to the *New York Times.*

Although there is a wealth of opportunities out there, there is an equal number of potential land mines. To avoid these, a CEO must develop a sixth sense for accurate valuation of IP.

In the experience of Mark Peterson, CEO of Robinwood Consulting and an expert in IP valuation, a useful working definition of IP is protectable distinctiveness.

"People today often refer to IP as being anything from training, customer lists, patents, trade names, and everything in between," says Peterson. "In valuation, however, protectable distinctiveness determines in large part how valuable an asset is. IP value is really the competitive advantage you get over the next best alternative."

If you are dealing in the international market, one of the first variables to consider is what kind of protection you can expect to be granted. Peterson has found that most of the value of technology comes from those areas of the world with strong IP rights. "If you're doing business in a country without strong IP laws, be very careful. The value you should assign to an asset when you have no way to protect it most likely needs significant discounting as compared to a protectable asset."

I second the notion that foreign IP entanglements can prove to be risky global business. Remember that U.S. patent protection stops at our borders. Bangalore is not Silicon Valley. If you are getting your R&D done in India or another foreign country, don't assume that the ownership rules are the same as they are in Silicon Valley.

Stephen J. Frank, a leading patent attorney with Goodwin Procter LLP, warns of recent cases of offshore buyer's remorse. In "Out Goes Development, In Come the Risks,"[9] Frank notes, "When proprietary technology gets loose in jurisdictions with poor enforcement records, it often spreads quickly and elusively. Underground businesses can spring up and compete with an IP owner

[9] Frank, Stephen J. "Out Goes Development, In Come the Risks," *IP Advisor* (Goodwin Procter newsletter), October 2005.

on a worldwide basis, zapping stolen software, for example, to anyone with an Internet connection and a credit card."

This can even take place when development is done at home in the United States. "An outsourcer's first step is always due diligence," Frank counsels, listing procedures a company can implement, from vetting an offshore partner for physical security measures to asking whether employees can take source code home to determining legal jurisdiction in the offshore partner's home country.

In Chapter 2 of this book, Edmund Walsh, an intellectual property attorney at Wolf Greenfield, and former Chief Patent Counsel at Teradyne, offers his view of maximizing business value from IP through various business models. According to Walsh, applying the value equation at each point of the decision process can lead to the best investment of the limited resources available to developing and maintaining an IP portfolio.

Walsh's chapter provides a battlefield-style analysis of your options in this competitive war. At one extreme is the licensing model, and at the other extreme is open source and antiproprietary, with most companies falling somewhere in between.

Today, businesses are also increasingly looking to generate IP value through a balanced protection of trade secrets and the new class of business method patents. In chapter 3, you'll learn from Karl Jorda, a professor at the Franklin Pierce Law Center and former Chief Patent Counsel at Ciba-Geigy, and Wayne Jaeschke, Patent Counsel at Connolly, Bove, Lodge, & Hutz, and former Chief Patent Counsel at Henkel, the critical distinctions between these two, and how some savvy companies are utilizing these forms of legal protection to leverage IP value.

> Certainly, taxation issues are another key variable in the IP calculus. "Accounting treatment can change the cash flow of a deal and thus affect the price of the deal," says Peterson. "However, the mere fact that a licensing deal is expensed on the P&L statement while an M&A deal involving the same technology is only referenced on the balance sheet is only one of many factors when deciding between the strategic use of licensing vs. M&A."

In this rough and tumble disruptive innovation world, however, fear of falling victim to creative destruction is driving some companies to slavishly jump on the innovation bandwagon and in potentially suboptimal ways.

General Electric may be one example. Eric Mankin, Executive Director of the Babson Research Center on Innovation and Entrepreneurship, analyzed the difference between GE's full frontal top-down model versus Best Buy's "popcorn stand" bottom-up approach.

The question in Mankin's mind is whether GE's top management–driven model will crowd out bottom-up innovators within the organization. Operating in its famous disciplined strategic style, GE's top brass has selected four strategic areas for their innovative push.

"GE's approach revolves around picking winners—determining the areas where the company should be making major investments so as to have big new businesses in the near future," observes Mankin. "It is concerned about initiatives that have the ability to 'move the needle'—specific kinds of innovations that can deliver big economic benefits within a reasonable period of time."

In contrast, "Best Buy customizes its innovations by store and even by sales associate. Each innovation on its own has a small impact, but the many new initiatives add up to strong growth in sales and earnings."

Mankin sums up GE's top-down model as a few big bets leading to big success in a few markets, but with a low level of iteration focused on hitting the right target. In contrast, Best Buy's bottom-up approach is based on many small bets generating results via many successes, but with a high level of experimentation.

"Bottom-up innovations often reflect a deep operational understanding of the business and its current customers," asserts Mankin. In his view, innovations descending from on high reflect strategic decisions by senior executives. While the two approaches are not mutually exclusive, he suggests most companies will want to use a combination.

Mankin concludes that Best Buy utilizes both approaches. "Its overall 'customer-centric' strategy is driven from the top, and entails systematic remodeling of its stores and selling approach. The top-down customer-centric approach complements the bottom-up experimentation that the company encourages."

As I think about the varied paths a company can traverse, the seemingly heretical Nagoya model also comes to mind. According to the *Wall Street Journal*, the very same heavy industries suffering from cheap overseas competition in the United States are thriving in this region of Japan—a country certainly no longer "low wage."

"Nagoya's manufacturers have kept them [competitors] at bay with a maneuver now being copied by producers across Japan," reports Jathon Sapsford. "They moved production of low-end products overseas, but continued to make lucrative high-end goods at home. Demand is growing for such products, which range from engines for hybrid cars to micro-robots for industrial use. To maintain its competitive edge, Nagoya spends robustly on research and development."[10]

[10] Sapsford, Jathon, "Japan's Economy Gains Steam from Manufacturing Heartland." *Wall Street Journal*, October 11, 2005.

While pressure for consistent earnings deters high R&D spending by U.S. counterparts, Nagoya companies like Toyota have been frugal. They've also kept to the conservative Japanese customs of lifetime employment, seniority, and cozy shareholder agreements that many economists blamed for the country's slump during the 1990s.

Sapsford maintains that at most Nagoya firms, shares are still held by affiliates, suppliers, or other loyal allies. "The intricate web of cross-shareholding that ties many of them together makes it easier for them to set aside capital for such long-term purposes."

Toyota is a prime example. By owning shares in many of its suppliers, when Toyota chooses to invest in R&D instead of paying a dividend, those suppliers probably won't object. As Paul Sheard, an economist at Lehman Brothers in Tokyo, sees it, the Nagoya strategy doesn't necessarily result in a lack of shareholder returns. "It means you have the freedom to make the best cars, and you don't have the capital markets breathing down your neck."

The Nagoya story also caught my eye because it's in that context of the Big Three patent counsels' concern about losing our manufacturing heft. It's not an economic concern. It's U.S.-centric. Maybe you can make more money selling Mickey Mouse brands over the Internet, but then no one here will be able to weld the axle in the drive train of your car. The collective of a tech company is a tech nation, and that is something we have to ponder in the rush to become a service economy.

Another lesson of Nagoya for CEOs is that if you are doing some of the final innovative assembly and a lot of that value is held back in "your Nagoya," whether that is in Kentucky or the Argentine Pampas, then what competitors "borrow" isn't as valuable. It's a component of the innovation but doesn't stand alone.

Already, hallmarks of leading innovative companies have emerged that can serve as guideposts for CEOs. These firms are translating their enhanced creative platform into increased growth and profitability.

Hallmarks include, first and foremost, developing and executing a synthesized, balanced approach to innovation. A strategic, cross-disciplinary approach leads to increasing their rate of innovation, shortening the time to market of new products and services, and increasing sales, with a concomitant reduction in development and production costs.

To accomplish this, companies often must find a way around traditional internal roadblocks such as a poorly designed incentive structure, an entrenched corporate cultural mind-set, and a fuzzy strategy when it comes to innovation and their IP portfolio.

Interestingly, studies show that the size of a company, per se, has no bearing on whether an entity can become the leading innovator within its industry. The most effective innovators achieve a higher rate of return more through deft management of the innovation process than merely throwing RD&E resources against the wall. Another hallmark is superior market intelligence. Attracting and retaining a top creative talent pool is also vital.

I'm a great believer in innovation by example—companies that those in the know have ranked as the most admired and successful innovators in the business world today. Polymath CEOs need not despair, for best business practices abound. For instance, Google allows engineers to spend up to 20% of their time on a project of their choice, subject to an oversight-and-approval process.

Google may think their brainchild original, but for me, it's back to the future. Google simply took a page—or should I say sticky note—from 3M, which long ago had their 15% rule, allowing employees to devote 15% of their time to projects of their own concoction, from which whole new businesses were created. When some engineer discovered that a particular adhesive wouldn't work properly, in a 15% "Eureka" moment he saw a potential use and invented Post-It® notes.

To give you a more precise picture of the two basic organizational models a CEO can choose to create for IP and R&D management, in later chapters of this book, two well-known corporate IP experts provide detailed descriptions of their particular setup.

Chapter 5, by Damon Matteo, Vice President of IP Commercialization at PARC in Palo Alto, presents a refreshingly decentralized and embedded IP asset distribution sensing system. PARC was famous (or perhaps infamous) at Xerox years ago as the place where everything was invented but no money was made. Now a subsidiary of Xerox, PARC is a veritable powerhouse of IP commercialization.

Playing counterpoint is Abha Divine, President and CEO of AT&T Knowledge Ventures Inc., the strategic IP management arm of AT&T. The model SBC adopted represents a more centralized system than PARC.

These two discussions provide a glimpse into two differing styles of managing your RD&E and resultant IP. Although one company might have a few hundred R&D scientists, and the other a few thousand, both are large enough that they give you an idea of the choices you have in strategic IP management. Both govern the flow between divisions—including those external to the company—and deals. That is always going to be a vital part of the cross-boundary process, whether it involves cross-divisional, cross-corporate, or cross-national or -international boundaries.

In the final analysis, polymath CEOs will have to take the pulse of the business they are going to be in and make a decision as to whether IP will be held closely or given away to drive business to your door and whether IP is a disruptive kind of business practice or technology or just a modest change. You will have to filter all of those factors through your strategic prism before you get down to choosing a Matteo or Divine style for managing large swaths of your RD&E in a larger organization.

Open Innovation and Disruptive Technologies

For a CEO to fathom open innovation and disruptive technology, he or she must first know this: Invention is not innovation. Understanding the difference is critical.

As Henry Chesbrough once elucidated in *Optimize* magazine, we should think of invention as new discovery. A discovery could be new to the world or new to industry, but it consists of something we did not know before. Furthermore, inventions are the province of people with scientific training or who are answering questions like how and why. They're plumbing the depths of difficult, long-term questions that result in fundamental new knowledge.[11]

Innovation, by contrast, is applying knowledge to a real-world problem and taking an idea to market. You may not have any customer in mind during a process of discovery and invention, but ultimately a customer is critical to the process of innovation.

In many cases, a company owns the rights to an invention, but innovation doesn't take place until they figure out how to package it, market it, sell it, and devise a business model that wraps around the invention.

Christensen points to the classic case of Xerox: The fact that you invented the Xerox machine doesn't mean anything until you come up with the leasing business model that meets a customer need and makes that copying machine profitable in the marketplace.

Anticipating the innovation, not just the invention, is the name of the disruptive technology game. That being said, the ability to scan the horizon and spot disruptive technology before it topples your business may sound like a mission impossible. But in Chapter 8 of this book, Dr. Bruce Vojak, a professor in the Department of Engineering at the University of Illinois, and Dr. Frank

---

[11] Chesbrough, Henry. "Are You Open to Innovation?" *Optimize*, July 2003.

Chambers, a former innovation director at Eaton, present a heuristic methodology for road-mapping disruptive technology threats.

Instead of relying on ESP or tarot cards, the senior technology visionary and his or her junior cohorts can use the authors' methodology based on observations of past patterns of changes in complex, technology-based subsystems to guide their intuition and predict the future of technology.

It is unlikely that Vojak and Chambers' modeling or the best general principles of Christensen and or Chesbrough can keep companies ahead of the relentless curve of change and the oh-so-elusive "disruptive" factor.

But three principles can be applied that keep a company, regardless of industry or size, more likely to be thinking outside of the lagging perspective of even its own customers, marketing people, and scientists:

1. Application of "open innovation" architectures across the entire corporate enterprise.
2. Using the beauty of small-scale initiatives (cf. Mankin) based on outside developed intellectual assets, often at smaller entities, via strategic alliances.
3. The use of outsourced, "out-of-the-box," and cross-disciplinary scientist businesspeople has been advocated and is increasingly being adopted. P&G's decision to tap InnoCentive's worldwide coalition of 80,000 technologists and scientists to originate half of its new product innovations is a prime example.[12]

An outstanding example of the first principle has taken shape at Air Products and Chemicals, Inc., a company that has evolved the open innovation model in a profitable manner. In Chapter 9, Dr. John Tao, Air Products' corporate director of technology partnerships, and Vince Magnotta, technology transfer manager of technology partnerships, outline the organizational structure and process begun in 1995 to centralize their external technology efforts and implement best practices across the company.

At Air Products, partnering is a cornerstone, mostly external. As the authors quip, "The best R&D is not an individual sport." They explain how solutions are identified and accelerated utilizing partnering strategies such as university R&D alliances, global R&D insourcing, external providers, licensing-in, and joint development. Case studies are reviewed covering university alliances, working with a Russian institute, and measuring external research programs.

[12] www.innocentive.com, Press Release, February 10, 2003.

I should note here that Dr. Tao says that Air Products inspired Chesbrough's work on open innovation almost as much as Chesbrough inspired them. Although these two may good-naturedly claim precedence over the other, notwithstanding Professor Chesbrough's original grounding in his hands-on industrial management experience, Air Products has implemented the principles throughout a large industrial entity. Of particular note is their significant foreign partnering in Russia and China.

In any event, based on my career in IP, I think the evolution of Air Products' open innovation model is a healthy and natural one, which may or may not have arisen from the Chesbrough theory.

The second operational principle is exemplified in Dennis McCullough's discussion of how ABB Lummus has used small-scale initiatives as a key growth strategy. He argues that small-scale initiatives provide low-risk entry to new markets. (Once again, the careful executive should observe the implicit cautionary against large company focus on a few big bets.)

McCullough explains how intellectual assets of others, nurtured through the disparate skill sets of larger and smaller partners in strategic alliances, can be made to work for both entities. His insights into specific techniques for "load leveling" in the alliance—giving the innovative lead to the small party and the developmental tilt to the larger party—are great teaching for the corporate leader.

The third operational principle of getting your future thinking into "left field" by using people from "left field," was discussed in an interesting McKinsey work from 2001.

Although that work discussed utilizing these on-call specialists for helping with out-licensing—an endeavor not nearly so mission critical as strategic in-licensing—the concept will work ideally for discovering, analyzing, and exploring development paths for available external technologies, which may prove to be the basis for the healthy internal disruption.

While discussing "how to out-license," the McKinsey work advocated the creation of teams of on-call knowledge partners, both broad-based technologists and industry specialists.

This 2001 idea for using these types of people to suggest applications for "leftover" or "excess" technologies across a range of technologies and industries had been applied by EKMS, Inc. since 1989.

At EKMS, on behalf of many *Fortune* 500 organizations, we had bred such a knowledge partner pool for strategic IP in-licensing, partnering, and out-licensing. At EKMS we dubbed these out-of-the-box thinkers "doctors of dangerous eclecticism" (or affectionately, DDEs)

The polymath CEO will recognize the need for pools of cross-innovating thinkers, scientists, and businesspeople who can look across fields as diverse as pollution controls and telecom and see the unexpected value connection.

Sustainability becomes less a matter of picking the right model than it is of developing a corporate environment that learns to be one subject to continuous reinvention of the very manner in which it innovates.

Generating value from innovation through cross-functional invention teams is a subject covered in Chapter 7 by Carsten Wittrup, Director of Global Technology at the BOC Group. To him, the internal and external connection network is vital because innovation is performed by people connecting with people in a creative and boundary-breaking process in which they are free to challenge rules, practices, and traditions to strive for and reach new and higher ground. His chapter provides a lot of grist for managing the "softer" side of the innovation process.

If you are the CEO reading this and realize that you aren't a right-brained type, what do you do?

You can open your organization to such types in the highest ranks of innovation management. These people will make tangible in an organization the realization that innovation is best achieved by people making connections in both internal and external networks in a creative and boundary-breaking process. As CEO, you need not be the person who inherently challenges rules, practices, and traditions in an ongoing effort to change more rapidly.

Ultimately, all innovation comes down to the human element. The leadership of the enduring tech company will take a village. It could be a committee of three to five people, some with an emphasis on the financial piece of the equation, some on sourcing of ideas, some on team leadership and innovation. But the person who leads that group must be a synthetic thinker, more right-brained than left-brained, and that may be a big shift.

Merger Mania vs. Tech Transfer

The urge to merge is back. Apparently, the mergers and acquisitions (M&A) world still possesses the same seductive powers that lured so many companies into disastrous relationships during the 1980s and 1990s. Never mind that every study conducted, including those by leading consulting firms like McKinsey & Company and PriceWaterhouseCoopers, have documented the shockingly high failure rate of this strategy.

"The stats on M&A failure, in fact, might be gloomier than the American divorce rate," observes the Caxton Group, a Cleveland consulting firm specializing in the needs of emerging companies. "Depending on whether success is defined by shareholder value, customer satisfaction, or some other measure, most research places the merger failure rate somewhere between 50% and 80%."

Flanagan Consultants of Stamford, Connecticut, places that figure even higher. "Depending on the particular time period and industries studied, the failure rate for M&As ranges from 60% to 90%."

There's not a lot of room to succeed in those percentages, which argues that smart CEOs would realize it imperative, as Santayana cautioned, to learn from history so they are not doomed to repeat it.

Interestingly, the Flanagan report noted that one in-depth study of 497 companies concluded that CEO overconfidence was the primary culprit. While other studies posit numerous other reasons for the demise of so many business entanglements, my own experience in this field prompts me to believe that leadership is certainly key to the question of how and when to merge to leverage IP growth.

I surmise the twenty-first century corporate rush to get back in the M&A game is driven by the resurgence of the high-tech sector. For some executives, it may be simply a lingering desire to return to the good old heady days of the 1990s when initial public offerings (IPOs) and M&A dominated headlines and drove stock prices through the roof.

For other CEOs, however, the driving force is the opportunity for market share and profit in a start-up tech rebirth that this time appears grounded in real-world business plans.

According to *Business 2.0*, the reappearance along the Silicon corridor of major players like venture capitalists, IP law firms, and investment bankers spells billions to be made. "What is on display in Palo Alto—indeed, increasingly in all of the nation's tech centers, from Seattle to Austin to New York—is the early stage of a new technology boom of potentially unprecedented power and durability . . . And this time, even some circumspect observers of the tech scene believe, the industry could soar to greater—and more sustainable—heights than ever before."

The article states that money invested in early-stage start-ups could top $1.5 billion in 2005, up 50% from 2004. The average seed investment in 2005, $4.4 million, is three times what it was the year before and larger than it was in 2000, which means that venture capitalists (VCs) are valuing start-ups at higher levels than at the height of the first boom.

Some veterans of the first go-round aren't buying, apparently suffering a case of start-up fatigue. But other big corporate names are jockeying for position in what they perceive as a rosy path to sustainable revenue growth.

How quickly they forget. Take XROS, a sure bet that Nortel eagerly ponied up $3.25 billion for at the time of acquisition. No matter that XROS had only $3 million in net tangible assets. That particular fiber-optical illusion has the honor of contributing to Nortel's world record $12.4 billion write-down in June

2001. Or consider Lucent's acquisition of optical networking systems developer Chromatis in 2000. The price tag—$4.7 billion in stock—was an unprecedented sum to pay for a start-up with any realized revenue. Even as the stock market bottomed out, investors still yielded a robust 1,600% ROI.

When you look back at the telecom boom, people should have screamed when Nortel stock was worth $100 billion. The XROS technology was bought by Nortel for multibillions of dollars after only a couple of rounds of VC funding.

People in licensing know that an idea by a university professor at Weitzmann Institute three years earlier would never have gotten licensed by anyone in corporate R&D at those telecom companies for even $100,000. Why? If the last 500 feet of fiber to the curb was so important that it was worth $3.25 billion, isn't there something wrong? XROS strikes me as a prime example of the puzzling CEO penchant for buying a whole company for $2 billion instead of licensing a much wider array of technologies and having a great deal of cash left over for moving them forward in a measured manner, and funding those that prove to be the better candidates—diversification over that "one big bet."

Outsized stock market rewards for M&A; financial disincentive to patent acquisitions; and lack of ability to assemble development teams to test, sort through, and scale only the winners all tip conventional practice toward acquiring a fully integrated technology company rather than placing, via license, discrete, multiple technology bets.

As the public markets continue to rebound, now is the time for the visionary CEO to at least consider that 100 technology licensing bets, complete with "portable" R&D teams, could be made for the price of one M&A deal.

Your stock price is inflating, but so is the price of the smaller but rarely VC-funded company that has some reduction to practice and initial beta sales.

Most VC operations finance later-stage ventures, keeping strong technologists with poor business prospects, very hungry for the larger company's advances.

Wide IP Vision as an Antidote to Trolls

A resurgence in M&A activity has occurred at the same time that much attention is being paid to the vexing problem of the patent troll.

The ability and willingness to practice "open innovation," to broadly and regularly survey the IP landscape of seemingly irrelevant invention activities in (seemingly) nonrelated industries, and to add strategic in-licensing as a business development complement to M&A could go a long way in reducing the rising threat of the patent troll.

Trolls, a term invented by Peter Detkin while he was at Intel, refers to a firm whose sole purpose is to assert allegedly fundamental, infringed patents against those technology firms shipping products that allegedly practice those patents' claims.

Owners of these fundamental patents would rather use the term *legitimate enforcement operations* rather than the more commonly used *troll*.

But as evidenced by the $600 million-plus settlement that ended the RIM (BlackBerry)-NTP battle, this is a growing problem for companies shipping products.

These patents picked up by trolls did not start life, for the most part, with assertion in mind. They were the embodiments of would-be technology products that, for one reason or the other, never got off the ground.

Failed technology product companies, whose only remaining value is a few patents filed years before, have no other monetization avenue than assertion. Certainly, many of those patents are not truly seminal. In those cases, these patents, handled by skillful assertion pros, can still, after cleverly gauging the cost of defense, set the price tag accordingly and collect several hundred thousand dollars per patent set, per licensee, without ever testing the substance of the issued claims—not good for innovation.

However, some of the patent "resurfacing" and assertion painfully in the here and now could have been picked up much earlier. A healthier mix of strategic in-licensing to complement M&A could have been a vaccine against some of these trolls.

An open innovation corporate culture will lead inevitably to a wider strategic view, better skills at landscape assessment, and more proactive in-licensing.

Had the telecom bubble not burst and an XROS succeeded, how many patents would have lined up to collect? And whether XROS should have been worth not 3.25 billion, but even $325 million, how many acquiring companies would have defensively and aggressively in-licensed related patents at the same time, as complement to the larger product acquisition?

In looking at the buying habits of an M&A-active company how many seminal patents were turned down while avoiding the "early-stage risk" of a tech transfer partnership with a small firm?

Most companies conduct "freedom of action" studies (patent clearance) before launching major product initiatives, but how much do most invest in in-licensing those patents that lie around the periphery of their otherwise "cleared" product?

Sustainability Requires Constant Change

The original title of this book was not *Innovate or Perish*; it was *Adaptive Innovation*. Not only must twenty-first-century CEOs adapt innovation to the globalized world, but they must continuously adapt their own internal innovation models to ever fast-changing circumstances.

CEOs of enduring technology companies must not only redesign the organizational structure to foster IP cross-pollination, they must also reengineer the business model for acquiring and productizing intellectual assets.

Polymath CEOs will have to take the pulse of each product initiative they are going to launch and make a high-level decision as to whether it will be held closely or given away to drive business to their door. These variables will have to pass through your prism before you can decide on the functional style for combining disparate operational elements on this particular subventure.

Traditional and even recently reengineered business models will not survive long; that's just the reality of a flattened world. The time-honored practice of listening to your customers for new ideas won't get you that leapfrog product or service because the customer doesn't necessarily anticipate the future. The existing market won't have the disruptive suggestion you're searching for because they want stability, too. This is why, as Chesbrough and Christensen have cautioned, the incumbent gets surprised.

Even if you ask your major customers, they will tell you to keep giving them that proverbial mimeograph machine. An invention alone without the innovative construct has no real value, however. To stay with the mimeograph machine analogy, no one will buy a $50,000 Xerox machine when a perfectly good mimeograph machine exists. But if they can lease it per usage, that changes the whole equation. This distinction is critical in understanding the difference between a great idea and an innovative construct that can open new markets. That is the now seemingly simple teaching of Christensen and Chesbrough—even your customers don't know when they want the next great thing.

Inspiring an environment in which a brainchild like Post-It® notes can be brought to life requires CEOs to ensure that a creative atmosphere permeates every aspect of their organization. 3M's Post-It® notes are the billion-dollar byproduct of management commitment to the value of free thinking. Granting employees time to engage in scientific experimentation may sound like a new thing, but it's basically letting people engage in a random walk.

It is those random walks that spark the rich associative process that leads to innovation. As a global technology leader, you must understand how to train your organization to identify disruptive technology from anywhere and decide how to link your company's complementary R&D to it. At the same time, you must determine what style of workforce and compensation structure will allow people to support that type of thinking. A CEO must also decide what kind of geopolitical role his or her corporation's country of origin and its economic policy plays in relation to all this.

The only way this transformation in leadership and culture at technology companies will take place is if everyone—including stakeholders—sees it as a business opportunity. Perhaps the ultimate innovation would be an innovative financial model that would account for and reward creativity and imagination. For example, a company might create a separate set of books or even stock—GE green might attract certain types of investors over regular GE stock.

One thing is certain: The revolutionary approach of the open innovation model is not without risk. But as Sir Francis Bacon observed, "He that will not apply new remedies must expect new evils, for time is the greatest innovator."

In closing, I deliver to you on stone tablets my Five Simple Commandments for Managing the Enduring Tech Company:

1. Make sure your incentive structure lets scientists build on other people's technology with an equal reward as if they had invented it in house.
2. Be cognizant that your archrival in one field may be your key technology partner in another product line.
3. Don't panic when you see a great national technology economy merging like a Brazil, India, or China. See only opportunity. Don't fear the danger. Learn to work with a gift.
4. If you do not understand it, that does not make it unimportant.
5. Governments, regulators, and stakeholders of all types are already demanding the longer view. If the lowest common denominator of the short view is to be found in a Houston courtroom, why not anticipate society's rewards for the company that builds transformative value for today and tomorrow?

PART 2

INTELLECTUAL PROPERTY MANAGEMENT

2

The IP Toolkit: Maximizing Business Value from Intellectual Property

Edmund Walsh

The early 1980s marked the beginning of the modern era of intellectual property (IP). In the prior era, IP rights were distrusted, being equated with monopolies, which were viewed as "evil." As a result, IP rights were often not enforced; there was no predictability, and IP rights were not a tool on which businesses could rely.

By the early 1980s, perceptions of IP had changed. The federal circuit court was established to hear appeals from all patent cases, with the hope of creating more predictability in patent enforcement. Along with the predictability came a willingness by the courts to recognize and enforce the value of IP.

Businesses responded by attaching greater importance to IP. Many began to affirmatively plan IP strategies. Early strategies were basic, focusing on either offensive or defensive use of IP, meaning that IP either would be used to block competition or to deter competitors contemplating enforcing their IP rights. With the increased utilization of IP, strategies were developed with the intent to extract value specifically focused on "mining" existing portfolios.

More recently, there has been a recognition that value can be increased by integrating IP and business strategy. Following are some rules for identifying the value of IP within an organization and methods of capturing that value.

The First Rule of Value: Intellectual Property Doesn't Do Anything (on Its Own)

IP owners must take *action* to turn their IP into value. An IP strategy that ends with acquiring patents or other IP, without accounting for how the IP will be used, is unlikely to be successful. There are two facets to action. First, IP is merely a right to exclude others. Action is needed for the IP rights to have any practical significance. Second, exercising the right to exclude—standing alone—harms others but does not generate value for the IP owner. There is more that needs to be done to capture a benefit to the IP owner from the exercise of the right to exclude.

The Nature of IP Rights

There are multiple types of IP "tools" that a business can use. Each tool has different characteristics, but they have in common that each can be used to exclude others from some action. They differ in the precise actions that can be excluded.

Patents are often the most valuable tool in the IP tool kit. A utility patent is a grant from the government of the legal right to exclude others from making, using, officering for sale, selling, or importing an invention. An *invention* can broadly be considered anything under the sun made by humans, including traditional machines, chemical compositions, industrial processes, and less traditional inventions, such as software, business methods, and genetically altered nonhuman life forms. Copyrights are another tool, providing their owners the right to exclude others from copying or performing their "works," such as books, movies, music, software, blueprints, and instruction manuals. Trade secrets provide a right to exclude the use of secret information if it has been wrongfully obtained. Trademarks represent the right to exclude others from using product names or slogans in connection with competing products.

However, the right to exclude does cause exclusion. In the United States, as in most countries, the government does not get involved in enforcing the rights to exclude, except in very limited ways. In some cases, government officials may seize infringing products. There are also criminal penalties for infringing some forms of intellectual property rights.[1] Theoretically, the government could move on its own initiative to stop infringement of IP rights. However, as a practical

---

[1]*See, e.g.*, 18 USC §§1831–1839 ("The Economic Espionage Act," making it a crime to misappropriate trade secrets and giving the attorney general the authority to seek injunctive relief in civil actions or fines up to $10 million and jail terms up to 15 years in criminal actions.); 17 U.S.C. §506 (making willful copyright violations a crime); 15 USC §1124 (requiring the Customs Service to exclude from importation into the United States goods with infringing trademarks, and allowing trademark owners to notify the Customs Service of their trademarks); Digital Millennium Copyright Act 18 USC §1343 (providing criminal penalties for circumventing copyright protection mechanisms); Interstate Transportation of Stolen Property Act 18 USC §§2314, 2315; and unauthorized computer access provisions of the Computer Fraud and Abuse Act of 1986 18 USC §1030.

matter, the government leaves enforcement of rights to IP owners. If the government does use its power to enforce IP rights, it is usually the result of urging and substantial assistance from the IP owner. On a more pragmatic level, the government's role is limited to providing legal mechanisms for IP owners to enforce their exclusive rights.

Of course, resorting to legal mechanisms to enforce IP rights does not always involve seeking product seizures or criminal sanctions. Less than 5% of IP enforcement is criminal.[2] Legal action usually involves a civil suit seeking damages and/or an injunction.

Sometimes the IP owner does not have to affirmatively enforce its IP rights to cause a change in behavior by others or may not need to pursue the matter to a court verdict. Fewer than 2% of civil suits alleging IP infringement are resolved by a court verdict.[3] A large percentage are actually disposed of by private settlement.

Moreover, the possibility that an IP owner will enforce the right to exclude by suing for infringement may be enough to cause others to change their behavior. Many companies perform patent clearance studies as they design products and may decline to introduce a product or change its design when the study finds IP rights that could be enforced to block the products. Likewise, due diligence prior to an investment in a company typically includes an effort to assess IP risks to the company, and investors may shy away from investing in companies that run too high a risk of infringing the IP rights of others.

However, others changing their behavior to avoid the risk of IP enforcement does not itself generate value for the owner of the IP rights. A willingness to enforce IP rights is just the beginning of what is needed to extract value from the intellectual property. Somehow, the exclusionary effect of IP must be coupled with a business action of the IP owner in order to generate value.

Business Actions that Generate Value

A traditional way to generate value from the exclusionary rights provided by IP is to use those rights to block competition to the IP owner's own products or services. When a business sells a product or service based on the intellectual property, excluding competitors may translate into more sales or higher margins

[2]Motivans, Mark. *Intellectual Property Theft, 2002*. NCJ 205800, October 2004. Available online at http://www.ojp.usdoj.gov/bjs/pub/pdf/ipt02.pdf.

[3]Id.

on the same amount of sales. Even with this relatively straightforward application of intellectual property, the IP by itself is not generating value for its owner. Rather, it is the business action—selling products or services—that captures the value.

Another traditional approach to extracting value from IP is to license the IP rights in exchange for monetary payments. License payments provide an obvious mechanism to convert the exclusionary action IP into benefit for the IP owner. Again, the IP itself does not generate value; rather, it is the action of finding a licensee and entering into a license agreement.

There is an inherent conflict between licensing and enforcement that makes successful implementation of licensing programs difficult. If competitors were licensed, they could not be excluded. Because selling a product often generates more profit than can be collected in royalties if a competitor sells the same product, many businesses had a strong bias against licensing programs. To resolve this conflict, views on licensing programs evolved to focus on surplus or noncore IP. Such programs are premised on the idea that businesses, particularly large companies with big portfolios, likely have some IP, particularly patents, which are not valuable to the owner's business, but could be much more valuable to another company. By mining the portfolio for these nuggets of value, a greater return on the IP can be obtained.

Beyond Portfolio Mining

Intellectual property licensing has received much attention following stories of the large fees collected by companies such as IBM. At first blush, portfolio mining seems like an excellent way to maximize value. The numbers make a compelling case for portfolio mining. Companies are being granted patents at record rates, leading to a buildup of the number of patents in force. Exhibit 2.1 shows that the number of U.S. utility patents in force has nearly doubled in the last 20 years, with most of that growth coming in the last ten years.[4] Many companies have large patent portfolios, often for no clearly defined purpose. While portfolio mining presents an excellent alternative to latency, such an action should have more clearly defined business objectives beyond the collection of licensing fees.

[4]Data obtained from the U.S. Patent and Trademark Office Web site at www.uspto.gov. Several simplifying assumptions were made to create Exhibit 2.1. It was assumed that patents have a 17-year life, if all maintenance fees are paid. It was also assumed that patents expired for failure to pay either the 4-, 8-, or 12-year maintenance fee at a rate of about 15%, 20%, and 17%, respectively.

EXHIBIT 2.1 U.S. Patents in Force

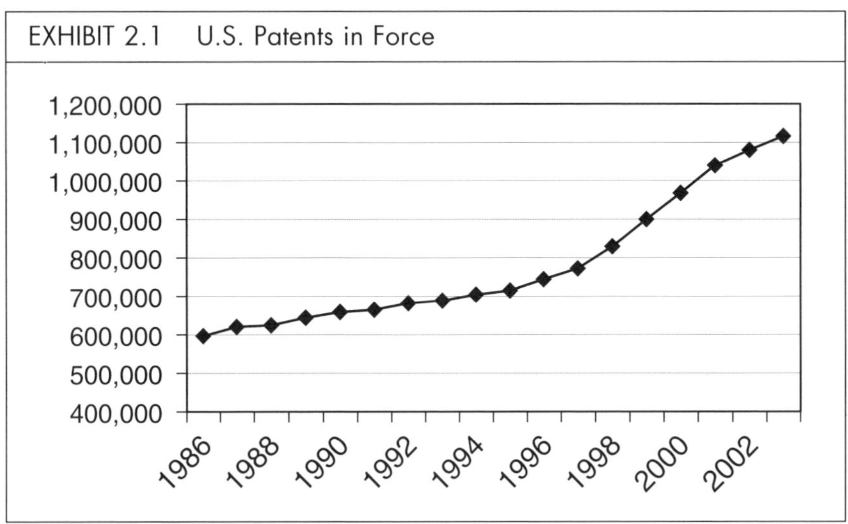

Portfolio mining is not without a downside. Every request by a patent holder for license payments carries with it an implied threat of legal action if the payments are not made. Even though a small percentage of licensing disputes result in the filing of litigation, and an even smaller percentage result in walking up the courthouse steps, the costs of litigation can be substantial.[5] The cost of defending a patent infringement suit has been estimated at $2 million to $4.5 million.[6] In addition, patent litigation consumes the time and attention of a company's most creative employees, exacting a high opportunity cost.

The cost of acquiring and maintaining a patent portfolio can also be cost sink. Exhibit 2.2 shows how expenses of developing a portfolio by filing 100 patents per year build over time. In the first year, there is only the expense of filing that year's patent applications. In subsequent years, there is the same cost for filing new patent applications in addition to the expenses incurred prosecuting or maintaining patents previously filed. In addition, the global nature of today's economy makes it necessary for patents to be filed in other countries.

[5]The American Intellectual Property Law Association (AIPLA) Economic Survey 2003 found that parties to patent infringement suit spent on average $2 million, inclusive of all costs, when there was between $1 million and $25 million at risk.

[6]Varian, Hal. "A Patent that Protects a Better Mousetrap Spurs Innovation," *New York Times*, October 21, 2004.

EXHIBIT 2.2 Cost of a Portfolio (100 Patents per Year)

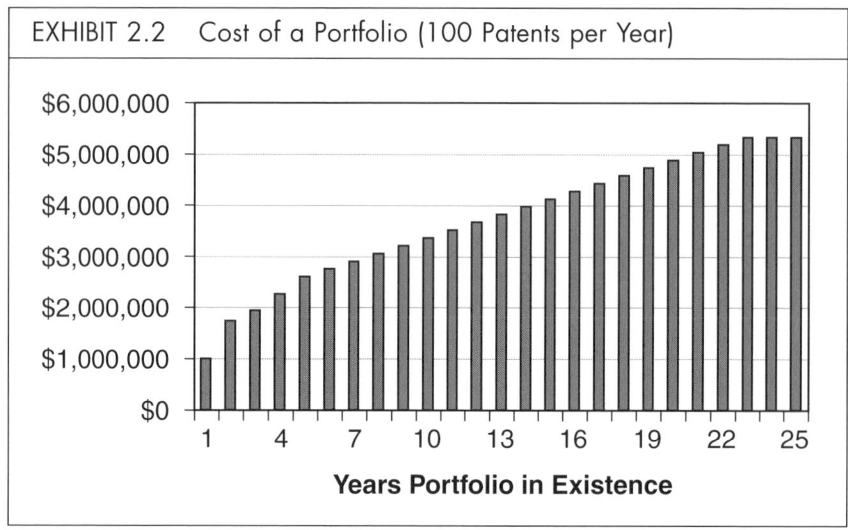

Patents outside the United States can add substantial cost, most of which is incurred in the years following the filing of a U.S. patent.[7]

IBM, distinguished as the leader in generating licensing revenue (over $1.5 billion per year), has also been the top patent recipient for many years, averaging over 2,500 patents per year.[8] While IBM's licensing revenue sounds impressive, Exhibit 2.2 puts into context the cost of maintaining its massive patent portfolio, without considering the $5 billion annual research and development (R&D) costs required to generate the underlying technology on which the patents are based.[9] This clearly illustrates that amassing an IP portfolio in the

[7] Exhibit 2.2 includes many simplifying assumptions. It is assumed that filing a U.S. application costs $10,000, with additional costs of $4,000 to prosecute the application over three years. Exhibit 2.2 assumes that foreign patents are filed to correspond to 30% of the applications filed in the United States. It is assumed that when foreign patents are filed corresponding to a U.S. patent application, they are filed in three countries at a cost of $10,000 over five years in each. It is additionally assumed that every patent has a maintenance cost of $800 per year. The exhibit does not show savings that may be realized by abandoning patents or applications that are found to have no value. Many companies with large patent portfolios do some form of "pruning." Patents in force are periodically reviewed, and those judged to be unsuitable—based on whatever criteria the company uses to measure "suitability"—are abandoned to avoid further costs. But, even with pruning, the costs of maintaining a portfolio can be substantial.

[8] IBM was the top recipient of U.S. patents in 2001, with 3,411; in 2000, with 2,886; in 1999, with 2,756; in 1998, with 2,657; in 1997, with 1,724; and in 1996, with 1,867. *Source:* USPTO *Patenting by Organization* reports, available at ftp://ftp.uspto.gov/pub/taf/.

[9] IBM had RD&E expenses of $4,750 million in 2002, $4,986 million in 2001 and $5,084 million in 2000. IBM 2002 form 10-K, p. 90.

hopes of reaping a windfall from licensing royalties is unlikely to be a winning business strategy.

While portfolio mining or even a strategy of developing technology to license can generate revenue, the real question is whether utilizing the IP in a different way could create more value. In fact, IBM gets more value from its IP by integrating it into its business. IBM has a business strategy of differentiating itself from its competitors through innovation and leveraging its investments in R&D in other business actions.[10] For example, IBM's patents played a role in over $30 billion worth of original equipment manufacturing (OEM) agreements.[11]

The Second Rule of Value: Rational People Don't Sue Themselves

Companies often build IP portfolios by protecting IP in their own products. Such a strategy runs the risk of missing the mark. Often, more value can be generated with patents on *competitors'* products. After all, there is likely more to be gained by suing a competitor than suing oneself.

For those companies that select inventions to patent based on whether the patents cover technology being actively utilized in their products, the strategy is not entirely irrational—it just reflects a narrow view of value. The objective in building a patent portfolio should be to get patents on inventions that are valuable. In practice, companies are limited to patenting things they know about. Therefore, businesses are limited to patenting things at the intersection of what they know and what they believe has value. Product development efforts at many companies will be focused at this same intersection of knowledge and value. In addition, many companies are unlikely to assert their patents unless goaded into action by a competitor who has copied their products. Thus, the technology used in a company's own products is a good starting point for building a valuable patent portfolio.

But a broader view of value is required to maximize value from IP. A vibrant business should generate IP beyond what is reflected as features in its own products. A business cannot turn every valuable idea conceived by its employees into a product it makes. A business often lacks the resources to develop or manufacture multiple products simultaneously or may already be committed to a product strategy and is unable or unwilling to introduce other products that are inconsistent with the strategy. Yet ideas not incorporated into products may well be as useful as the ideas built into products and are a source of valuable IP.

---

[10] IBM 2002 form 10-K, p. 45.

[11] http://www.research.ibm.com/resources/news/20000111_patents99.shtml.

Threats and Opportunities

More generally, IP should be aligned with the threats it can diffuse or opportunities it can generate. Valuable IP that is not directly incorporated into a business's products may be generated during work that is collateral to product design. A business may generate valuable IP in the process of exploring ways for customers to use its products or ways for vendors to make components it will buy. As another example, process-related ideas or technology used in the design or manufacture of products may be a key source of value for a business. And all IP may not be in the form of technology applicable to products. A business may get substantial value from nontechnical information, such as where to buy components or who is willing to buy its products. Opportunities to obtain IP in these areas will be overlooked if a business has too narrow a view of IP.

However, an overly expansive view of what IP should be protected carries with it the risk that the IP portfolio will be diluted by patents that are never needed by the business. To avoid this pitfall, the IP program should seek to consider the full range of IP, but focus on the IP that can generate value for the business.

In cases in which there is a substantial threat of product copying, a product-focused IP portfolio would provide value. But the largest threats to a business may not come from companies who copy products. For example, a product that meets customer needs in a different way may pose a greater competitive threat. A manufacturer of transparency film for making slides used in business presentations likely loses more customers to manufacturers of projectors that can be attached to computers than it loses to other manufacturers of transparency film. In this case, building an IP portfolio to exclude others from copying the product, rather than using IP to control the solution of the ultimate customer need, results in a portfolio that does not address the most serious threats to the business.

Sometimes a patent portfolio focused on a company's own products will not deliver business value because customers do not make purchase decisions based on differentiated products. In some markets, purchase decisions are based purely on price, or presale or postsale service may drive the purchase decision. Other times, a company's reputation as a trusted manufacturer of quality products or its ability to put products on the market quickly once a need is identified may be more significant in generating value for the business than being able to exclude others from copying its product features.

In cases such as these, where the largest threat to the business is not from competitors who offer products with similar features, using IP to exclude competitors from selling such products does not maximize value. Other tools from the IP toolkit would be more effective at adding value to the business. Where reputation of the supplier matters, a vigorous trademark program may be the primary focus of an IP program. Where time to market matters, value is likely being generated by process knowledge within the company. Information about the infrastructure used to design and release products or the list of the suppliers and subcontractors that can respond rapidly could be the critical enablers for the company's business. These are things that are better protected with a trade-secret program.

To maximize the value that can be obtained from IP, it is necessary to have a broad view of how the IP tools may be used for business advantage. The goal is to obtain and apply IP to defeat a threat to the way the business generates value.[12]

The Spectrum of Business Models

There is a spectrum of business models, and integrating IP into a business may mean different things depending on the business model used. At one end of the spectrum are companies that acquire IP for no reason other than to license it. Their only product is IP itself. Rambus is a company that develops semiconductor memory interfaces and gets over 90% of its revenue from licensing those interfaces to companies that manufacture semiconductor chips.[13] In 2002, Rambus had revenues of nearly $100 million and profits of $24 million.[14]

But these results are not without risks and other factors that may make others unwilling or unable to duplicate them. A Virginia jury found Rambus guilty of fraud by participating in setting standards for memory chips, secretly patenting features that would likely be used by those implementing the standards, and then using those patents to collect licensing fees as the standards were implemented. Fortunately for Rambus, this finding was overturned on appeal—but not because Rambus was innocent of the acts of which it was accused. Rather, the appeals court held that Rambus's conduct did not meet the technical definition of fraud because the standard-setting group had not

[12]IP can also be used to create an opportunity for the business to generate value. However, the thought process is the same. An opportunity is created by diffusing a threat to the way the business wants to generate value.

[13]Rambus, Inc., 2002 form 10-K, p. 22.

[14]*Id.*, p. 19.

insisted that participants disclose patenting activity.[15] With standard-setting organizations now sensitized to the issue, it appears that similar strategies will be less successful in the future. Rambus is still facing enforcement action by the Federal Trade Commission for its conduct.[16]

At the other end of the spectrum are companies that are "antiproprietary." They do not want to exclude competitors. Companies that make a standards-based products and those that participate in the open source software movement are generally antiproprietary. Standards and open source software are both premised on there being no restrictions to anyone making or using such products. Seemingly, antiproprietary companies should not want any proprietary rights. But there is a growing recognition that IP rights can be traded for anything of value, which may include standardization or promulgation of open source terms.

Most companies will fall somewhere in between, generating value by selling a mix of products, services, and IP.

Exhibit 2.3 shows this idea as a matrix. In the matrix, every square represents a specific threat to a business using a particular business model. A business may use more than one business model, but no business will use all business models simultaneously. Nor will a business face every type of threat. Thus, for any specific business, it is important to identify the intersections of the business models and the threats that matter to that business (i.e., which squares in the matrix matter for the business). It is at these intersections that IP can provide the most value to the business.

The matrix of Exhibit 2.3 is constructed by listing across the columns ways a business may generate value. The list is not exhaustive but shows common business models. Broadly, a business may make money by selling products, services, or IP itself. Within each of these categories, businesses may take different approaches to win customers or support premium pricing. Exhibit 2.3 shows the possibility that a business sells more products by successfully competing on price. A business may also increase sales or charge more for its product's functionality, quality, or customer convenience, such as flexible delivery schedules. Timing, such as being the first to market with a product, can also generate advantage.

The matrix also lists business models that are not strictly tied to product superiority. In some cases, good marketing is enough to win sales. Other times, personal relationships drive sales. In yet other instances, businesses get sub-

---

[15] *Rambus, Inc. v. Infineon Techs. AG.*, (Fed. Cir. Nos. 01-1449, -1583, -1604, -1641, 02-1174, -1192, January 29, 2003).

[16] *In the Matter of Rambus Incorporated*, File No. 011 0017, FTC Docket No. 9302.

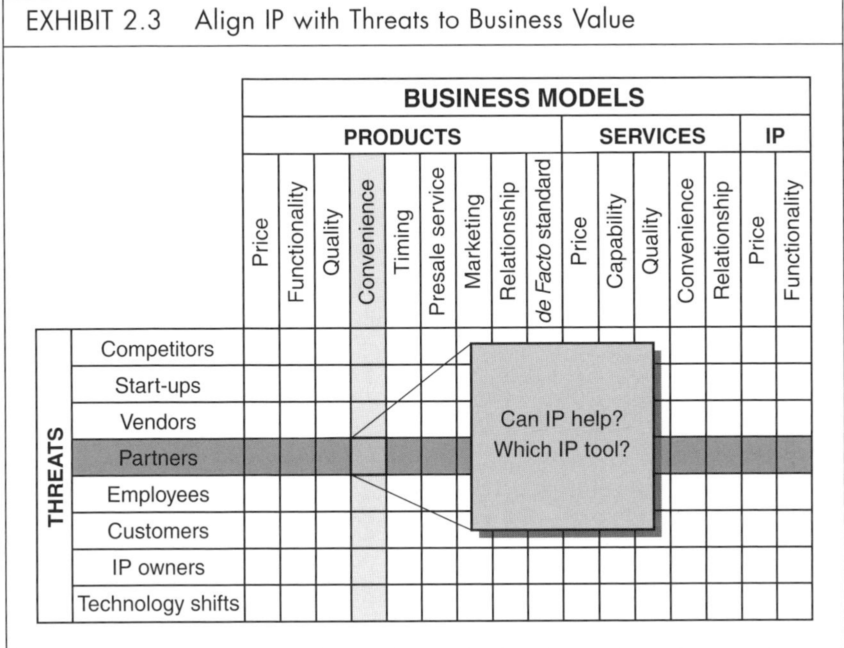

EXHIBIT 2.3 Align IP with Threats to Business Value

stantial advantage from having their products adopted as a de facto standard. For example, in the computer industry, many software packages have come into widespread use and are de facto standards. Because of the need for computer users to share files and data, very few computer users would buy anything but the *de facto* standard, even if a product with superior features were offered. Thus, Exhibit 2.3 includes all these as possible models under which a business will operate.

Analogous business models also exist in which the "product" is actually a service or even IP itself. Examples of ways a business may make money by selling these types of "products" are also listed in the matrix.

The second dimension of the matrix is formed by listing threats to the business down the rows. For example, existing competitors are a common threat to a business. Start-ups are listed as a separate type of threat because competitors of different sizes or varied business strategies may require diverse countermeasures.

Other sources of threats include vendors or technology partners. Vendors have an incentive to maximize their value, which may require actions that do not align with the interests of their customers. They may want to charge premium prices for their products or expand their markets by leveraging their learning in selling to your business in order to sell to others similarly situated (i.e., your competitors). Technology partners also pose a similar threat, though the greater degree of collaboration with technology partners creates greater opportunities for diverging interests.

Not all threats to a business are from people or other businesses. A technology shift could wipe out the need for a product entirely. Less than 30 years ago, vacuum tubes were a thriving product and are now virtually nonexistent because of the technology shift to semiconductors.

The intersections of the business models that generate value for a specific business and the threats to those models are the starting point for decisions around IP. If IP can help defuse the threat, it can bring more value to the business. These intersections where IP can help achieve business advantage define the value equation for the business. The value of IP is maximized by obtaining and using IP effectively against those threats that intersect the business model.

In the example of Exhibit 2.3, a column is highlighted to indicate that the business operates under a model of selling products by offering customer convenience. A row is highlighted to indicate that the major threat to continuing a profitable business comes from development partners. The value equation is maximized by seeking IP that defuses the threat to the business from technology partners.

A situation in which this condition may exist is a business that sells products that do not, standing alone, fully meet a customer need. The full customer solution is provided by combining those products with products offered by a technology partner. In the computer industry, this happens where one company sells a hardware product but relies on another company to provide software to process data captured by the hardware product. The hardware manufacturer has a lot to lose if its software technology partner signs an exclusive license with a competitor. Without access to the software, the hardware product becomes unusable. Loss of access to the software, which could completely end product sales, is a bigger threat than increased competition in the sale of the hardware, which would only reduce sales or profits. In this case, the hardware manufacturer gets more value from IP that excludes the software provider from dealing with competing hardware providers than having patents on its own products.

With the recognition of the magnitude of the threat provided by the technology partner, the hardware supplier can focus on IP tools that may defuse that threat. While the hardware vendor may still seek patents on its product, it may place greater emphasis on patents covering the system made by combining the hardware and software products. Such patents would exclude the software supplier from selling its product, thereby creating leverage for the hardware supplier in a negotiation. Likewise, business method patents relating to the use of the software or patents on the method of controlling the hardware could all create leverage in a negotiation with the software supplier. Quasi-IP protection provided through contracts may also provide value, such as a long-term supply agreement, an exclusive license to the software product, or a noncompetition agreement.

In summary, Exhibit 2.3 provides a graphical depiction of the mind-set for maximizing value. A business must understand its value equation—how IP can generate value to defuse threats to its business model. With this mind-set, the business can then turn its attention to the practical problems of creating an IP position that maximizes its value equation.

The Third Rule of Value: "Patience and Diligence Remove Mountains"—William Penn

An IP program does not generate instant value. Most forms of IP require some time to acquire. The U.S. Patent and Trademark Office typically takes two to three years to grant a patent, and coverage in some foreign countries takes even longer. Years could pass before there are any valid patent rights to enforce.

However, the time to acquire patents is only part of the reason why an IP program cannot deliver value immediately. Intellectual property is premised on the creation of something new. A patent requires an invention. A trademark requires the creation of a product name or image that becomes recognizable by customers. A trade secret requires the creation of information that is protected as a secret. It takes time for such "creation" to ensue.

Further, just making the creation is only the first step in having valuable IP. Because IP rights provide only the right to exclude, they do not have value until others recognize the risk of being excluded. Intellectual property rights in a creation do not become valuable until another business either copies the creation or recognizes the benefits of it and wants to use it. Therefore, no matter how clever a creation is, there is inherently a delay until IP rights in it are valuable.

One practical implication of this inherent delay is that building an IP portfolio takes patience and a long-term commitment. But an equally important lesson is that when measuring value, that value should be measured in the marketplace as it will exist sometime in the future—possibly three to five years. Market trends are more important than current competitive struggles.

While the rule may seem simple, it is difficult to apply in practice. In making value judgments, people are more likely to think in the comfortable framework of what they know rather than to speculate about the future. It is difficult to integrate technical views about what will be possible with marketing views about what customers will want or the marketplace will be like. It is easier to think about the features in a product that has just been released than about what customers will want or competitors may be selling.

Creating a future-based mind-set is not unparalleled. The revolution in product quality during the 1980s was based on just such a change in mind-set. Businesses had to abandon the comfort of building products to meet concrete manufacturing specifications and instead learn to think about building products to meet latent requirements—requirements that their customers did not even know they had.[17]

In the same way that a focus on future requirements greatly increased the quality of manufactured products, a focus on how IP will be used under future market conditions can significantly increase the quality of an IP portfolio and increase the chance that IP will have value when the time comes to use it.

Top-Down and Bottom-Up Execution

The most difficult part about creating an IP strategy that maximizes value often is getting individuals to take the time to consider the possibilities. The value of IP generated today is always in the future. But individuals are always going to be faced with many short-term and immediate demands.

Creating a mind-set of IP value maximization requires integration across the entire business organization. High-level management support is essential to make individuals feel comfortable diverting even a small amount of attention from immediate problems to focus on long-term value. Further, a value equation must be communicated to those who have the ability to influence the generation and capture of IP. Of particular importance is the need to foster communication among those who define business strategy, those who develop technology, and those who execute on the day-to-day business operations.[18]

---

[17]Shiba, Shoji, Graham, Alan, and Walden, David. *A New American TQM: Four Practical Revolutions in Management* (Portland, OR: Productivity Press, 1993), pp. 1–14.

[18]A discussion on the theory of implementing management initiatives or even the various organizational models that may be used is beyond the scope of this chapter. Initiatives can be driven top-down. The initiative could be centralized or decentralized. Many companies, particularly larger ones, have a director of IP or person with a similar title who is primarily responsible for driving such an initiative. Many smaller companies have a visionary who is influential in the business who drives the initiative. But initiatives can also be driven bottom-up. Likewise, the initiative could be driven with procedures and infrastructure to audit and enforce compliance, or it could be based on communicating the desired result and empowering individuals to select how to achieve those results. The most effective method of implementation for any business will likely depend on the character of that business and its experiences implementing other management initiatives.

But each piece of IP is inherently unique. No matter how much top-level planning or strategizing is done, there is ultimately a need to select specific inventions, ideas, or other creations to protect and to follow through. Selection and protection of IP at the tactical level involves detailed knowledge of technology, business, and the law. Once the right mind-set is created, it must be applied in a series of tactical decisions throughout the life cycle of IP. It should be applied during both the acquisition and the utilization of IP. The precise way in which it will be applied depends on many factors, not the least of which is the personality of the business.

For businesses that have a reactive approach to IP strategy, the value equation can be used to filter out IP that is not worth the investment. At many stages in the life cycle of IP, decisions are made about continuing or pursuing IP protection. For example, many businesses collect invention disclosures from their engineers, and an invention review committee decides what to patent. The value equation can be used to bring focus to the work of the invention review committee in prioritizing inventions. In this way, investment can be made in only the most valuable ones.

Similar decisions are made throughout the life cycle of the patent. Decisions must be made about whether the expense of foreign patents is warranted or whether to pay periodic maintenance fees to keep a granted patent in force. Applying the value equation at each decision point can lead to the best investment of the limited resources available for maintaining an IP portfolio.

Analogous decisions are made about other forms of IP. For example, a business may be faced with a choice of imposing restrictions on its manufacturing process to increase secrecy or losing its trade-secret rights in the process. Knowing the value that the trade secret may generate will allow such decisions to be made rationally.

For businesses that have a more proactive personality about IP, the value equation can actually be used to guide the acquisition of IP. Where employees are not disclosing invention or other creation leading to IP that maximizes the value equation, a business can actively seek out such inventions. Or the business may be even more proactive and encourage the creation of inventions that will lead to valuable IP.

An even more proactive approach is possible. The patent law does not require a working model of an invention to be built before it can be patented. Thus, patents can be filed on purely theoretical inventions, and some companies claim to be able to generate inventions to meet a specific demand.[19]

[19]*See, e.g.*, IPCapital Group, Inc. *Invention on Demand*. http://www.ipcapitalgroup.com/services/consulting/create.htm.

Corresponding choices also apply to the utilization of IP. The value equation can be used as a guide to decide how or if IP should be used in a particular circumstance. For example, knowing that IP was acquired to be used against certain types of threats helps in evaluating a request for a license to the IP. A business would probably not want to license the IP to any company that represented such a threat, but the business would want to generate revenue where granting a license would not diminish the value of the IP against the threats to the business.

Or the IP can be used more proactively. For example, a business may train its purchasing organization to use IP as leverage in negotiations with vendors or technology partners, or the sales force may be trained to use IP in the selling of products.

Each business will have its own ways to apply the value equation, but the common objective is to use the value equation to define the kind of IP the business can use to generate value and to set up an infrastructure to acquire and utilize IP in that fashion.

Conclusion

Maximizing the business value of IP comes from having a broad view of the way IP can be used. The views that lead to traditional strategies, such as of portfolio mining or product-based patenting programs, should be broadened in two respects. First, the ways in which IP may be used should be evaluated. Threats and opportunities to the business, beyond the traditional notion of competitors selling similar products, should be considered. Second, the relevant time frame should be broadened. A business should look into the future when the IP it is investing in now will be available for use. This broader perspective should be integrated into the business and guide decisions regarding the acquisition and utilization of IP to maximize value.

3

Harvesting New Intellectual Assets: The Role of Business Method Patents and Trade Secrets in Strategic IP Management

Karl Jorda and Wayne Jaeschke

The Fusion of Marketing, Technology, and IP in Integrated IP Management

The harvesting and evaluation of "inventions" are often confined to scientists and intellectual property (IP) or patent attorneys, with little marketing participation. This is especially true in large organizations for reasons that are partly philosophical, namely, the predilection that inventing is confined to the technological fields and patent protection can be granted only on technology innovation. However, the reasons are also practical. Business and marketing people conduct different activities at locations and schedules at variance to scientific personnel, and communication among these functions is sporadic. Such a disconnect is accepted practice and not likely to change in the absence of some incentive. A change in culture would occur if management were to be persuaded that valuable and patentable innovation could be extracted from sources beyond the traditional research and development (R&D) setting and that the resulting IP could be enforceable in the future.

Innovative entrepreneurs often are successful when there is a natural fusion or integration of the inventor and market mover in one person or close collaboration within a small group. Entrepreneurs generally work quickly and effectively with IP counsel in protecting their "brainchildren." As companies grow and become compartmentalized, communication becomes less intimate between the business and technical functions, especially where IP protection duties are abdicated by business and assigned principally to the technical unit.

Business method patents (BMPs) provide a good example of a natural fusion of business, technical, and IP functions. Adoption of this IP tool by *Fortune* 500 companies whose core businesses are most readily adapted to business method coverage may provide a helpful model for others who are examining the potential benefits of a closer fusion of marketing/business, technical, and IP functions.

The BMP was pioneered in the financial and e-commerce industries. Prior to the federal circuit court's decision in *State Street Bank v. Signature Financial Group*,[1] which demolished legal barriers and held that business processes are patent-eligible subject matter where a tangible or concrete result is achieved, business methods were deemed unenforceable. Large financial institutions, such as banks and stock exchanges, have since been required to pay large sums of money for employing methodology within claims asserted by nonuser patentees (also known as "patent trolls"). Such activity has created a widespread pejorative association and characterization of BMPs as trash.

Leading *Fortune* 500 innovators, nevertheless, have quietly embraced business method patenting for the protection of their core business interests. Among the major users of the business method format are leading software, electronics, imaging, communications, and document management organizations whose business models are most readily adapted to the fusion of marketing, technical, and IP functions. Some of the major users are identified in Exhibit 3.1.

Other established product and service companies have been more cautious, perhaps even subtle, in their adoption of BMPs to protect their core interests. Among the latter group are manufacturers and marketers of construction and farm equipment, automobiles, chemicals, pharmaceuticals, and personal care products. A cross section of these organizations is identified in Exhibit 3.2.

Many companies are simply nibbling at the edges until they determine whether the business method model is sufficiently tasty to justify a bigger bite.

---

[1]927 F. Supp. 502, 38 USPQ2d 1530 (D. Mass. 1996).

EXHIBIT 3.1 Major BMP Users

Company	*Patents*	*Applications*	*BMP Examples*
Accenture	42	34	**6,895,383** Overall risk in a system
General Electric	52	20	**6,901,406** Accessing multi-dimensional customer data
Hewlett Packard	96	37	**6,865,548** Virtual publishing
Intel	61	12	**6,850,899** Online purchases using a rule-based transferable shopping basket
Kodak	41	43	**6,938,004** Providing photofinishing credit
Lucent	60	6	**6,744,891** Ensuring royalty payments for data delivered over a telephone network
Microsoft	108	148	**6,185,534** Modeling emotion and personality in a computer user interface
Oracle	22	29	**20050137981** Personalization and identity management
Pitney Bowes	257	131	**6,517,265** Loss of funds prevention for postage meters and personal computer meters
Siemens	48	61	**6,839,678** Computerized system for conducting medical studies
Sony	86	105	**6,938,006** Selling tangible and intangible products
Xerox	45	63	**20010008997** Element organization support and storage medium

The numbers for the patents and patent applications were obtained in a course of the online patent search by the U.S. Classification Index 705 designated for business method patents (Federal Register, Vol. 66, No. 108, June 5, 2001, p. 30168) and also by the key words "business" and/or "marketing" in the claim(s) language. The BMP patents are since 1998 and the applications since the inception of publishing applications to 2004.

As leaders begin to emerge and enforce their business and marketing method claims in selected fields, competitors need to reexamine available strategies for the protection and defense of their own core businesses.

EXHIBIT 3.2 Other BMP Users

Company	*Examples*
Bayer Healthcare	**20040073464** Data management in patient diagnoses and treatment
BASF	**20050015297** Marketing photopolymeric sleeves for flexographic printing
Becton Dickinson	**6,294,999** Monitoring patient compliance with medication regimens
Black & Decker	**20050187783** Personalized combo kit of tools and accessories
Cargill	**20030195792** Method of animal feed market analysis
Caterpillar	**20040073468** Managing a fleet of machines
Dana Corp.	**20020087345** Tracking user certification and training
Deere and Co.	**20050004682** Management of the processing of an agricultural product
Dow	**6,345,259** Integrating business and manufacturing environments
DuPont	**20040054633** Electronic order entry of photomask orders
Ecolab	**6,576,298** (claim 95) Reduced-risk food packaging
Eli Lilly	**5,898,586** Method for administering clinical trial material
General Motors	**6,405,106** Enhanced vehicle controls through wireless information transfer
Halliburton	**6,931,378** Acquiring data to update a geophysical database
Honeywell	**6,574,581** Profile-based method for deriving a temperature setpoint
L'Oreal	**20030065636** Use of artificial intelligence in providing beauty
Monsanto	**6,865,556** Recovering licensing fees from growers of seeds or plants
Procter & Gamble	**6,862,585** System and method for managing product development
Rohm and Haas	**6,882,980** Chemical product commerce network
Steelcase	**6,002,855** 3-D spatial graphical user interface for querying and manipulating a relational database management system for order-entry applications
3M Innovative Properties	**6,780,220** Generating pollution credits while processing reactive metals

EXHIBIT 3.2 *Continued*

Company	*Examples*
United Technologies	**20020188494** Method and apparatus for managing an operation
Ortho Pharmaceutical	**5,509,064** Call routing and handling system for conveying confidential medical test result information to anonymous callers
McNeil-PPC	**20060020175** Method for managing deselection of medicine

See note under Exhibit 3.1, which is applicable.

State Street Bank Leads to an Explosion of Financial and E-Commerce Patents

Prior to the *State Street Bank* decision, previous courts held that methods of doing business were nonstatutory subject matter and, thus, not entitled to patent protection. The landmark opinion of Judge Giles Sutherland Rich caused the innovative fires already smoldering in the financial and e-commerce fields to erupt in a blaze of patent-protected innovation. Patents granted under U.S. Patent and Trademark Office (USPTO) Class 705, which contains most of the business model and e-commerce patents, "more than tripled" for several years following the *State Street Bank* decision.[2] Activity reached its peak of over 8,000 applications in 2001 and leveled off at about 6,000 published applications per year for 2002–2004. However, BMPs that were actually granted following examination ranged only between 900 and 1,000 from 2000 to 2004,[3] following the initial surge.

The Internet-related activity associated with prominent business method protection fueled an enormous increase in the stock price of many venture companies. An article in *Forbes* painted a picture of Walker Digital's Jay Walker as

[2]Stobbs, Gregory A. *Business Method Patents* (NY; Aspen Law & Business, copyright 2002).

[3]Basis is search of PTO site for 2002–2004 and Wagner's paper, page 4, 2001.

a modern-day Edison, heralding his ownership of 12 BMPs with 240 pending. *Forbes* pointed out that two of Walker's patents protected the name-your-own-price airline ticket business of Priceline.com.

Building on precedent, the 3–2 decision of the USPTO Board of Patents and Interference Appeals in *Ex Parte Lundgren* held that there is no judicially recognized separate "technological arts" test that a patent examiner can properly apply to deny a patent. The decision further confirms that a "technical effect" is not required for patent eligibility under U.S. patent law. Leading IP experts have expressed diametrically opposed opinions as to the potential impact of the Board's decision. Many say it properly opens the door to patenting innovation of all persons, thereby fueling inventive genius that might save the world. On the other side, experts contend that *Lundgren* might create a massive flood of junk claims that would sink the USPTO.

The Debate over Patenting Business Methods and Nontechnical Subject Matter

Whether the holding of *Lundgren* and removal of the technology connection from patents will withstand scrutiny over time is a matter of debate. Meanwhile, applicants applying for BMPs will be encouraged to seek even broader claims from the USPTO, not limited to computer enablement. Courts are not bound by the rulings of the USPTO Board, and the issues will be hotly contested in litigation, for example, based on the dissent in *Lundgren* and arguments on the side of State Street Bank in their losing battle.

Jeffersonian Liberal Encouragement of Innovation

Both *State Street Bank* and *Lundgren* clearly encourage creative genius beyond technical fields, including innovations in marketing, finance, human resources, e-commerce, and beyond. Judge Giles Sutherland Rich struggled to find that the data processing claims of Signature's patent 5,193,056 were within a statutory class of patentable subject matter, yet the result is consistent with the broad-based encouragement of all forms of innovation from our Founding Fathers and Supreme Court precedent:

Article I, Section 8 of the U.S. Constitution gives Congress the power "to promote the progress of science and useful arts by securing for limited times to authors and inventors the exclusive right to their respective writings and discoveries." Thomas Jefferson wrote, "Ingenuity should receive a liberal encouragement." Abraham Lincoln, who was the only president to hold a patent, described the patent system as one of the three most important developments "in the world's history." Authored in part by Judge Giles Sutherland Rich, the 1952 revisions to 35 U.S.C., section 103, clarified that a "flash of genius" is not required for patentability, stating that "patentability shall not be negatived by the manner in which the invention was made."

Further liberal encouragement is found in *Graham v. John Deere*[4] wherein the Supreme Court sanctioned the use of secondary evidence, such as commercial success, to uphold as patentable any invention that is otherwise very close to the prior art. In 1980, the Supreme Court supported fledgling biotechnology research, holding in *Diamond v. Chakrabarty*[5] that microorganisms produced by genetic engineering are not excluded from patent coverage. The decision was handed down, despite strong opposition from the USPTO, which contended that such subject matter was not within the patentable statutory classes. The Court cited reports in back of the 1952 patent revisions that Congress intended patentable subject matter to "include anything under the sun that is made by man." Title 35 U.S.C. 101 includes both inventions and discoveries within patent-eligible subject matter. The Harvard "mouse patent" (U.S. patent no. 4,736,866) is an example of living subject matter that is patentable since it is the result of man-invented genetic manipulation.

These principles of liberal encouragement of innovation underlying the patent laws of the United States provide rationale for the inclusion of business and marketing input and innovation in integrated IP management. On the other side, others might prefer more traditional, technology-based IP scenarios by reason of the uncertainties and concerns described below.

The Doomsday Scenario if Nontechnology Patents Are Not Reined In

The encroachment of business methods, marketing, and nontechnology innovations into the long-established sphere of patent-eligible subject matter is fraught with practical concerns and troublesome to many. Experts believe there

[4]383 U.S. 1 (1966).

[5]0447 U.S. 303 (1980).

are many potentially adverse ramifications, and that Congress, if not the courts, needs to better define and arrest this intrusion. Some of the arguments include:

- Insurmountable difficulties of the USPTO in examining business methods and nontechnical inventions, including lack of examiners skilled in nontechnical arts such as insurance or human resources and the lack of appropriate databases as prior art.
- Unacceptably poor quality of patents granted on business methods, especially in nontechnical fields, which will render highly uncertain the validity and infringement of such patents.
- Huge backlogs of unexamined applications and delays in granting patents that are unacceptable for businesses and ventures because the USPTO is already faced with a deficiency of resources.
- A flood of unwarranted litigation and harassment of legitimate operating enterprises by "trolls" seeking to make a quick buck on hastily constructed patents of doubtful validity, causing a significant drain on business productivity.
- The patent bar will be opened up to nontechnical personnel contrary to USPTO rules.
- A further canyon of disharmony will be opened up between U.S. business methods and nontechnical patents and patents in Europe and Asia. Judge Klaus Melullis of the German federal court leaves no doubt in his paper presented at the Intellectual Property Owners Association's (IPO's) International Judges Conference (October 24–26, 2005) that in his view, BMPs should be limited to circumstances in which there is a nonobvious technical effect at the point of claimed novelty.[6] A contrary view is presented in a 2004 paper by Stefan Wagner of the University of Munich School of Management, in which the author states that "there has been a widespread misconception based on the imprecise wording of ART. 52 of the European Patent Convention (EPC) that the protection of business methods by patents is prohibited in Europe." Wagner identifies numerous patent equivalents in Europe to U.S. Class 705.

The U.S. Supreme Court may soon broadly review the types of subject matter that are eligible for patenting. This was evidenced when the Court agreed to

[6]Mellulis, Klaus. Paper presented at the IPO's International Judges Conference, Washington, D.C., October 24–26, 2005.

review the patentability of a medical test method arising from a 2004 decision of the federal circuit, *Laboratory Corp. of America Holdings v. Metabolite Laboratories, Inc.*[7] Metabolite's patent claim includes "correlating" an elevated level of homocysteine with a vitamin deficiency. Would any doctor who merely thinks about the relationship after looking at test results infringe such a patent? The opinions of the Supreme Court will significantly impact the subject matter eligible for medical and business method claiming in the future.

Litigation of Business Methods

In 1999, in *AT&T v. Excel Communications*, the federal circuit reinforced *State Street Bank* as to the patentability of the business and financial methods claimed in U.S. patent 5,333,184. The Court noted that the criteria of usefulness, concreteness, and tangibility of the claimed invention is decisive for patentability, not the technicality of the underlying invention.

Further in 1999, Amazon.com was granted U.S. patent 5,960,411, covering its "one-click" ordering method. Amazon sued Barnes and Noble, and after a hearing, was granted a preliminary injunction barring Barnes and Noble from conducting online activity during the busy Christmas season. While this action spawned national controversy, the potential value of such patents was indelibly etched into the IP landscape. When Priceline.com sued Microsoft for infringement, it was unable to stop the competing Expedia "name-your-own price" service; however, Microsoft reportedly agreed to pay a royalty.

The value of such patents and related technology has been confirmed by the courts and in numerous settlements. On June 4, 2001, it was announced, essentially on the steps of the courthouse, that Hewlett-Packard would pay Pitney Bowes $400 million for both the imaging technology and rights expressed in U.S. patent 4,386 272. This further illustrates the value of covering technology, via patents and know-how, maintained as trade secrets in an integrated IP strategy.

[7] 370 F.3d 1354 (Fed. Cir. 2004).

Using Business Method Patents to Protect Core Market Interests beyond Finance and E-Commerce

Major Users

Among the major users of business method patenting practices are *Fortune* 500 companies in business communications, document management, electronics, imaging, and software whose business models most readily fit the format of the business method patent. These organizations are creating new processes and methods for communications related to purchasing and selling, document classification and file management, enhanced security of information and currency, and so on. Proprietary hardware or software often forms an integral part of the business method. Unlike fluid flow in the chemical and petroleum industries, business processes involve the flow of information that is not contained in physical conduits. Yet the protection of these "information-flow" processes is as important to assure encouragement and protection of business innovation of the twenty-first century as fluid flow processes were in the twentieth century.

Pitney Bowes owns a large number of BMPs and applications and are a recognized leader in BMP's.[8] The company has transformed from a postage-metering company to a leading provider of a wide range of business office solutions that help companies communicate with their customers. Their innovative methods are well suited to protection by BMPs of USPTO Class 705. Pitney Bowes files counterparts of their U.S. business method claims in the European Patent Office.[9] Angelo Chaclas, deputy general counsel at Pitney Bowes, stated that, "Business method patents are critical to our strategy to maintain our leadership position in this area."

Former director of the USPTO, Q. Todd Dickenson, observed, "The substantial cost of filing, prosecution, and maintenance of these business method patents and applications is justified on the basis of protecting freedom to operate in core areas of interest to ongoing businesses." These patents are key to creating defensive space surrounding products and services on which companies depend for their ongoing profitability. Seldom are these investments justified on speculative interests in potential licensing of third parties, although circumstances often arise wherein such patents may serve as bargaining chips or as the basis for venture activity. Sanjay Prasad, former chief patent counsel at Oracle,

---

[8]USPTO White Pater and Wagner's paper at U of Munich 2004.

[9]*See* Wagner's paper.

confirmed the reliance of core software companies on BMPs to maintain freedom to operate.

Other Users

Many *Fortune* 500 manufacturers of goods and services in chemicals, pharmaceuticals, farm and construction equipment, automobiles, consumer products, and medical equipment are "experimenting" with the use of BMPs. The number of BMPs is small, but published applications suggest that usage is increasing. Chemical and hardware inventions always have been eligible for patent coverage. Hence, there is less incentive to adopt the more controversial BMP format. More subtle or less visible protection is available where BMP claims can be asserted in the same application as traditional product and process claims. The resulting patents and applications are often assigned to a USPTO class other than the main BMP Class 705.

Procter & Gamble (P&G) actively integrates marketing, technical, and IP functions and is forging ahead with BMP coverage of core products. P&G's business method claims relate to marketing of dog food, coffee, and cleaning products. P&G's 6,862,585 patent, identified in Exhibit 3.2, may be of greater interest, however, as it defines a novel method of managing product development. Granted claim 1 could be employed widely in the development of consumer products and illustrates the potential potency of claiming marketing innovation more generally.

The BMP format adds another level of protection of creative market genius that is not limited to specific new compositions, chemical processes, and specified equipment. Here, the innovative process of development itself is claimed. Of course, if such a claim were to be asserted in court, while it is presumed valid, the federal circuit court of appeals would have the last say in interpreting its scope of coverage for infringement. P&G's published BMP application 20030177055, entitled "Virtual Test Market System and Method" further illustrates coverage of creative marketing methodology.

L'Oreal's published 20030065636 application illustrates use of business method claiming in marketing cosmetics and beauty products. According to claim 1 of the L'Oreal application, tailored beauty treatment advice is dispensed to a user by accessing a structured database where personal information from the user is compared with stored, reference data via "an artificial intelligence engine." The method is not limited to specific beauty products. The disclosure of this marketing method, whether granted or not, will assist L'Oreal in defending its core business in beauty products. If granted as a patent, the method could be a concern to competitors in a wide range of marketing activities. L'Oreal's published application could also stimulate others to improve the method or apply it to other markets.

The Bayer Healthcare and Becton Dickinson BMP examples in Exhibit 3.2 illustrate creative methods of tracking patient care and medication. A large backlog exists in the USPTO for the examination of business methods in the medical fields. Rohm and Haas, Monsanto, Dow, DuPont, and BASF are filing business method claims for a range of new marketing activities. Rohm and Haas's 6,882,980 patent relates to a network-implemented method useful for receiving purchase orders for and shipping custom tailored formulations to customers. Monsanto's 6,865,556 patent addresses recovering license fees for their "seeds" business. Dow's 6,345,259 patent merges business and manufacturing inputs. DuPont's 20040054633 application describes a creative solution to order entry in the electronic chemicals business. BASF's 20050015297 application targets improvements of flexographic printing in support of their core polymers business.

Johnson & Johnson affiliates, including Ortho Pharmaceuticals and the McNeil-Merck joint venture, are actively innovating in the management of medical information as shown in Exhibit 3.2. Phil Johnson, J&J's chief patent counsel, commented on the important role of BMPs as follows:

> Information is now at least as valuable to health care as the chemicals and devices that are used to deliver that care. In the future, traditional pre-market clinical tests are unlikely to meet our society's expectations concerning either the detection of rare but serious side effects or the identification of the sub-populations that will best respond to a given treatment. In the future, prescribers will want real time access to the collective experience with a given treatment, hospital administrators will want to understand the operational impacts of that treatment, and payers will want to understand its economics. Driven by these needs, we will experience an explosion of data that will need to analyzed, understood and acted upon. As this trend advances, more efficient business models will evolve that will avoid the costs of ineffective treatments. IP, including business methods IP, will play an important role in this future. Patent-mandated disclosure requirements will force the prompt sharing of vital information and insights, thus advancing our collective understanding. At the same time, the promise of IP protection will stimulate the incremental R&D investment needed to make personalized medicine a reality.

Ecolab's 6,576,298 patent (claim 95) claims innovative business aspects of a food-packaging process said to reduce business risk and insurance costs and illustrates inclusion of business method claims in the same patent with product and process claims. The resulting business method claims were classified by the USPTO outside of business methods Class 705.

Use of business method claiming for marketing innovation is also prevalent among smaller and entrepreneurial businesses. Sherrill and Richard Kelley of Shreveport, Louisiana, were granted U.S. patent 6,349,820 covering a marketing method using a book-shaped device adapted to provide herbs and spices matched to recipes for their use in desired cuisines. B&G Products of Wichita, Kansas, was granted U.S. patent 6,692,260 on a method for marketing automobile fluid replacement services. E-Harmony's U.S. patent 6,735,568, which covers a computerized method for matching people of similar personality traits, further illustrates the potency of merging marketing and IP techniques for the creation and protection of a successful business venture. Even the University of California is getting into the act. The university owns several BMPs, including published application 20030187763, which describes an intelligent interorganizational system for procurement and manufacturing.

In some instances, business method patenting may be the primary tool for covering innovation. However, backup protection is created when business method claims are granted together with conventional machine, composition, or process claims. A court might invalidate claims to the machine or composition itself. Yet patentability and infringement might be upheld for the business or marketing experts. Furthermore, the published disclosure of use of the claimed machine or composition in the marketing context might provide the basis of a successful defense against assertion of a third party's BMP. While recognizing the shortcomings, leading manufacturers are recognizing that business method patenting and claiming may be necessary for protecting their core business interests. William B. Heming, chief patent ounsel at Caterpillar, assessed the situation as follows:

> I recognize that many organizations are filing significant business methods. There is value to be extracted even though we all recognize the difficulties of establishing any new technique. I see parallels to when software first became clearly patentable. A lot of dust in the air and then things settled down. At first, both the PTO and the users are searching for the right way to proceed and struggling with the problems. There is not yet enough experience to know all the answers and that is frustrating. Quality control is clearly a problem in the PTO as examiners gain experience and the right databases are put in place. But like software and other new patent fields that have emerged, business methods may settle out in a positive way. In the meantime, we all must play the field.

Heming's comments emphasize the rationale for an established manufacturing company's employment of business method coverage and the need to "play the field" even though numerous uncertainties exist.

Dovetail Business Method Patents and Trade Secrets

It is certain that an integrated approach to IP coverage is likely to provide the best backup protection. This is no less true where marketing and business innovation are involved. As with filing traditional patent applications, the specification of a BMP must provide the "best mode" known to the inventor at the time of filing and contain sufficient information such that one of ordinary skill could carry out the claimed invention. All later-developed improvements of methods and machines, computers, software, documentation, product development specifications, scale-up engineering and designs, and the like may properly be protected as trade secrets. Many states have adopted provisions of the Uniform Trade Secrets Act wherein financial data and compilations are generally protected if properly maintained as confidential information.

The Role and Value of Trade Secrets in Conjunction with Patents

Literature and presentations on IP strategies, IP valuation, and other IP topics almost always speak to patents and patent portfolios. However, doing so overlooks the fact that legal protection of innovation of any kind, especially in high-tech fields, requires the integration of more than one IP category (i.e., dual or multiple protection). Focusing on patents as the only measure of innovation or vehicle for protection and licensing ignores the fact that they are often valueless or inadequate for commercializing viable products, absent associated, collateral know-how protected by trade secrets.

Professor Jay Dratler, in his book *Intellectual Property Law: Commercial, Creative, and Industrial Property*,[10] was the first one to "tie all the fields of IP together." According to him, from former fragmentation by specialties, intellectual property rights (IPR) are now a "seamless web," due to progress in technology and commerce.

Thus, we now have a unified theory in the IP world, a single field of law with subsets and significant overlap between IP fields. Several IPR are available for the same IP or different aspects of the same IP. Not taking advantage of the overlap misses opportunities or, worse, amounts to "malpractice," according to Professor Dratler.

---

[10]Dratler, Jay. *Intellectual Property Law: Commercial, Creative, and Industrial Property* (New York: Law Journal Seminars Press, 1991).

One IPR category, often patents, may be the center of gravity and more important than others. Other IPR categories are then supplementary but very valuable to cover additional subject matter, strengthen exclusivity, invoke additional remedies in litigation, stand up if a primary IPR becomes invalid, and thus provide synergy and optimize legal protection.

Regarding the importance of trade secrets, James Pooley proclaimed recently: "Forget patents, trademarks and copyrights . . . trade secrets could be your company's most important and valuable assets." Trade secrets are said to be the "crown jewels" of corporations. "Trade secrets are the IP of the new millennium and can no longer be treated as a stepchild," according to Mark Halligan.

Indeed, trade secrets are now gaining greater reverence as a tool for protection of innovation, and the stakes are getting higher. Injunctions have become a greater threat in trade-secret misappropriation cases and damage awards have been in the hundreds of millions in recent years. For instance, in a trial in Orlando, in which two businessmen were seeking $1.4 billion in damages from Walt Disney Company, accusing the company of stealing trade secrets for the sports complex at Walt Disney World, the jury awarded them $240 million. And misappropriation of trade secrets of Pioneer Hi-Bred International on genetic corn seed materials by Cargill, Inc. cost the latter $300 million. Similarly, Lexar Media was awarded $465 million in a trade-secret case against Toshiba for theft of controller technology, which enables a memory chip to communicate with its host device.

According to a 2003 IPO survey on strategic IP management, patents are often not viewed as a panacea but as a sideshow inasmuch as patents have limits—early publication, invent-around feasibility, and patentability requirements. However, proprietary technology is highly rated as a key source of competitive advantage, and the really important intellectual assets are skills and knowledge (88% of responses), which implicates trade secrets.

Moreover, patents are but the tip of the iceberg in an ocean of trade secrets. Over 90% of all new technology is covered by trade secrets, and over 80% of all license and technology transfer agreements cover proprietary know-how (i.e., trade secrets), or constitute hybrid agreements relating to patents and trade secrets. Bob Sherwood, an international IP consultant, calls trade secrets the "workhorse of technology transfer."

Finally, and very importantly, trade-secret protection operates without delay and without undue cost against the world, while patents are territorial and so expensive to obtain and maintain that they can be taken out only in selected countries.

Trade secrets are the first-line defense: They come before patents, go with patents, and follow patents. As a practical matter, licenses under patents without access to associated or collateral know-how have little commercial value because patents rarely disclose the ultimate scaled-up commercial embodiments. Hence, data and know-how are immensely important. The importance of know-how to technology transfer is confirmed by many leading industry practitioners:

- "In many cases, particularly in chemical technology, the know-how is the most important part of a technology transfer agreement." (Homer Blair, professor emeritus of Franklin Pierce Law Center).
- "Acquire not just the patents but the rights to the know-how. Access to experts and records, lab notebooks, and reports on pilot-scale operations, including data on markets and potential users of the technology, are crucial." (Robert Ebish, a freelance writer).
- "It is common practice in industry to seek and obtain patents on that part of a technology that is amenable to patent protection, while maintaining related technological data and other information in confidence. Some regard a patent as little more than an advertisement for the sale of accompanying know-how." (Peter Rosenberg, author of *Patent Law Fundamentals*).
- In technology licensing "related patent rights generally are mentioned late in the discussion and are perceived to have 'insignificant' value relative to the know-how." (Michael Ward, Honeywell VP licensing).
- "Trade secrets are a component of almost every technology license . . . (and) can increase the value of a license up to 3 to 10 times the value of the deal if no trade secrets are involved." (Melvin Jager, former Licensing Executives Society [LES] and LES International president).

Patents and trade secrets are not mutually exclusive but actually highly complementary and mutually reinforcing; in fact, they dovetail. In this context it should be kept in mind that our Supreme Court has recognized trade secrets as perfectly viable alternatives to patents: "The extension of trade secret protection to clearly patentable inventions does not conflict with the patent policy of disclosure" (*Kewanee Oil v. Bicron* (1974)) and further strengthened the bases for trade secret reliance in subsequent decisions (*Aronson v. Quick Point Pencil* (1979) and *Bonito Boats v. Thunder Craft Boats* (1989)). Thus, it is clear that patents and trade secrets can not only coexist, but are in harmony rather than in conflict with each other. "(T)rade secret-patent coexistence is well-established, and the two are in harmony because they serve different economic and ethical functions." (Professor Donald Chisum).

In the past—and even today—the question always was phrased in the alternative: "trade secret vs. patent protection," "trade secret or patent?" "to patent or to padlock?" But it is not necessary and, in fact, is shortsighted to choose one over the other. The question is not whether to patent or to padlock, but rather what to patent and what to keep a trade secret and whether it is best to patent as well as to padlock, that is, integrate patents and trade secrets for optimal synergistic protection of innovation.

Patents and trade secrets are indeed complementary, especially under the following circumstances:

In the critical R&D stage and before any patent applications are filed, trade-secret law particularly "dovetails" with patent law (see *Bonito Boats*). Provided an invention has been fully described so as to enable a person skilled in the art to make and use it and the best mode for carrying out the invention, if available, has been disclosed, as is requisite in a patent application, all associated or collateral know-how not divulged can and should be retained as a trade secret. All the massive R&D data, including data pertaining to better modes developed after filing, whether or not inventive, can and should also be maintained as trade secrets, to the extent some of the data are not disclosed in subsequent separate applications. Complementary patenting and padlocking is tantamount to having the best of both worlds, especially with respect to complex technologies consisting of many patentable inventions and mountains of associated know-how.

The conventional wisdom that because of the "best mode" requirement, trade-secret protection cannot coexist with patent protection, is a serious misconception. This requirement applies *only* at *the time of filing* and *only* to the *knowledge of the inventor(s)* and *only* to the *claimed* invention.

Patent applications are filed early in the R&D stage to get the earliest possible filing or priority date and the patent claims tend to be narrow for distance from prior art. Therefore, the specification normally describes in but a few pages only rudimentary lab experiments or prototypes, and the best mode for commercial manufacture and use remains to be developed later and often by others. The best mode requirement is thus no impediment to maintaining the volumes of collateral know-how developed after filing as trade secrets.

In Peter Rosenberg's opinion, "(p)atents protect only a very small portion of the total technology involved in the commercial exploitation of an invention. . . . Considerable expenditure of time, effort, and capital is necessary to transform an (inventive concept) into a marketable product." In this process, he adds, valuable know-how is generated, which even if inventive and protectable by patents, can be maintained as trade secrets, there being "nothing improper in patenting some inventions and keeping others trade secrets." And Tom Arnold asserted that it is "flat wrong" to assume, as "many courts and even many patent lawyers seem prone to do," that "because the patent statute requires a best mode disclosure, patents necessarily disclose or preempt all the trade secrets that are useful in the practice of the invention." (*1988 Licensing Law Handbook*).

Gale Peterson also emphasizes that "the patent statute only requires a written description of the *claimed* invention and how to make and use the *claimed* invention." He advises, therefore, that inasmuch as allowed claims on a patentable system cover "usually much less than the entire scope of the system, that the disclosure in the application be limited to that disclosure necessary to 'support' the claims in a § 112 sense, and that every effort be taken to maintain the remainder of the system as a trade secret."

In addition, as shown by case law, manufacturing process details, even if available, are not a part of the statutorily required best mode and enablement disclosure of a patent. And it is in this process area where best modes very often lie.

Exemplary Trade-Secret Cases

It goes without saying that technical and commercial information and collateral know-how that can be protected via the trade-secret route cannot include information and know-how, which is generally known, readily ascertainable, or constitutes personal skill. But this exclusion still leaves masses of data and know-how, which are the grist for trade secrets and additional improvement patents.

General Electric's industrial diamond process technology is an excellent illustration of the synergistic integration of patents and trade secrets. The artificial manufacture of diamonds for industrial uses was very big business for GE, and the company had the best proprietary technology for making such diamonds. Some of the patents had already expired, leaving much of the technology in technical literature and the public domain. But GE also kept certain distinct inventions and developments secret. The Soviet Union and a Far Eastern country were very interested in obtaining licenses to this technology, but GE refused to license anyone. Getting nowhere with GE, the Far Eastern interests resorted to industrial espionage, and a trusted fast-track star performer at GE, a national of that country, whom nobody would have suspected, was enticed with million-dollar payments to spirit away GE's crown jewels. But after a while the GE employee was caught, tried, and jailed.

The integration of patents and trade secrets is further demonstrated by Wyeth and their hormone-therapy drug, Premarin. Their patents on the Premarin manufacturing process (starting with pregnant mares' urine) expired decades ago, but Wyeth continues to hold closely guarded trade secrets. On behalf of Barr Laboratories, which had been trying to come out with a generic version of Premarin for 15 years, Natural Biologics stole the Wyeth trade secrets. Wyeth sued and prevailed, getting a total injunction, as it was an egregious case of trade-secret misappropriation.

The GE and Wyeth cases illustrate the value of trade secrets and, more importantly, the merits of marrying patents with trade secrets. Indeed, these cases show that GE and Wyeth could "have their cake and eat it too." Were GE's or Wyeth's policies to rely on trade secrets in this manner or, for that matter, Coca-Cola's decision to keep their formula secret rather than to patent it, which could have been done, damnable? Clearly not.

Other recent decisions, such as *Celeritas Technologies v. Rockwell International* (Fed. Cir. 1998) also demonstrate that it is now well established that dual or multiple protection for intellectual property is not only possible but essential to exploit the IP overlap and provide a fall-back position.

In *C&F Packing v. IBP and Pizza Hut* (Fed. Cir. 2000) for instance, Pizza Hut was made to pay $10.9 million to C&F for misappropriation of trade secrets. After many years of research, C&F had developed a process for making and freezing a precooked sausage for pizza toppings that had the characteristics of freshly cooked sausage and surpassed other precooked products in price, appearance, and taste. C&F had obtained a patent on the equipment to make the sausage and also one on the process itself. It continued to improve the process after submitting its patent applications and kept its new developments as trade secrets.

Pizza Hut agreed to buy C&F's precooked sausage on the condition that C&F divulge its process to several other Pizza Hut suppliers, ostensibly to assure that backup suppliers were available to Pizza Hut. In exchange, Pizza Hut promised to purchase a large amount of precooked sausage from C&F. C&F disclosed the process to several Pizza Hut suppliers, entering into confidentiality agreements with them. Subsequently, Pizza Hut's other suppliers learned how to duplicate C&F's results and, in turn, Pizza Hut notified C&F that it would not purchase any more sausage without drastic price reductions.

IBP was one of Pizza Hut's largest suppliers of meat products other than sausage. Pizza Hut furnished IBP with a specification and formulation of the sausage toppings, and IBP signed a confidentiality agreement with Pizza Hut concerning this information. IBP also hired a former supervisor in C&F's sausage plant as its own production superintendent but fired this employee five months later after it had implemented its sausage-making process and Pizza Hut was buying the precooked sausage from IBP.

C&F then brought suit against IBP and Pizza Hut for patent infringement and misappropriation of trade secrets and the court found (1) on summary judgment that the patents of C&F were invalid because the inventions had been on sale more than one year before the filing date and (2) after trial that C&F possessed valuable and enforceable trade secrets, which were indeed misappropriated.

What a great example of trade secrets serving as a fall-back position where patents fail to provide any protection! Indeed, a patent is a slender reed in light of the existence of dozens of invalidity and unenforceability reasons and many other potential patent attrition factors, such as:

- Doubtful patentability due to patent-defeating grounds
- Narrow claims granted by the PTO
- "Only about 5% of a large patent portfolio having commercial value" (per Emmett Murtha, ex-IBM and former LES president)
- The average effective economic life of a patent being "only about five years" (Emmett Murtha)
- Enforcing patents being a daunting and expensive task
- Only very limited or no coverage in existence in foreign countries

Connecting Business and Marketing with Innovation and IP Protection

While the decision in *State Street Bank* reinforced the connection between business and marketing and protection of IP, entrepreneurs and many successful business organizations have recognized the importance of maintaining a close connection between innovators and business personnel. Unfortunately, some organizations with large R&D centers have experienced difficulties in the past as the business movers and technical innovators were isolated in different organizational silos. The results were disappointing. Without adequate interface between the businesses and the technical units, many worthwhile discoveries were patented in fields unrelated to the core business interests of the company. Since IP personnel were often placed in close proximity to scientific personnel, there was less catalysis and little harvesting of business innovation. Important lessons of "management by wandering around" were violated. As chronicled in books such as *Rembrandts in the Attic*,[11] thousands of patents that were produced in areas of little or no interest to the sponsoring company were sold off for pen-

[11]Rivette, Kevin G., and Kline, David. *Rembrandts in the Attic: Unlocking the Hidden Value of Patents* (Boston: Harvard Business School Press, 1999).

nies on the dollar. While with adequate "spin" this might have seemed to be a windfall for the then current chief executive officer or chief financial officer, shareholders were not adequately rewarded in these circumstances.

Business, Technical, and IP Partnering to Pollinate the Seeds and Harvest the Fruit

Many business organizations began to restructure their technical development and business interfaces in the early 1990s to become more responsive to customers and market needs. Research and development specialists were more closely integrated with technical sales and marketing personnel so that "necessity" or real-world problems once again could be the "mother" of useful innovation in the organization. R&D sharpened its focus in line with the core business missions to create innovation more directly benefiting key products and services of the company.

Since many patent departments were closely aligned with R&D, as those organizations more closely interfaced with business and marketing, the patent or IP functions also grew closer to those functions. As management perceived the potential shareholder value, CEOs and top-level managers encouraged closer integration of IP functions with both marketing and technical functions.

At the inception of the twenty-first century, Robert Lurcott, entrepreneur and retired president and CEO of Henkel Corporation, observed, "Patents are a powerful marketing tool to sustain competitive advantage." Lurcott further suggested that "patent groups should partner with technical and business personnel to develop the broadest coverage to protect the company's core proprietary positions; and, this team approach helps to develop new and non-infringing pathways around the patents of competitors."

Suggestions for improving connection of marketing and business personnel with technical and IP specialists include the following:

- Management should request that the business or marketing leader attend those parts of patent committee meetings, together with IP and technical specialists, (1) where new filing decisions are made on invention disclosures and (2) where decisions are made on maintaining or pruning pending applications or patents.
- Management should encourage IP seminars for business and marketing people, together with technical personnel, to educate all potential innovators as to business and technical patenting and IP possibilities, values, processes, and requirements. It is not likely that either R&D or marketing

and sales would immediately recognize the types of business method inventions that are potentially patentable without assistance from IP. The IP department should point out to business and technical personnel examples of the patented business method inventions of others (e.g., Exhibits 3.1 and 3.2).

- IP departments should circulate advisory and news memoranda or newsletter items beyond technical groups to include business, marketing, human resources (HR), and the executive suite, and ask for feedback.
- IP managers should challenge executive managers, marketing, business, and HR personnel to submit their innovative ideas for IP consideration and to actively support wide participation in the IP programs. Innovation is everyone's job.
- IP attorneys should be encouraged by business managers to selectively participate in a wide range of business as well as technical meetings and development planning so that they can bond with and better support the overall business mission.
- Business development and investment teams should include IP representation as well as marketing and technical people when feasible.

Capturing All of the Innovation for Added Shareholder Value

Intellectual property leaders of Dow Corning, Oracle, and Procter and Gamble were panelists and presented papers under the heading "IP Scorecarding—Demonstrating and Maximizing Returns on IP Investment" at the Association of Corporate Patent Counsel (ACPC) summer meeting in June 2005. Steve Miller illustrated P&G's "open innovation" model, which he styled as "connect and develop." He reported that development teams, including IP specialists in addition to technical and marketing personnel, were successful in reducing costs for deodorants, improving revenue sharing for storage bags, extending brand equity from perfumes to vitamin sales, and improving retailer relationship and sales for the Swiffer Sweep+Vac® system. IP's intense participation in their venture with Royal helped P&G shift the Swiffer® product from placement in the vacuum device aisle to the higher-exposure detergent aisle, thereby doubling sales volume. As an integral part of the team, the IP representatives were able to more rapidly recognize and provide timely solutions to problems of disclosure of information and protection of inventions. In the past where IP representatives were not an integral part of the team, faulty and secondhand communications often derailed venture projects. Mr. Miller further pointed out the following:

> Today's competitive environment requires companies to leverage and protect the creativity of all employees, not just the output of their R&D organizations. At P&G, we look to create holistic IP strategies that plan for the IP needs of the businesses, developing a portfolio of IP rights to protect more than just the great way our products perform. Today's P&G IP portfolio must include protection for the exceptional look, feel, taste or smell of our products; business method patents protecting how we sell these exceptional products; and trademark protection that goes beyond P&G's strong existing brand names. And these IP strategies must be global in scope, tailored to the regional business needs and IP rights available in the regions of interest. Without close collaboration between the IP attorneys and the business teams, many of these opportunities would be missed.

In relation to the importance of business method patents, Miller further observed,

> Business method patents open the opportunity for every employee of P&G to be an inventor. We've seen the importance of these patents to the businesses and look to make them an even bigger part of our patent portfolio.

Over the years, manufacturers have been faced with an array of problems wherein the solutions likely would have been expedited to the mutual benefit of all concerned by closer teamwork of the technical, business, and IP functions. One illustration involves the tug-of-war that developed between a company that invented and marketed advanced chemical treatment compositions critical for prevention of rusting and adherence of paint on automobile bodies. The company recommended high dosage rates to ensure maximum protection and maximize sales. As more autos were produced and Environmental Protection Agency regulations required more and expensive wastewater treatment, the company and automakers were at loggerheads. The problem was complex and involved a range of legal and IP, marketing, and technical issues. Eventually, the automakers and suppliers agreed that the chemical supplier would be compensated based on a fixed fee per automobile treated rather than the rates of chemical used. This provided incentive to fund the research needed to reduce chemical consumption to minimum levels and relieved the need for expansion of wastewater facilities. This example occurred long before *State Street Bank*, and there was no protection for the brilliant compensation method. The incentive created by the eligibility to patent such solutions might have greatly increased the speed of the interactions needed to solve this important problem and clearly could have increased the speed of its adoption throughout the automobile industry. Publication of this elegant solution likely would have fueled the fires of genius in other industries with similar problems.

Marc Adler, chief IP officer at Rohm and Haas, recently commented, "We have and do file on business method inventions, especially in connection with new means for delivering chemical products and services. I believe that such process inventions are complementary to thorough IP strategies developed by multifunctional teams, including IP, technical, and business/marketing personnel."

Adler's comments sum up the desirable fusion of marketing, technical, and IP functions in developing and implementing a fully integrated IP strategy.

4

Giants Can Be Nimble: The SBC Story

Abha Divine

One clear trend in global markets is the shift over time from production-based economies to service economies to the new knowledge economies. The past century has witnessed incredible growth and change in the basic framework of the U.S. economy and workforce skill sets. This shift forms the backdrop for increased emphasis on intellectual property (IP) assets and the related skills required to fully mobilize them.

Shifts in Innovation

Beginning in the early twentieth century, the hallmark of the U.S. economy has been industrial goods and production technologies that can churn out millions of an item with the least unit cost. Businesses achieved these capabilities through standardization of manufacturing processes, initiating the reliance on relatively broad labor skills to staff and operating mass production capabilities. However, where firms once derived value from production efficiency—brought through standardization and scale operations—markets soon shifted to reward improved flexibility to meet customer demand and the ability to deliver an improved customer experience. This resulted in a shift from a focus on production innovation toward service innovation based on improved marketing, sales, and customer support. Later, this evolved to focus on increased customization of product and experience through enhanced knowledge of the customer and through technological improvements in information technology (IT), requiring a more highly skilled workforce and improved IP treatment for business methods and software-based technologies.

Valuation of IP Assets

Employment trends over the past 60 years bear this out: in 1939, 60% of U.S. workers were engaged in goods production.[1] In 2000, this had fallen to only 20%, with 80% employed in "services production." The capital markets have also recognized the growing impact of a strong IP portfolio and other intangible assets in an increasingly "knowledge-based" economy. A recent Brookings Institute study indicates that a substantial shift in the drivers for a firm's market value has taken place over the past two decades.

As a result, it is clear that by properly harnessing and managing IP assets a company can directly influence and drive overall valuation (see Exhibit 4.1). This has a direct impact on shareowner value and company performance. In fact, in the absence of clear information about a company's IP strategy and operations, the markets develop an implied view of a firm's IP effectiveness and worth. This has been documented in a variety of studies, including one[2] that uncovered the cost to firms of improperly managing their intangible asset base. Baruch Lev's work documents a downward spiral in some firms. It begins with a lack of clear information regarding the value and use of IP by a firm, causing investors to undervalue intangibles/IP. This results in a higher cost of capital for such firms, causing the firms to underinvest in IP development and commercialization. Thus, these firms bypass opportunities for increased value creation and return, creating more pressure from outside investors. Similarly, investors sometimes err on the side of overvaluing IP, resulting in misalignment or errors in capital deployment. Recent history shows us one such example—markets wildly overvalued intangibles in the dot-com boom, resulting in inefficient and wasted capital deployment.

The under- and overvaluing of IP and other intangibles seems to stem from several sources. First, companies themselves often do not have an accurate and efficient means of measuring IP management practices and results because they simply haven't tracked their portfolio and its use; this leaves the market to try to handicap future performance of such assets without seeing how the assets are utilized (or not) for the business. Second, by their nature, these assets are

---

[1]http://www.smartecon.com/articles/new_economy/service_economy.asp.

[2]Lev, Baruch. "Sharpening the Intangibles Edge," *Harvard Business Journal*, June 2004.

EXHIBIT 4.1 Why Focus on IP Now?

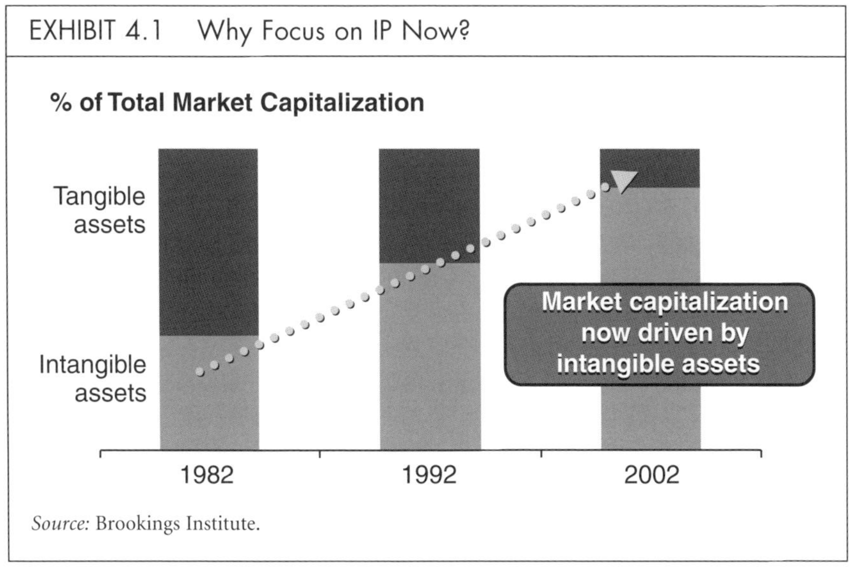

Source: Brookings Institute.

unique, making typical market-based pricing or industry trend analysis difficult. The return on IP is often tied closely to the owner and the application of the IP. Thus, IP assets have suffered from the lack of a broad and transparent market for price setting and evaluation. Ready buyers are often not able to find ready sellers of the IP they require. Resolution of this last issue, however, has witnessed some progress with the growth of monetization and commercialization vehicles (e.g., asset securitization, IP sale/lease-back financing, IP auctions, and private equity firms specializing in IP spinouts).

These value-impacting factors and others have spurred firms to more actively focus on IP management. In fact, studies indicate that more than 50% of *Fortune* 500 firms proactively manage and leverage their intellectual assets to create incremental profits—though how a firm defines *incremental profits* varies somewhat from company to company. Given the various means by which IP can impact firm value, measurement of IP value merits a broader assessment than top-line revenue. The variety of IP management models in place in industry seems to underscore this very point.

Intellectual property management techniques span a spectrum of approaches, each one tailored to different objectives and priorities for the underlying business with which they are associated. Each one delivers real value for the business, but realizes it in different ways; thus, a firm interested in establishing an IP business area needs to first assess its core objectives, both strategically and operationally, in order to find an approach that fits best.

IP Management Styles

In looking at the IP environment more closely, most companies view and manage their investments in intellectual property in three primary ways: "defend and protect," "develop and drive," and "market and commercialize." The following sections will describe each of these approaches in greater detail, including the benefits and issues associated with each one. By clearly aligning to a core strategy for IP management, business leaders can then effectively establish an implementation strategy that is much more likely to achieve predictable and desired results. In other words, ensuring consistency between expectations and approach will ensure that the team charged with implementation knows what to deliver and has the tools necessary to do so.

Defend and Protect

Managing IP in a defensive posture is perhaps the most traditional and basic form of IP management. In essence, the second that a company opens its doors for business, it is in the position of defending itself against outside IP claims. Firms that focus primarily on this aspect of IP management tend to view the function as a reactive one—responding and mobilizing only when threatened or asserted against. Clearly, effective defense against such claims is value producing for the company, as it limits or eliminates financial and operating exposures. Recent American Bar Association figures suggest that, on average, defending a patent litigation suit costs between $2 million and $6 million. This does not include damages that might result from a finding of fault. Thus, any activity that reduces the number of patent suits that a firm defends against produces a measurable value in expense reduction, and one that in particularly litigious industries could have a real impact on profitability.

Develop and Drive

The second way companies have historically leveraged their IP is by driving its use inside the business. More proactive than the first category, the business reaps increased value by capturing and deploying IP back through the business to improve performance in a variety of areas, including operational efficiencies, unique product and service capabilities, better tools for service delivery and management, and so forth. This activity is best characterized by the kind of work that research and development (R&D) or engineering teams undertake.

At companies that enjoy scale in operations or production, process, and know-how, IP often represents significant value and a source of competitive advantage. These firms further capitalize on the benefits of this IP by instituting standardized approaches across business units, thereby reducing costs of operation or improving quality and reliability in product or service delivery. Recent history has shown how some firms have used such IP as a direct driver for market value and shareholder return. One such example is Dell Computers' "direct" model of sales and customer management via the Internet. Though Dell expanded its product and customer segment focus to encompass consumers to enterprise customers and computers to peripherals, the company appears to have been steadfast in standardizing on a direct model of customer interaction, ordering and product fulfillment (rather than use of third-party retail channels), resulting in cost savings and operational efficiencies.

Many firms have attempted to emulate their approach with varying degrees of success, demonstrating the value of investing in IP, rather than just waiting to emulate others' innovations. As noted, this type of IP is closely linked to R&D investment; however, using R&D expenditure as a proxy for a company's IP performance or health yields an incomplete picture. Instead, to fully gauge a company's effectiveness in using IP to develop and drive product and operational improvement measurement of R&D, return on investment (ROI) is required. When companies focused on driving value through this type of IP management monitor and manage against ROI, they are better able to guide resource allocation among projects and determine adequate R&D spending levels.

Market and Commercialize

Clearly, the first two categories are important business practices that add value to the organization. But there is a growing trend among companies today to do even more with IP to extract *all* of the value from the asset and maximize its potential. This approach views IP through a broader business lens—IP is used not only for defensive purposes and for enhancing products and operations, but also as a direct means of revenue generation and competitive positioning. This approach exercises a firm's IP for both internal improvement and external commercialization, requiring consideration and valuation of IP's impact strategically to the firm and tactically in the broader market so that a determination of the maximum value path may be assessed. In other words, the prime objective is to maximize value by placing IP where it will have the most impact. In general, this results in valuable IP quickly being deployed to the marketplace, either by the innovating company itself or by others who are better able to deliver the technology or innovation to customers. In such a model, the interests of all constituents—IP developer and investor, IP-based product deliverer, and consumer—are aligned. Thus, active IP management based on solid financial and strategic measures serves as an incentive for better and faster innovation, since all parties find economic benefit in participating.

In this manner, effective IP management is a business engine that can improve a company's product offerings, enhance its market position through new partnering or licensing arrangements, deliver noncore but valuable IP to consumers efficiently, and enable innovators to capture fair returns on investments that become widely used. Moreover, increased focus on IP value generation and measurement by firms should provide a more visible marketplace for buyers and sellers of IP to come together (see Exhibit 4.2).

EXHIBIT 4.2 IP Licensing Dynamics

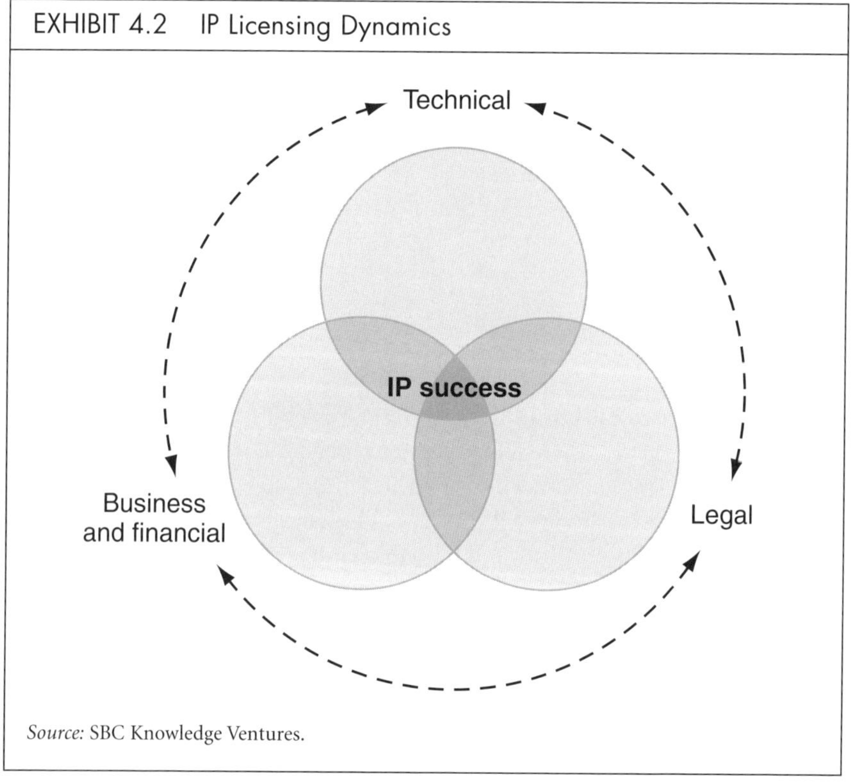

Source: SBC Knowledge Ventures.

THE SBC COMMUNICATIONS STORY

SBC Communications, much like other *Fortune* 500 firms, responded to this increased emphasis on intangible value and created a separate unit for IP management. This unit, SBC Knowledge Ventures, is charged with managing and commercializing SBC's IP portfolio—software, trademarks, patents, and other know-how. In executing on these objectives, SBC Knowledge Ventures has had to develop broad IP programs for the corporation, and establish processes for mining and management of IP assets and approaches for internal teaming in commercialization activities. Furthermore, this has driven SBC Knowledge Ventures to adopt a specific structural design and functional roles within the organization and, further, to staff these roles with specific skill sets and capabilities to deliver operational and financial results for the corporation. At the same time, the very nature of IP assets and their commercialization requires a "nimble" process for decision making and execution to be successful.

First and foremost, implementing any of these strategies requires certain tactical elements, beginning with organizational design or approach. An effective organizational model aligns with the business strategy and objectives to ensure that resources are efficiently deployed to meet defined business objectives. This alignment is a crucial step in launching and operating an IP business activity within a large firm and ensuring that the entity is equipped to deliver the desired results. Returning to the three models of IP management, the first step in implementing an IP management function is selecting the primary strategy. Once selected, several characteristics of organizational approach emerge for each strategy.

With the "defend and protect" strategy for IP management, the primary objective is risk mitigation. This objective seems best aligned to an IP management model that is a support function to the overall business operations. This type of organization requires a small set of specialized legal experts that assist clients throughout the corporation with IP capture and development (i.e., patent and trademark filings, markings requirements, etc.) and manage external IP issues related to in-licensing. The general structure operates as part of a "service" entity for the other business areas of the firm; its operations are generally part of the larger legal cost center. Primary metrics focus on freedom-of-operation results for the client organizations, and (secondarily) cost management. The other business areas do not integrate IP considerations and planning directly, relying primarily on legal to manage and mitigate impact to the core business activities of the firm.

For the second model, "develop and drive," firms can benefit from centralized management of IP to lower costs of operation and introduce best practices across the company and better ROI through extended use of their IP. Such objectives lend themselves to a structure that closely aligns IP management with R&D and engineering activities, and positions IP management as a complement to business unit (profit center) operations. Often, such functions will be housed in the R&D part of the business, and may have close ties to procurement and other "make/buy" decision makers who require guidance on IP needs and availability.

IP management in such environments requires specialized legal expertise as before, but also benefits from technical expertise that can identify core technologies for reuse or extension. As noted earlier, value is returned to the business unit operations themselves in the form of improved efficiency, cost reductions, or better time to market, and the IP function operates as a cost center function. Beyond product improvement and efficiency measures, this approach to IP management may also be measured on cost management against the function's budget. More sophisticated implementations of this approach, however, do focus on assessing R&D internal return measurements to drive future investment and project selection within the R&D function.

The last model, "market and commercialize," is most aligned to firms with a strong focus on ROI of the IP portfolio as a whole and revenue diversity. Given the strong financial drivers behind this model, the IP function is best operated as a separate unit with a multidisciplinary staff skilled in transaction formulation and execution, along with legal experts in IP. Such operations should be expected to be self-funding and measured accordingly. Organizational models suited to these objectives focus on establishing a stand-alone, centralized business operation for IP mining, opportunity development, and licensing. Such organizations can be placed as a core operating area under the chief operating officer (COO), placed within other asset management and transaction areas (such as corporate development or corporate strategy) or under the direction of the chief financial officer (CFO).

Fundamentally, the IP unit must have autonomy to pursue disposition approaches that deliver the highest value (measured in revenue or expense reduction) for the firm. Assessment of value must account for strategic or competitive benefits derived from the IP, as well as straight top-line results for the IP entity. In other words, while measured against its own earnings before interest, tax, depreciation, and amortization (EBITDA) goals, the IP entity must maintain the broad perspective of corporate value resulting from enhanced market position, customer satisfaction, or product profitability (not business unit value alone). The remainder of this chapter will focus on this last model for IP management and the tactical elements of instituting this type of IP operation in a large enterprise.

As noted above, a "market and commercialize" IP management approach is best suited to a stand-alone business unit structure within a firm. By creating a centralized management organization, efficiencies are gained in transaction speed, effectiveness, and consistency since an IP-focused team of experts manage all transactions relating to IP. This is particularly important since the underlying strategy aims at business partnerships to bring internal innovation, brand strength, and other IP value to the marketplace via implementation or channel partners.

To speed time to market of IP, the autonomy of the IP business unit should be balanced through significant internal partnering efforts by its leadership team. In contrast to the other strategy models, which are more "client-provider" in nature, this IP management model operates as an equal partner with other profit center or operations-focused areas of the business. As such, the IP management leadership team must rely on peer organizations to cultivate, identify, and support IP development and extraction within their business areas. In turn, the IP organization must provide leadership in this regard by establishing and articulating the "market and commercialize" IP strategy and its tactical implications for the company, including specific and measurable goals for IP creation, identification, and protection. Moreover, the IP unit will meet with better time to market and execution success in its out-licensing programs through strong relationships with key areas such as marketing, engineering/IT, and procurement. From close interaction with these areas, the IP leadership team can establish a clear picture of specific partners and vendors involved in enabling future market offerings, delivering key infrastructure components and systems, and deploying complementary services and products. This understanding can provide the IP business development team with valuable insight into potential partners' market capabilities and strengths, and areas for enhancement that could be enabled through IP.

Centralizing IP management and responsibilities also results in lower risk, as specialized and experienced transaction teams lead negotiations to mitigate common IP issues such as indemnity, product development and launch time lines, market performance by licensing partners, and use restrictions for the IP. With a core team focused on managing license rights on IP, each negotiation for out-licensing or in-licensing of such assets can be completed quickly, while ensuring that the corporation's interests are protected since the nuances of key IP issues do not have to be learned anew for each agreement. Importantly, this core team approach also ensures that transactions do not interfere or conflict with one another or other business interests of the company.

An IP organization pursuing the "market and commercialize" approach should be comprised of a multidisciplinary staff in order to effectively identify, assess, and market the IP assets of the firm. This staff should include technologists, attorneys specializing in IP issues and transactions, financial and economic experts, and marketing and business development professionals. Each asset and transaction requires attention from key members of each functional area to build a complete picture of the asset's scope, application, or use; market value; and licensing partners. In particular, this staffing and structure aims to leverage specialized skills for specific results, while ensuring that each function "plays position." Thus, the technical team is charged with asset evaluation and characterization, focusing on the technical and operational underpinnings of the asset. Once the technical team has developed a detailed picture of the asset's scope and technological applications or use, the marketing or business development team steps in to develop an assessment of the commercial impact of the IP. Based on this broader market analysis, the financial team establishes a financial assessment—often relying on several techniques—to assist in prioritizing transaction efforts and setting pricing levels. Throughout, the legal team provides advice regarding the status of IP rights, risks, and options for exercising the IP. Based on the synthesis of inputs from the various perspectives, disposition plans are developed and executed by the business development team.

Certainly, all areas provide support to the transaction activities, but the primary negotiation responsibilities fall to the business development team. Still, the business development, finance, legal, and technology teams serve an important "check-and-balance" role for each other for each IP transaction. How these teams operate in a complementary fashion and accomplish this check and balance for each other is described later in this chapter as each functional area is described in detail, as well as the consistent and methodical processes for completing analysis, asset disposition recommendations, and valuation.

Organizational Approach

As noted above, the "market and commercialize" IP management strategy is best implemented under a functionally diverse organizational design. The key functional and skill areas include portfolio management, business development, finance, and legal.

Portfolio Management

Portfolio management is the most technical of the functional areas, drawing on staff members with significant technical training and experience. These experts provide the underlying technical and operational diligence and planning related to asset commercialization. To do so, the team draws on extensive experience in bringing technology from concept to market delivery to ensure a realistic assessment of the IP's scope and uses, and how best to realize deployment ready solutions. Particularly with early-stage innovations, lab results and implementations are a long way from market-deployable offerings since they often rely on very controlled environments or narrow parameters to operate. Moreover, the market opportunity may require extension or integration with other components or capabilities. This integration and development effort must be defined in terms of functional or development needs, estimated in terms of time and cost, and a determination made of dependencies and resource requirements to implement the commercial version of the IP. Accuracy in these estimates is important to determining the potential market timing of product introduction, costs incurred by a partner or licensee to commercialize the IP, and risks that may hinder market delivery.

In the case of software solutions, the IP may be very widely deployed internally, demonstrating its ability to scale and operate in a typical customer environment. Further, internal use may provide significant data regarding value via cost savings or operational improvement. However, the technical team must undertake a similar analysis of the underlying IP both to catalog the breadth of assets (software, know-how, associated data or processes, etc.) and to determine compatibility of the development environment and platforms with broad market requirements. Further, the portfolio management team reviews the software solution for its flexibility and capability for integration with complementary solutions already available in the marketplace. Based on these detailed design reviews, the portfolio management team produces a similar assessment of required additional development time and cost, features and "road map" enhancements, and other elements required to commercialize the IP. While such internal software IP has proven operational hardiness, what may be lacking is detailed documentation for users and operators alike. The asset may also require additional development to improve the ease of maintenance by the provider.

Clearly, the better these estimates and analyses, the better the potential for quick market delivery through licensing or partnering. Without a detailed understanding of the IP's extent and potential complementary elements, business development may not accurately target the right partners—those whose product line would benefit from the IP's addition and those who have the resources to dedicate to develop and market the final product. For these reasons, it is vital that the portfolio management team have deep experience in technology introduction or product deployment. It is insufficient to have strong technical knowledge; rather, these staff members must additionally possess tactical business knowledge related to criteria for successful market delivery, market adoption, and long-term product success. Often, this implies a strong systems engineering expertise, along with experience in recommending or defining requirements or architectures for complex business needs.

Interestingly, some of the strongest individual contributors for R&D or IT development are not the best suited to the portfolio management role because they may be unaware of the activities and effort required to take a working instantiation of IP to general market availability, they may be too narrowly focused in a particular discipline of interest, or they are unable to objectively assess the market's interest or demand for a particular capability or IP. Objectivity in IP analysis is crucial to prioritization of efforts and focus for the IP team as a whole, and requires that portfolio managers maintain the discipline to look beyond technology for "technology's sake" and be capable of seeing the worth in powerful but less groundbreaking IP.

As might be expected, the portfolio management team serves as the first stop for IP assets—both those for extraction and those ready for commercialization. Therefore, it is important that these experts have the technical and operational experience noted above; such expertise when accompanied by business acumen provides a strong basis of technical and market characterization of the asset base and what the long-term state of the portfolio should be. The portfolio management team and its leadership have primary responsibility for establishing and communicating the overall IP portfolio strategy and objectives, such as key areas for development and mining, based on a thorough understanding of the market and technical landscape and the scope of the firm's IP asset holdings.[3] By maintaining a strong understanding of the market dynamics, the portfolio management team provides a road map for the long-term vitality of the IP portfolio, ensuring that asset areas of strong commercial interest and impact (both internally and externally) are encouraged and actively mined. This portfolio shaping also benefits from effective pruning by a well-informed, strategi-

[3]Portfolio management oversight of the IP portfolio focuses on patents, software, trade secrets, know-how, and other related IP. It does not include the trademark assets, which are managed more directly by the business development team.

cally minded portfolio management team. By establishing near-term and long-term road maps for the portfolio, the portfolio management team is able to evaluate assets for ongoing focus and protection. In the case of patents, for example, the pruning exercise coincides with patent maintenance periods to ensure proactive review of ongoing protection efforts. In the absence of such strategically guided reviews, firms may fall victim to one of two extremes: Either they automatically pay all maintenance fees over the life of the patents, thereby incurring higher expenses overall, or they may arbitrarily let IP rights lapse through nonpayment of maintenance fees, resulting in the loss of potentially valuable assets. The latter is a likely outcome in firms that are undertaking across-the-board expense cutbacks, resulting in an unwitting destruction of value for the business.

To be effective in its cataloging and mining efforts, the portfolio management team must be well connected to internal peer organizations. These organizations must be brought in as partners to the overall corporate objectives relating to the IP portfolio. Inside large firms, this often requires a mix of clearly articulated goals for the partner organizations and strong outreach in communication, training, and mining by the IP group. This partnering support is also achieved through involvement of the peer organizations at touch points throughout the IP identification, capture, and commercialization process. In particular, while the portfolio management team leads various IP evaluation committees (e.g., patent committee, other IP/innovation review committees), their efforts benefit significantly from participation on these committees by leaders and senior managers from other peer organizations, such as marketing, engineering, IT, and operations.

This mix of technical, market, and operational expertise is crucial to ensuring that the evaluation of IP for addition to the overall portfolio is aligned with the strategy for IP commercialization. In other words, this variety of viewpoints aids in the assessment of newly identified IP for its market impact and value. (More traditional IP management objectives, such as defensively focused strategies, may not require the broader insight such a cross-functional committee brings, since the primary criterion for evaluation is centered around internal use of the IP.) Moreover, the involvement of leaders from these other organizations integrates them into the IP operation and strategy, making them more aware of the value and importance of the IP generated in their organizations. Rather than enduring the existence of the IP unit, they are involved in the codification of the assets for the corporate portfolio and, as such, often become advocates for strategic mining efforts within their organization, resulting in the generation and capture of additional IP.

Near-term benefits to the peer organizations include the goodwill engendered in their employees in response to the formal recognition programs for IP development, which can include significant cumulative monetary compensation for the individual. Such programs should be administered by the IP unit (and budgeted there), but should engage the line management team in delivering the positive message to individual employees. Thus, the operational business areas are able to gain additional financial compensation for their employees, aiding in overall employee satisfaction, without incurring any direct budget impact.

Strategic mining efforts by the portfolio management team represent the proactive "pull" of IP from across the company to augment the "push" of IP submissions by the organizations and employees across the company. As alluded to earlier, strategic mining has two primary benefits: (1) mining in key strategic areas supports portfolio development in accordance with the overall IP portfolio objectives developed by the portfolio management team; and (2) it often results in higher volume and stronger IP assets. In general, these innovation sessions serve to marry the internal strategic interests of the business and the market opportunities for the resulting IP to maintain strength in the portfolio.

Most firms, especially those focused on the "develop and drive" strategy, engage in some form of strategic mining or ideation activities. Led by the portfolio management team of the IP unit, such sessions may bring together key players from marketing, R&D, engineering, systems/IT, and other relevant areas to discuss and codify a vision for future services, features, and architectures to support their deployments. By bringing together team members from a variety of areas, more detailed descriptions and approaches can be captured for these future offerings, including technical implementation and integration details. Alternately, strategic mining may be spurred by ongoing commercialization efforts within the IP unit and the identification of complementary technologies or IP areas. In this scenario, the portfolio management team would engage the specific teams across the company involved in developing or implementing such capabilities to capture additional complementary assets. The result may provide additional elements for the asset set under review for licensing, increasing the value to the licensee or reducing the risk in implementation. For example, a software asset focused on managing the selection and engagement of vendors or products might benefit from a complementary application aimed at payment authorization and remittance processing. It is the role of the portfolio management team to identify the potential synergy and initiate mining activities with the appropriate groups across the company, if the needed assets are not already characterized and cataloged in the IP portfolio.

Business Development

The business development team spans two key activities in the commercialization efforts: business analysis and planning and transaction execution. Based on the identification of high-priority assets by the portfolio management team, the business development team establishes a complete business "plan" and analysis for commercialization of the IP. This team moves the analytics from the technical relevance and depth provided by the portfolio management team to incorporate market factors, demand, and opportunity size for the IP. The resulting analysis is comparable to any investment-grade evaluation and plan for new product or service offerings, and includes consideration of risk and approaches for mitigating it.

The business development team accomplishes this rigorous, yet rapid, evaluation in an iterative manner. The intent is to quickly evaluate assets against a series of success criteria to enable quicker elimination of assets that are unlikely to result in a value-producing transaction at that time. This funnel pruning is an important factor in managing overall resource allocation and deal flow. The longer an asset stays in the funnel, the more resources it consumes in analysis and planning for commercialization; therefore, it is vitally important that assets that reach the deal stage have a very high likelihood of closing. This is somewhat counterintuitive to general sales philosophy, in which many "at bats" are required to close a single deal. However, the key difference is that each asset is unique in its analysis and disposition approach; essentially, each asset forms the basis for a full business case effort. Thus, maintaining low-probability assets in the funnel starves other, more favorable assets of licensing attention, resulting in longer commercialization efforts. Given that some of the value of the licensable IP is in time-to-market benefits, such delays could reduce the long-term value of the asset.

So, what analysis is appropriate for IP licensing? How does a firm ensure adequate review and diligence to properly value the IP it intends to commercialize, while still maintaining speed to market? As suggested earlier, an iterative approach is one way to improve time through the analysis process. The purpose of the business development team's evaluation and planning for each asset is to identify the value of the asset and its market application(s), understand the market dynamics and resulting value produced by the IP, determine the best commercialization path or approach, and identify key partner characteristics to improve the odds for successful market delivery. The analysis is aided by the technical assessment of the portfolio management team, the valuation analysis of the finance team, and the legal guidance from the IP attorneys.

The iterative analysis seeks to answer successively more detailed questions about the assets and marketplace. Initially, the business development team focuses on assessing the IP in the context of a preexisting market category or the extension to an existing market. In this manner, the business development team is able to begin to define the market trends and customer requirements, comparable capabilities or offerings in the marketplace, and the relative impact of the IP to the landscape. Ironically, the incremental IP assets may often provide the quickest path to commercialization, though they are likely to yield less value than the category-defining IP. A skilled business development team balances the mix of near-term opportunities and longer-term opportunities in the funnel to deliver against annual performance objectives.

Following this initial assessment, assets that demonstrate market fit and strong value proposition overall are further evaluated to determine how best to commercialize the IP. A growing number of approaches are available in the market today, including sale of the assets, licensing exclusively and nonexclusively, equity-based spinout, and others. The business development team assesses the market landscape to determine which approach yields the strongest results, while mitigating risk in outcome. For example, a concentrated market may point toward exclusive licensing as an appropriate means for capturing most of the market value of the assets, while potentially limiting the risk of a single partner, due to the broad market reach of that partner. In a more fragmented industry or one poised for consolidation, nonexclusive licensing may provide appropriate risk mitigation of dealing with emergent or smaller parties. Paired with an assessment of preferred partner characteristics, a specific "lead list" may be generated for prioritized licensing efforts in a later stage. For example, the IP may best be suited to commercialization by a firm that has in-house consulting services to augment delivery and integration of the base solution. Alternately, the IP may be aided by a commercialization partner that has a strong presence in key market segments.

This stage of analysis further evaluates risk of commercialization to the firm offering the IP. Among the considerations is a detailed review of strategic impact of the IP to the firm itself and the industry in general. In highly competitive industries, licensing may need to be restricted to external markets, secondary uses, or certain geographies. Or the IP may be held for exclusive internal use due to its high strategic benefit or ability to provide lasting differentiation in the marketplace.

Throughout the analysis, the business development team engages the subject matter experts related to the target industries, technologies, or product areas to garner valuable market data and insights and to validate assumptions regarding expected commercialization efforts or development needs for market delivery. Such discussions often provide valuable considerations for the strategic importance analysis described earlier; through these internal collaborations, the IP team is able to more accurately quantify the impact of the IP on the internal business activities and the value of maintaining exclusivity. Rather than a purely qualitative exercise, the same principles for external valuation are applied to assess internal value of the IP. This enables the IP team to rigorously and objectively assess when to commercialize and when to retain internally valuable IP by comparing the relative external return against the exclusivity returns (through better customer retention, reduced price erosion, etc.). It also serves to keep the peer business leaders involved and informed regarding the licensing plans for IP, reducing eleventh hour or postdeal friction over transactions.

Assuming that external commercialization is still the objective for the particular IP set following this analysis, the business development team formulates a detailed execution plan for initiating and completing an IP transaction. Many IP licensing efforts fail to invest in this planning stage, with resulting inefficiency and potential long-term relationship issues with their licensee. Thus, time saved in the short run may be multiplied in long-term time spent. This stage also provides another crucial touch point for internal socialization across the firm.

The execution plan focuses on developing a detailed project plan for engaging customers, negotiating terms, and closing the IP transaction. In particular, the plan identifies key steps, both internally and externally, toward completion to ensure rapid close and effective communication with stakeholders throughout the organization. In order to maintain support from key peer groups for current and future transactions, it is important to inform other leaders of planned execution time lines, disposition approaches, and potential impact on their business activities. In some cases, collaboration and integration of independent transactions with the same third party may help streamline the process for all concerned or deliver increased value to the parties. For example, the IP unit may be in discussions with a technology provider to license and commercialize IP in the form of software and data. At the same time, the engineering team may have an interest in outsourcing the next-generation implementation for related IP. By integrating the two negotiations, a more cohesive arrangement of licensing and product license-back can be accomplished, while still preserving appropriate ownership rights of the IP for the firm. The licensee may benefit from this arrangement because they can ensure an "anchor client" for future sales and potentially lower licensing fees in return for the license-back of the commercial implementation. The engineering team benefits from the additional leverage (and resulting lower cost) for the implementation work sought. And all three benefit from a potentially faster transaction close.

To achieve this type of integration and benefit for the corporation as a whole, the IP unit and its peer business areas must communicate routinely regarding pending transactions, the expected outcomes, and parties involved so that opportunities to work together are identified early. It also serves to further cement the beneficial relationship between the IP unit and the other business areas, as key provisions for service, support, or updates to the base IP implementation are included in the terms negotiations on behalf of the operations areas. Moreover, relationship strength between the technology supplier and the various business areas of the firm can aid the negotiating and due diligence process for the IP transaction. Thus, communication with other areas of the business should be viewed as a means for accelerating IP transactions, rather than as bureaucratic overhead.

This phase also signals the shift from analysis to market engagement, and includes the development of appropriate communication materials. As with other complex sales efforts, effective "sales collateral" is a necessary component of engaging prospective customers and illuminating the underlying value proposition for the product. In this case, the product is IP assets, and the value proposition must therefore not only address how the IP is useful to the customer or its customer base, but also provide rational explanation of how the IP could be commercialized, marketed, and sold. Since IP assets may apply to a variety of industries and product categories, this marketing material is important to help customers clearly and succinctly understand how the IP is relevant to their own business operations and market objectives. Customer engagement may vary from relationship-selling approaches (i.e., recurring transactions with previous IP licensees) to broker-initiated communications to targeted customer calls. In each case, however, the marketing collateral provides an initial picture of the IP and its potential use or worth to the customer.

As part of the analysis in this phase, the business development team establishes pricing expectations and a proposed deal structure in collaboration with finance. The pricing reflects the specific risk-adjusted returns expected from a potential collaboration with a licensee, including both at-risk and guaranteed financial consideration. Moreover, the pricing links back to the overall valuation of the asset. Therefore, an outright sale of IP assets should garner at or near the valuation of the asset. Nonexclusive licensing, however, would reflect the expected market reach of the licensee in light of the overall valuation. In order to maintain the integrity of the valuation and licensing processes, the finance team's valuation provides a comparison point for pricing proposals and disposition alternatives pursued. The effectiveness of the licensing effort can be measured, in part, by how closely the overall returns track to the valuation of the asset.

Throughout the analysis and execution phases, the business development team works closely with IP legal experts, finance, and portfolio management to complete the strategic analysis, market positioning, disposition recommendations, and execution of the transaction. Each functional area contributes significantly to the development and completion of the transaction; the approximate magnitude of involvement at various stages of the IP funnel activities is depicted in Exhibit 4.3.

As noted, the business development team has primary responsibility for driving the analysis and preparation of IP assets for commercialization after initial prioritization and characterization by the portfolio management team. Successful IP business development staff members have a technical background and experience in technology-oriented industries augmented with substantial transactional expertise. This expertise is generally the result of specific training and experience in financial analysis, strategy development, or corporate development transactions. While technical sales and marketing expertise is also beneficial, IP business development requires complex transaction experience based on a structured approach to negotiation.

EXHIBIT 4.3 IP Funnel Stages and Functional Involvement

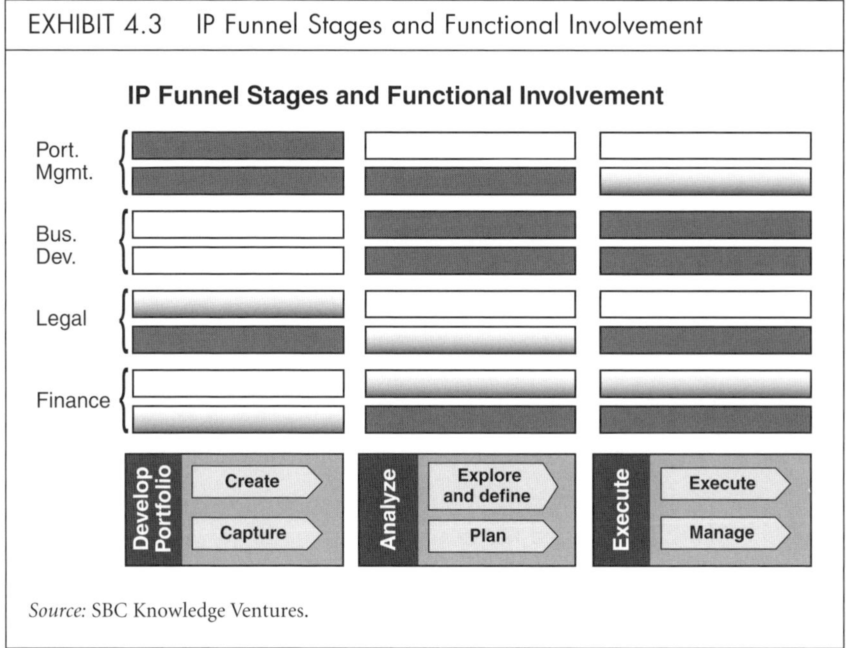

Source: SBC Knowledge Ventures.

IP deals are complex and multifaceted, requiring the ability to focus on a variety of details and their interdependencies. Further, given the specialized nature of IP and its status as an instrument of legal definition, skilled business development team members must work closely with and have a detailed understanding of the legal implications of deal structure, terms, and other contract elements. The business development team serves as the primary interface with customers, and so must also possess the ability to communicate effectively with a variety of stakeholders (technical, management, and financial leaders). Moreover, the business development team must have the ability to simultaneously balance strategic considerations and tactical details to achieve desired results since their work spans the marketing and business analysis activities to the sales and negotiation stages. One business development leader at SBC Knowledge Ventures, Juan Cordoba, sums up the licensing efforts as follows, "Successfully licensing IP assets is a combination of new-product development coupled with an M&A-type transaction. A licensing executive needs to articulate what a future product may look like and how it fits with a potential partner's existing solutions and future road map. Once the vision is effectively communicated, one needs to negotiate with the buyer to most effectively realize value for both parties."

Finance

Throughout the IP capture, characterization, and commercialization process, the finance and legal teams provide significant guidance regarding asset value and market options. These areas operate as an "overlay" function to the other areas, providing continuity and analysis through each phase.

With respect to the individual portfolio assets and their disposition planning and execution, the finance team has the primary responsibility for valuation and pricing of the assets for commercialization. In particular, this involves formulating specific models of the market environment and players, the IP's part in the overall landscape, and the resulting value generated by that IP. This analysis focuses on identifying key economic contributions of the IP to the overall marketplace. In some cases, this is the result of enhanced products and services. In other cases, it relates to savings resulting from improved operational efficiencies. Still other cases find the IP contributing to better customer satisfaction and retention; this can represent significant sources of value, albeit difficult to measure independently or directly. Thus, each model is unique to the IP and market opportunity to which it relates.

The financial modeling also takes into account the required investment, in time and money, to commercialize the IP. As noted earlier, this is drawn from the assessment of the portfolio management team regarding the scope of the assets and the development or other tasks required to make the solution market ready. Other factors for consideration in valuing the IP include the market stage of the IP; is it early stage or late stage in its development and operational use? Sometimes incremental IP that enhances existing applications or technologies may be easier to license quickly, since the market is somewhat mature and risk of adoption is lowered. Additionally, the finance team must consider the whole set of IP. While it is the role of the portfolio management team to identify other synergy assets, the finance team builds the comprehensive valuation of the set. Such related assets are an important consideration in the value of the IP, since they often are more than additive to the value of the overall asset group. For example, exclusive IP rights (such as those associated with patents) can overcome the basic replacement cost value or time-to-market value of nonexclusive IP.

What begins to emerge is a model that looks very much like a traditional business case discounted cash flow (DCF) analysis, complete with investment needs, timing, and sales expectations over time. The benefit of this rigorous and systematic approach to valuation is threefold. First, it provides the IP team objective means for evaluating the various business, market, technological, and legal considerations that have been reviewed and synthesized through the cross-functional analyses. Second, it provides a sound basis for future pricing analysis and evaluation of negotiation points in the transaction. A framework resulting from the financial and business analysis described thus far can be honed to fit the subset parameters of a particular licensee and market, thereby allowing the multitude of interrelated factors in a deal to be assessed against the "universe" of the economic value the IP could produce. This gives firm footing to the business development team in their licensing discussions as they negotiate the various gives and takes necessary to close the transaction, and enables the overall balance of risk and return to be equal between the parties. Finally, by developing formal analyses grounded in typical managerial and financial frameworks, the IP licensing effort becomes less alien to stakeholders across the business.

Managers accustomed to reviewing business cases for new-product launches, acquisitions, or investments in new technologies or capabilities can readily follow the business assumptions and plan represented in the DCF model, without having to formulate the elements of commercialization independently. These partners can better apply their own expertise and experience to the discourse on the commercialization plan through specific input on the key assumptions of the model: time lines, revenues, and expenses.

Sophisticated financial analysis must also incorporate risk to adequately assess the value of the asset. Some tools for incorporating risk into the model include decision tree analysis, Monte Carlo analysis, and adjustments to the discount rate. Individual firm approaches may vary in their uses of these and other tools, such as options based modeling, but the underlying intent remains to integrate multiple probable outcomes or value-effecting factors. Since the IP commercialization effort is often prospective in nature (i.e., a development or channel partner enhances the IP to make it market ready by adding documentation, support features, platform ports, etc.), incorporating the alternate future outcomes or *nonexecution risk* (discussed later in this chapter) in the analysis is an important element of valuation.

Decision tree analysis provides a means for tracking the results of multiple variables that are specific expected outcomes in the future. For example, if the IP relates to a particular approach for which the standard is still unsettled, the finance team may want to address the risk of a favorable outcome in the standards arena versus an unfavorable outcome by mapping branches of a decision tree to each alternative. The key element in this approach is that the future event is known to have one of several discrete outcomes.

Monte Carlo analysis provides a means for assessing the sensitivity of the overall valuation to particular assumptions within the model. Here, the finance team is concerned with uncovering the key drivers of the model and determining the most likely range of economic value delivered by the IP. For example, market timing may be critical to IP that relates to maturing technological solutions. Likewise, adoption rates may impact significantly the overall economic value of the IP, as in the case of products subject to network effects.

To balance the desired rigor of the financial analysis against the need to remain nimble and ensure proper distribution of resources on value-producing projects, the finance team mirrors the business development team's iterative approach. Initial valuation of assets is developed quickly, based on high-level parameters and a prestructured model focused on a "top-down" approach. The resulting "scorecard" provides a valuation range based on market size assumptions, adoption rate assumptions, and expense expectations related to commercialization. Standard industry rates for margin; sales, general and administrative (SG&A) costs; and other broad business factors are applied within this early model to derive the initial valuation range. The purpose of the scorecard results is to allow for asset prioritization within the portfolio, and initial elimination of low-return asset opportunities. While the valuation is directional in its guidance, it is not relied upon as a complete and final valuation for the IP.

At the second stage of business analysis, the finance team initiates the customized model and structure for the asset set. This model takes into account the specific findings from the technical and business analyses to define the key assumptions and dependencies. In particular, specificity is brought to the elements of the business operation and investment required for the commercialization effort. For example, the IP may be marketed broadly to the end consumers at relatively low-unit-price points. Such a product generally should have very different sales cycle time frames, costs, and staffing requirements than an enterprise-oriented product that requires significant investment and integration effort on the part of the customer. Moreover, the finance team also incorporates market dynamics and trends into the model at this stage, providing a more accurate environmental backdrop for the IP's pricing, adoption, and life span.

The differing economics of these and other relevant business characteristics for the IP and resulting commercial offering are developed in a "bottom-up" approach. This stage of financial analysis also provides comparative views of alternative disposition approaches under consideration by the business development team. Therefore, risk assessment is included in the analysis, as described earlier. The result is a more detailed and rigorous valuation of the IP based on its economic impact to the marketplace and the risks associated with various commercialization approaches. The IP leadership team uses these results to guide decision making for appropriate disposition approach by balancing risk, return, and time lines against overall funnel opportunities.

Finally, the finance team provides similar leadership in pricing analysis. Before describing this phase in detail, the difference between pricing and valuation should be noted. Valuation reflects the economic value and return resulting from the IP in a given market or industry application. It reflects a macro view of the market. Pricing, however, is specific to a particular set of terms and partner characteristics. For this reason, execution risk, which results from the specific characteristics of the parties engaged for commercialization, should be factored into the pricing analysis, not the valuation analysis.

Pricing analysis, another critical responsibility of the finance team in support of IP transactions, aims at adapting the framework for the "market and commercialization" approach developed in the valuation model and applying it reflect the specific circumstances of a particular development or channel partner. Thus, the pricing model should reflect the overall market reach, position, and effectiveness of the partner within the chosen industry. Moreover, resource availability and expected development time frames prior to launch of the commercial solution based on the IP should be incorporated into the model. Execution risk, as noted above, should be included here—most likely in the discount rate. For example, if the partner is a stable, large market participant with ample access to needed capital, customers, and other success factors, the discount rate should be lower. The resulting pricing model should be a dynamic tool used throughout the commercialization negotiations.

As the terms are modified through discussion between the parties, the model can reflect impact to the overall expected returns from the transaction. In a similar fashion, the model can provide specific guidance for counterproposals in the negotiations. For example, if the development partner prefers a graduated royalty rate that declines over time, the model can provide guidance on royalty rate changes to achieve such a goal. The finance team also provides structural guidance (along with direction from the legal team) for the transaction. Often, structural changes can be made to accommodate both parties' cash flow or risk-mitigation needs.

As expected, the rigorous financial analysis outlined above requires well-qualified specialists in finance and economics. Dave Elliott, one of SBC Knowledge Ventures' finance leaders, summed up the results of the finance team's work as follows, "Valuing intellectual property serves as an integral component of the analysis process. From a high level, it creates an independent risk-adjusted financial view of each IP asset. This helps to effectively allocate and prioritize resources among many IP assets. From an individual opportunity level, it allows us to value not only the asset as a whole, but also the value of a particular deal with a potential partner. Finance also plays a role in structuring a deal in the best possible terms."

In staffing this area of a commercialization-oriented IP management organization, seek individuals with in-depth financial training, preferably resulting from graduate education in the area. Additionally, members of the finance team should have significant experience in venture financing, investment banking, product pricing, or other valuation-oriented activities. The finance team serves as the stewards of financial valuation and quantification of risk in the IP commercialization plans of the unit, an important element in managing operational results on annual and longer-term bases.

Legal

The legal function within the IP unit operates and supports the business functions in a manner typical of any IP legal staff. The IP legal team manages efforts to secure and prosecute IP rights, guide licensing terms and negotiations in support of commercialization efforts, and provide mechanisms for risk management in deal structure and terms. The legal team also provides significant insight and analysis related to asset scope and interpretation, to allow the portfolio management team to accurately characterize and assess the IP portfolio. Often, the legal team's detailed knowledge of certain aspects of the portfolio (due to involvement in securing and protecting rights for the assets) makes them an important partner for the portfolio management team as they prioritize, group, and identify complementary assets for commercialization. The legal team is an integral part of the IP unit, and in a manner similar to the finance team, provides overarching guidance to the operations and strategies of the IP unit and its commercialization activities. As such, one of the most important aspects of their guidance is in assisting the business and financial teams in translating legal risk to business terms, and assisting in formulating terms that address business objectives while mitigating the legal risks involved.

In outlining the various functional areas comprising the successful "market and commercialize" IP management model described earlier, the intertwined nature of functions in the asset analysis and commercialization process should have been evident. Moreover, while each functional area necessarily staffs with specialized talent, the project-oriented nature of the work requires each team member to draw on a broad range of skills spanning technical, strategy, financial, marketing, sales, and legal topics. For example, the business development team and portfolio management team must each draw on experience and knowledge of the legal considerations surrounding IP, how these rights may be exercised, and how to translate business intention into contract language. Moreover, it has already been noted that the technical members of the portfolio management team are well served to have significant business experience in product delivery, specification, or technical marketing to ensure a balanced perspective on the vitality of the IP under review. The finance team's modeling efforts should mirror the qualitative and quantitative findings of the business development and portfolio management teams. To accomplish this, the finance staff should be comfortable in the analytical approaches used by the business development team, and have experience to guide them in testing or questioning key assumptions. The legal team also must draw on a practical understanding of business relationships, negotiations, and motivations. In particular, experience in structuring sales or procurement transactions provides them experience in managing risk while still reaching consensus. Understandably, the business development team must bring marketing expertise to evaluate and define the market opportunities and customer needs, along with sales expertise in engaging and managing multiple customer interactions, effectively predicting close rates and time frames for active commercialization efforts in the funnel, and managing analysis and disposition activities to achieve appropriate funnel depth and transaction volumes. These additive elements in each functional area's approach and expertise are summarized in Exhibit 4.4.

EXHIBIT 4.4 Summary of Functional Skills

	Technical	Business	Financial	Marketing	Sales	Legal
Capturing role	●	◕	◑	◔	○	◑
Legal role	◑	◑	◔	○	◔	●
Analysis role	◑	●	●	◕	◑	◕
Licensing role	◑	◕	●	●	●	◕
Finance role	○	◕	●	◑	◕	◕

Source: SBC Knowledge Ventures.

Operational Controls

With a focus on a "market and commercialize" IP strategy, the IP unit must measure its success against specific financial and operating targets. The IP unit charged with value creation for the firm through external partnering and deployment of IP assets should adopt the business fundamentals of any profit center delivering products to the marketplace. In this regard, the first measure should be effectiveness in managing revenue and expense on a long-term basis, the implication being that the unit should be able to manage resources toward near-term objectives and that the leadership has the ability to forecast and achieve long-term, repeatable, and reliable results for the corporation. To do otherwise would yield erratic business results—some years up, some years down, and always a bit of a "lottery ticket." Such an operation does not qualify as a peer to the other profit center business units in the firm; rather, it presents an annual challenge to the managers across the business regarding required results to achieve corporate-wide performance objectives.

Financial results alone are not adequate to measure the effectiveness of the IP unit's commercialization efforts. As with other business areas, the IP unit should also measure itself against operational metrics related to the core business drivers of the unit. For example, in a manufacturing environment, a business measures (among other things) work-in-progress inventory and inventory turns as indicators of efficiency in the manufacturing process. Similarly, the IP unit must assess its efficiency in identifying strong opportunities, developing rigorous and fair valuations for the IP assets, and converting these opportunities to revenue over the near and long term.

Fundamentally, metrics provide the business leadership a means for monitoring progress, gaining and maintaining support, and ensuring performance. A widely repeated business adage encapsulates the role of metrics: "Expect what you inspect." Metrics vary from simple qualitative assessments to more complex calculations, but all focus on signaling the health and direction of the operation. Ideally, the leadership team is armed with data regarding both leading and lagging indicators so that proper remedies can be implemented as leading indicators indicate potential variance from expected performance levels, and appropriateness of the remedy can be verified through the lagging indicators' data. For the IP function, leading indicators include IP portfolio depth and growth rates, transaction funnel depth, and yield rates at various stages of analysis and execution. Lagging indicators include final transaction pricing to valuation ratios, time frames associated with various analytical stages and deal execution, and overall revenue strength.

Operational and Financial Metrics

SBC Knowledge Ventures has divided operational and financial metrics into three distinct categories: business value metrics, portfolio metrics, and asset opportunity metrics. Business value metrics aim to assess performance in securing and creating value through the active commercialization of the IP portfolio. In particular, these metrics include assessment of average licensing rates, overall revenue per transaction and cumulatively over the active portfolio, and valuation to price ratio noted earlier. Business value metrics also assess cost coverage ratio of the unit. This provides a basis for understanding how well the primary resources (human capital, in the case of IP management) are being employed to achieve the revenue results of the organization. A related metric under the asset opportunity category tracks the cost coverage ratio against valuation on an IP asset group basis. This metric provides an important guidepost regarding which transactions and assets merit further pursuit, or conversely, how much value must be returned to exceed the cost of the transaction. This is particularly important in ensuring that smaller transactions are managed to limit complexity and time to close.

The business value metrics provide valuable insight to the profitability of the IP operation and its contribution of value to the overall firm. In particular, these measures focus on the heart of the "market and commercialize"–oriented strategy by signaling how well the IP unit is building a long-term revenue platform from the deployment of IP into the marketplace. Furthermore, the balance of expense- and revenue-oriented metrics ensures focus on operational efficiency and cost management, important considerations in the broader corporate context of which areas to continue to sustain and which to abandon. The business value metrics also should attempt to capture tangential value related to the IP strategy; such returns include lower cost of operation or purchase of products from partner suppliers and improved customer retention and market position through IP exclusivity. Finally, the comparison of valuation to achieved pricing provides a tangible measure of the finance team's accuracy in valuation of IP assets and the business development team's effectiveness in business planning and negotiations.

Portfolio metrics assess the utilization and effectiveness of the IP portfolio and related commercialization activities. They provide the management team with an overview of the quality of IP assets, both historically and prospectively, and ongoing business potential. They also serve as a qualitative measure of the portfolio management function's effectiveness. Portfolio metrics include volume of IP disclosures generated from the various business areas, portfolio growth in key focus areas, number of annual patent filings, number of other IP assets cataloged and characterized, and active asset funnel depth. These metrics provide valuable insight into the effectiveness of the IP communication and training programs, and the breadth of employee involvement in IP production, identification, and capture. As noted earlier, a key indicator of the long-term success of the "market and commercialize" IP strategy is the ongoing strength of employee involvement in IP protection and identification from all areas of the business, not just traditional sources such as engineering and R&D. The number of communication and training events provides a leading indicator of employee involvement. It has been consistently demonstrated that IP strategy and objectives communicated through training sessions result in measurable increases in ideation rates, IP submission rates, and IP licensing awareness and support by trained employee groups. The training provides a first step in the virtuous cycle, being reinforced through the innovation and IP recognition programs instituted by the IP unit. It should be noted that the communication of IP goals must take place at all levels of the organization—from thought leadership by senior executives (e.g., Ford Motor Company CEO Bill Ford's recent statement that "innovation is going to be the compass by which this company sets its direction."[4]) to

[4]Bill Coughlin in remarks at joint webcast of the National Knowledge and IP Management Taskforce and the Conference Board on October 6, 2005.

operational expectations regarding the need to protect *all* assets of the business, to concrete goals for employee contribution to the IP portfolio, to educational training for employee groups. The IP unit obviously has a strong hand in enacting this multitier communication, but must rely heavily on other leaders to also carry the message to their teams. Engaging leaders from across the business as partners in the IP effort is important to the overall success of the IP unit.

The portfolio management team's effectiveness can be traced somewhat directly to the volume of assets characterized, cataloged, and mined by the team, and the depth of the IP asset opportunity pool that exceed the business value metrics discussed earlier. At steady state, an IP operation can measure its long-term profit potential through the portfolio metrics related to utilization of the portfolio, in terms of both active asset opportunities and assets involved in closed transactions.

Asset opportunity metrics relate to the business analysis and execution aspects of the IP unit. In particular, these metrics focus on operational efficiency and accuracy in decision making. Metrics tracked include time to close transactions (beginning with initial asset identification and opportunity development), disposition approach mix, yield rates at each stage of analysis and execution, and overall revenue mix. Additionally, the type of assets involved in commercialization transactions should be tracked to provide insight into what types of asset bundles yield the strongest results for market entry and portfolio utilization. Moreover, the disposition mix and transaction mix provides an indicator of the strength of the long-term revenue platform. Given the prospective nature of the IP commercialization efforts, many transactions should result in recurring revenue for the firm. Thus, over time a strong annuity base can be developed for reducing volatility in annual financial performance. Finally, measuring the expenses associated with a particular IP commercialization effort against overall expected value provides an ongoing metric for guiding how to approach disposition, execution, and risk management. This not only ensures profitable operations overall, but assists business development, finance, legal, and portfolio management personnel in managing time allocated to analysis and customer engagement and complexity of terms and structure.

Conclusions

An IP commercialization strategy has the opportunity to unlock value from under-utilized assets within a firm and spur innovation across industries; however, it also has inherent risks, some of which can be mitigated and others that cannot. Firms considering an IP strategy focused on "market and commercialize" should acknowledge the similarity in purpose to venture capital investing. In the case of IP commercialization, firms are investing IP as capital, rather than cash. However, the model is in large part a "success-based" model such that the financial success of the IP is linked to the execution success of the commercialization path. In many cases, this will require performance by a third party, the licensee. Thus, commercialization agreements should focus adequate attention on mitigating risks associated with the performance of the development partner. For example, providing the development partner with needed pricing flexibility while ensuring a minimum return from unit sales manages risk that the partner will understate the value of the IP in a broader package or set of offerings to the end customer. Additionally, IP owners may consider stipulating specific investment levels by the development partner for marketing, development, and other activities necessary for bringing the IP to market. Finally, risk in missed market opportunity due to longer-than-anticipated development activities on the part of the licensee can be mitigated through specific performance milestones and thresholds. Failure to meet such elements could be remedied in a number of ways, including increased up-front payments or reversion of IP rights extended to the development partner.

Several studies have indicated that less than 5% of the global intellectual property value is realized.[5] Using this as a rough proxy for the individual firm portfolio, managers should set realistic expectations regarding the scope of licensing opportunity and return from the IP portfolio. By employing more sophisticated and integrated analytical processes to evaluate and qualify IP assets for commercialization, a firm may well be able to exceed this level. However, even a doubling or tripling of performance would put the IP commercialization activity on a similar success rate to venture capital funds. Venture capital funds traditionally expect 10% of their portfolio to exceed expectations, or produce "home run" results. These few stellar performers provide the bulk of the performance and return for the fund. An IP commercialization strategy aimed at deploying IP to the market through partnering and new-product introduction should be expected to realize similar results. For this reason, the volume of transactions is important, and consequently the efficiency and accuracy of the business analysis process is a fundamental element of long-term success. It is the balanced outcome of nimble decision-making strategies and rigorous business planning to improve the odds of successful IP commercialization.

[5]Dr. Steve Henning in remarks at joint webcast of the National Knowledge and IP Management Taskforce and the Conference Board on October 6, 2005, citing results from a British Technology Group study.

5

Innovation Asset Portfolio: The Intellectual Property Muse Gets an MBA

Damon C. Matteo

Innovation has pulled off perhaps its greatest inventive feat ever—it has reinvented itself as chic. Perception has long relegated research and development (R&D) and innovation to the dark basement hallways of corporate research labs, roamed only by "nerds" with thick glasses and the hapless few who got lost on their way to somewhere that was actually important. Well, the lights are on now; perhaps they have always been, and we've only just noticed. Either way, the spotlight is tightly focused on innovation as a keystone of corporate fitness, and in many cases its survival. So, it's not surprising that there is a lot of new (and renewed) interest in innovation. We see it everywhere now, not just in dusty esoteric journals, but in the fashionable press as well, and it even conspicuously adorns the corporate logos of well-known companies (e.g., Hewlett-Packard's "Invent"). How much more mainstream can you get? As is often the case, however, new attention is easier to focus on a subject than are new skills. Often, newfound passion leads us to start painting before we even know how to hold the brush. Skills and the requisite contextual sensitivities with which to apply them need to be cultivated over time. This chapter is a response to those lag effects and an attempt to improve our artistic endeavors in realizing value from innovation with a "paint-by-numbers" jump-start, so to speak.

All of this interest in innovation isn't really surprising if we look at the current environment in which corporations need to operate: Margins and product life cycles are shrinking, competitive pressure is growing, the need for speed to market and distinguishing functionality has never been more important, and the costs of R&D continue to skyrocket. The list goes on, and this litany of market conditions means that companies don't simply operate anymore—they compete, and the competition is fierce. Companies are looking for an edge, or at the very least a life jacket. Enter, innovation.

Finding Value in Innovation

From high-tech to lowest-of-tech, companies are scratching their heads trying to figure out how to satisfy that pressure to find additional value, and now they are looking to innovation. Many are forming intellectual property (IP) commercialization programs in response. Typically, this means either licensing/assigning their IP assets or asserting them against another company. Assertion has recently become a tool of choice for many organizations. But, again, we often see that interest in value extraction exceeds our skill to effectively realize it. As we react, the pendulum swings too far in one direction—both in terms of exceeding companies' ability to execute with appropriate skills and resources and even often beyond what is in its best interests. The "new" interest in realizing innovation value often takes the form of a single-minded focus on exploiting the near term and "free" money from assertion and licensing. Companies can unknowingly exhaust their innovation assets in this type of feverish short-term exploitation, or worse, see those precious assets naively squandered. This can leave companies without the "found" revenue they are counting on in the future, but more importantly leave them without the necessary innovation assets to support their current or future core business.

As in many reactive situations, the sense of long-term balance between opposing forces can be skewed by near-term pressure. The forces out of balance here are familiar to us all: extraction versus investment. Attendant to the manifest pressure to extract additional value is the need to reduce costs, so R&D budgets are shrinking at the same time demands on innovation are on the rise. If this trend continues, there is real danger of consuming innovation resources faster than you can replenish the supply. It's hard to strike that balance without an understanding of the context, the key parameters, and the opportunity costs associated with the different scenarios. As I've suggested, the lag-effect disparity between interest level and skill level often gets in the way of identifying and striking the appropriate balance. In addition, the near-term extraction focus of most of this activity tends to view innovation assets as a *fait accompli* (as opposed to focusing on creating assets better suited to the demands of this new environment) and as an inexhaustible resource (more of that "free money" mania). What we begin to lose here is the appreciation that innovation assets need also to be carefully created and strategically nurtured—keeping the pump primed, so to speak. Make no mistake about it, there is new money to be had from innovation assets, but it is far from free.

Moving R&D into Accountability

We see what is driving the new interest in innovation: intense competitive pressure, which immediately translates into pressure to extract additional value. And *value* is cast in terms alien to many research organizations, but quite familiar to most business functions: investment and returns. Bringing innovation into the return on investment (ROI) part of the business equation is a good thing. Innovation has perhaps begun to atrophy and languish in the land of sunk costs, and given today's competitive pressures and limited R&D budgets, there seems little alternative to moving R&D further into accountability.

In this kind of an environment, research functions become R&D organisms, which have to sustain themselves as such, and are unique in that virtually every element of the innovation food chain is open to them and increasingly required of them. So research organizations can no longer afford to live in the isolated (or, perhaps insulated) world we have come to expect, but in reality theirs is more of a hybrid world, where all things are possible and sometimes even necessary. Much of what we read in the press, and much of what companies are now furiously engaged in doing with their innovation assets involves value extraction. The pressure to extract value is clear and palpable. Rising to that challenge means recognizing the need to operate with equal facility in multiple domains and be accountable for that activity in order to be successful.

Yet there is an opportunity resident in this obligation that shouldn't be ignored. Stepping back to look at innovation assets as the product of research affords an expansive and rich view of all of its potential applications and the myriad vehicles available for realizing its value. However, this requires a fundamental change in the perception of the business of R&D—the realization that it *is* a business. There is also an opportunity to view R&D as an investment, and like any investment we want to nurture it—place it where it will grow most effectively and provide the greatest returns (and change our ideas about how to measure returns). Making these fundamental changes in the perception of R&D has incredible power: to make money, to make research more relevant, and to create a vibrant and sustainable enterprise of innovation. Empowering that perspective shift and executing against it is at the core of what we'll call the innovation asset portfolio (IAP) approach.

Everyone knows the term *portfolio* when speaking about intellectual property. Again, the popular press has made much of portfolio comparisons, most commonly on the basis of pure patent "headcount"—a blunt instrument for comparison, which rarely takes you beyond the "mine is bigger than yours" level of sophistication. By this measure, all companies have an IP portfolio, and by implication, more is better. Well, that is not really "portfolio" in the true sense, and certainly not in the IAP sense that we will be developing. It is simply an aggregation of intellectual property. Not all IP is created equal. Therefore, we can safely assume that not all patent portfolios are equal. As George Orwell accurately observed, some are more equal than others.

Our objective is to secure some of that advantaged inequality in our own portfolio, and our framework for doing so is the IAP approach: an operating context for creating and sustaining value from innovation. IAP focuses on innovation assets, but as vehicles for realizing broader corporate objectives, not as independent assets themselves. So the first-order goal is always to identify the corporate objectives at issue (e.g., revenue, savings, or strategic advantage). The second-order goal is to divine and develop areas of IP that confer advantaged positions for realizing those objectives, by virtue of, for example, leveraging multiple competencies, identifying multiuse technology, mapping IP coverage to support product interests, and identifying blocking positions against competitors. When deciding which individual pieces of IP to actually seek and secure, this notion of ROI (return on innovation) figures prominently in our IAP thinking (i.e., on the margin, how this incremental investment serves the greater objectives). It may seem slightly counterintuitive that the IAP approach, admittedly an innovation asset methodology, does not serve the greater good of innovation first and foremost. Yet, by invoking *asset* as part of the methodology, it calls the innovation into the service of a higher purpose: achieving the broader corporate objectives. IAP is about creating optimal innovation assets for realizing corporate strategy.

As with any ideal investment portfolio, an IAP portfolio is diverse—it strives to hedge against risk and minimize investment, and endeavors to identify assets that will best appreciate in value. An IAP portfolio, however, achieves diversity in a different way: by spanning the many types of IP (e.g., patent, copyright, and know-how), by including early- and late-stage research, by placing investments across multiple technology domains, and by contemplating multiple commercialization vehicles for realizing value. An IAP portfolio also seeks to minimize investment. All of this is formative and speaks to the targeting and creation of innovation assets, and cannot be solely reactive to extant innovation assets. For innovation, that often translates into increasing research efficacy through better targeting, and also by obviating bad investments in technology or application areas that hold little promise or are strewn with obstacles. Finally, and principally, an IAP portfolio is designed to maximize returns—where the measure of returns can be as varied as the landscape of companies and markets a portfolio might serve. The return could be providing a leveraged IP position in a key market, reducing costs through process technology improvements, and/or using IP to block the trajectory of a competitor. Since viewing innovation assets as elements of a true portfolio is in many ways a new endeavor in the research community, we return to the necessity of skills. Creating and managing this kind of IAP portfolio requires specialized skills and the strategic framework for practicing them. It requires that we broaden and refine the measures by which we gauge their value and develop strategies for optimizing that value. The number and complexity of the moving parts here suggests a definite need to proceed from conscious design, rather than rely on serendipity.

A New Methodology

If the goal is conscious design, how do we raise our consciousness? We need a model that comprehends the nature, requirements, fragility, foibles, and objectives of the innovation asset. We need a methodology conceived with the notion of innovation as an *asset* at its very core. But, as suggested, innovation assets are unique, and so the IAP approach will also necessarily employ elements of traditional IP management. If you look at how lightweight and strong composite materials are, you realize that power derives from the blending of different materials. The power of the IAP approach also rises from the synthesis of several complementary materials: IP management and investment management methodologies. We will develop a methodological framework and the tools necessary to create and maintain a powerful IAP portfolio. The portfolio itself—and just as importantly, the exercise of its development—supports, informs, and shapes commercialization interests with the anticipation and goal of realizing value from that asset as its focus. Most, if not all, of the methodologies; resources; and, in particular, solutions and tools employed to develop an IAP portfolio in a research organization easily generalize to many operating scenarios.

On the more traditional IP management side, you can think of the IAP approach to innovation as having five key operational elements and one unifying element. As you might expect, each element helps inform and shape the other; this is not a serial process, but rather one that operates in parallel, iteratively, and with myriad "feedback" loops. While the demarcation between these elements is subjective (if not illusory in many ways), for convenience, we can think in terms of:

- *Capture.* As the name suggests, this ensures that all valuable assets are captured and properly codified so that they can be easily recalled, not using corporate memory, but databases, lab notebooks, invention disclosures, and filing systems. When best practiced, capture includes not just knowledge formally rendered in instruments like patents and copyrights, but also the more diffuse know-how that is often the key to implementing and realizing value from the patents and copyrights.
- *Protection.* Based on the evaluation, educated choices can be made about which assets to protect and how to protect them. The options here include seeking no protection, statutory protection, or protection by virtue of secrecy, more commonly referred to as *trade secrecy.* Statutory protection for innovations generally takes the form of patents, copyrights, and mask works. In the realm of statutory protection, the best option depends on the unique nature of the innovation, the target market, and the budget available.
- *Management.* This is the unifier, the synthesis—the strategic management of the innovation asset so carefully and lovingly produced by the other five elements of the process. At its core is the quest for optimization of resources, assets, and returns.

Since our stated goal isn't just the management of IP but the management of innovation investment assets, we need to meld investment management principles with these IP management methodologies. A purely IP management–based analysis reveals the myriad research options that potentially lead to advantage. But, if taken no further, these amount to little more than potentialities, and far more of them than most mortal R&D budgets could hope to pursue. So when IP management succeeds in filling our arms with potential, how do we identify which among the many IP goodies are most worthy of investment?

Measures of Value

No investment principle figures more prominently than stepping back to understand the fundamental reason(s) for establishing the portfolio in the first place. Of course, these objectives vary by company, industry, market segment, corporate culture, and even a company's maturity. Each organization will have its own, and the important thing here is to focus on two key elements of the organization: its principal objectives and how it gauges success against those objectives. So how do we take our innovation targets that we have so lovingly nurtured and winnow them down to the precious few we can truly call investment-level IP? When looking at IP, there are several measures of value that merit investigating for each innovation asset and are the key criteria for IP to gain entry into the IAP portfolio. In aggregate, they gauge how well a particular innovation asset succeeds in realizing stated objectives (a notion we will return to discuss). You can think of these measures as broadly reflecting the characteristics of the innovation asset that impacts its value in the legal, technical, and market domains. In essence, these represent the many different worlds in which the innovation needs to live, breathe, and, if necessary, defend itself.

Legal

Legal measures of value tend to be instrument-centric. They focus on the instrument (e.g., patent or copyright) that embodies or conveys the rights to the innovation asset. Alone, that kind of focus can have tragic implications for the commercial impact of the innovation asset. However, taken in conjunction with the other measures of value, this focus operates as one perspective in a complementary set of views of the same asset. The other measures of value and their own perspectives on the asset fill out the entire picture and bring it to clarity. When looking at a legal instrument like a patent, you quickly realize that there are myriad metrics that are used to evaluate patents. Some of these metrics include the patent's pendency at the U.S. Patent and Trademark Office (USPTO), the number of claims (independent and/or dependent or their ratios), the number of citations, attorney time content, and the length of the specification. One attorney actually advanced the notion of using the PTO's payday as a useful metric, the principle here being that if you could time your submission or office action to hit the examiner's desk just after payday, he would be happier, and thus give your work a more favorable read. While certainly creative, its utility as a metric for patent quality is suspect. This is an admittedly extreme example, but the truth is that many of these metrics have an arbitrary nature to them if applied outside of the context of the patent's purpose. Commonsense guidelines exist, but they are of limited utility and often blunt instruments or, worse, misleading. The most telling reading of a legal metric is context sensitive. For example, consider the specification of a patent. A long specification is considered by some to open the patent up for attack, as it is overly expansive and may include more art than the patent itself can sustain. Yet a short specification may be leaving too much on the table and represent a missed opportunity for additional patent coverage. A long or short specification is neither good nor bad in and of itself Only in the context of how well it supports the invention and desired protection does the measure reveal value. Again, we have a recurrent theme of coupling the measure with context and objectives. In terms of patents, some of the broader objectives they might support include assertion, enablement (direct-to-product consumption), and licensing. Each of these introduces its own sensitivities and its own priorities in terms of measuring the potential value of the IP. For example, ease of infringement detectability might not even be on the radar for a patent destined for use only in the company's products. However, even if that is the primary use of the patent, the IAP approach suggests casting a broader net around potential value. The additional desire to assert the patent (for either strategic of monetary benefit) under the IAP model might raise detectability significantly in importance.

Technical

With regard to technology measures of value, there are also a number of different objectives that can be served. An obvious set of goals is to establish a foundational or unique position in a technology space to provide the basis for current or future products, or one that blocks the progress of a competitor. Less obvious are the investment-oriented objectives that are well served, if not only served by an IAP portfolio. An important IAP principle is to distribute the innovation investment. Distributing the investment has the potential to improve the chances of success and reduce risk. For example, technology, like most things, matures. Early-stage research often first eventuates seminal innovations that lay the fundamental groundwork in a technology space. Later, more application-focused innovations might be targeted at a particular way to use or extend the technology for a specific purpose, and then perhaps fully mature with product-specific implementations of that technology: a product. Generally speaking, the more tightly coupled the innovation asset is with a product, the stronger the protection it confers with respect to that element of the product. Seminal inventions may anticipate or provide the foundation upon which a product was built, but they often do not cover the product-specific implementations from which market advantage often derives. For example, foundational work in semiconductor materials may have laid the groundwork for the DVD players that were to follow, but don't capture the "product implementation" as a consumer electronics device. So, groundbreaking though these seminal innovations may have been, there may be no value to capture from them. However, merely focusing on product-specific innovations means running the risk that a seminal innovation by someone else might underlie and be required by your product (i.e., the seminal patent is "dominant" and blocks anything built upon it). Take the example of using the fundamental development of the blue semiconductor laser for that DVD player. There are a few companies with those foundational and blocking positions in blue lasers (e.g., Nichia), and by and large, any company that wishes to make advanced products employing them can do so only under a license to those foundational innovations. Distributing the innovation investment across this spectrum of technology maturity has the potential for covering all of the bases on your product. Laying the groundwork with more seminal innovations serves several investment objectives. It increases the potential for success by helping ensure a foundation upon which your anticipated products may later be built, and may be sufficiently broad that they enable multiple paths to productization (i.e., a hedge against a line of research that does not prove out). It may also be sufficiently broad that it can operate to hinder or keep competitors out of a product space entirely. Further up the technology maturity spectrum, where more risk has been eliminated, product-specific innovations have the potential to protect your particular value-add. This more specific type of later-stage innovation is often best focused on functionality that maps directly to the sources (e.g., unique functionality) of market advantage.

Market

Identifying those points of market advantage and mapping innovations to them is the goal of the market measures of value. This secures a place in the market for the innovation, but hopefully an advantaged position as well. It is often useful to look at the innovation asset in terms of whether it provides an entrée into an entirely new market or solidifies a position in an existing market. Another key element in achieving market success is often being able to identify the pain/pleasure point for consumers. Market measures of value suggest the extent to which an innovation captures the salve for the pain or the allure for the pleasure. Innovation assets that map directly to these sources of market advantage rise to the top of our investment list, and ones for which we seek to establish an advantaged IP position. In our previous DVD example, the ability to move to a shorter wavelength (i.e., blue laser), significantly increases the storage capacity of the disk and provides a compelling salve for the pandemic pain of too much data to store. In a very real sense, this translates to realizing the objectives of market research through innovation research: Find the need in the market, and find the solution through innovation. This principle is at the heart of the IAP approach—using innovation assets as vehicles for realizing higher objectives. One additional reflection of market value here is the exclusivity of the innovation asset. Establishing an IP position that gives you the ability to render some functionality is powerful, but if there are truly no other ways to provide that functionality, such a blocking position adds value far beyond just its enabling nature. When this market-advantage filter is applied, special attention might also be given to innovation assets with no or difficult work-arounds. Monopoly power works in the realm of innovation as well.

Linkages and Dependencies

There are linkages and dependencies among the legal, technical, and market measures of value, so weakness in one often diminishes value or viability in another. This negative dependency tends to propagate negative properties of innovation across value boundaries, while the positive elements tend to be more narrowly confined. Imagine an innovation around a new "killer app." Further imagine enormous demand, and that the technology developed addresses the market need perfectly. Yet, if there is no way to get a position in the IP that supports and enables the technology, then there may not be a killer app after all. Prior art can kill your killer app, or perhaps just dilute your returns because you need to secure rights from third parties to practice your technology (as in our blue laser example where another company had blocking fundamental IP). Powerful advantage in both the market and technology measures of value is stymied by a weakness in the legal measures of value. An IAP portfolio, by its nature and purpose, attempts to anticipate and understand exactly this type of linkage scenario and enable educated decisions at an early stage of innovation investment about how to avoid or mitigate them: a simple, but powerful distinction between *anticipating* circumstances and later *reacting* to them. Getting to the value of the innovation asset is really a journey through all of those different worlds, and only then into the domain of value: a confluence of legal, technical, and market measures of value. Like any good investor, we've established our measures of value. We now turn to how and where to apply them in service of our broader objectives. For this we need context.

That means going back to fundamental principles, and treating the costs and output of research as what they are: investments and (potential) returns. An IAP portfolio is an IP portfolio with a slightly different flavor, more of an investment portfolio. As with any portfolio, there is cost (R&D budget), returns (for which the IP is the vehicle), and risk. The guiding principle of managing any portfolio is to minimize cost, optimize returns, and obviate risk. Hardly rocket science at its core, yet rarely is it applied effectively to IP portfolios. The other investment principle is that of marginal contribution, that is, incrementally, how much more is gained by the portfolio from adding this one additional piece of IP or entering this new realm of research. The measure of value here is how well it incrementally serves the objectives of the portfolio and to what extent it is expected to contribute to the portfolio ROI (return on innovation). Another unfortunate similarity to other types of investment portfolios is that IP portfolios rarely live up to promised returns. (You need only look at my own stock portfolio to know that returns are far from guaranteed.) Identifying the objectives and their relative priorities is the first step, and the weighting of the measures of value flows from the specific objectives the innovation needs to serve. Not surprisingly, though, these efforts often fall into service of only a handful of basic objectives. These include profit/revenue, cost, and risk. Generally speaking, a solid IAP portfolio will support all of these objectives to varying degrees, but often there are one or two that rise to a greater level of import for a corporation. Depending on the corporation's current state, either revenue generation, risk management, or even cost containment might be of particular import. We'll look at each of these individually.

Profit/Revenue

Profit is a fundamental objective loved by one and all, and not surprisingly so. Profit drives everything from the company's very existence to its growth and, appropriately enough, its innovation investment. How, then, can an IP portfolio support profit objectives? Answers to that question become the IAP filters for screening our myriad innovation opportunities. In a fiercely competitive environment, perhaps one of the key ways to preserve market share is to improve extant products and services. Let's say you offer a streaming data service to cable modem and DSL subscribers, which provides up-to-the-minute weather information. You've executed so well on this product that you are a victim of your own success—you've captured the lion's share of the market, and growth has stalled because there is no more market to get. A deeper look using some of the IAP methods may suggest that performance improvements like better compression to support faster data transmission could enable you to move the service downmarket into low-bandwidth devices like cell phones and wireless personal digital assistants (PDAs). This is an enormous market opportunity, and the IP necessary to support it needs to find expression in the portfolio commensurate with the scope of the opportunity and tailored to secure the IP protection necessary to provide the advantaged position. This is a direct mapping of innovation assets to commercial objectives, with IAP as the enabling bridge between them.

As with any investment, there is a measure of risk associated with seeking to create a new innovation. Depending on the level of risk (and reward) associated with a particular line of research, a company may wish to open a second line, with a slightly different approach. When considered as a formative part of the new research strategy rather than after the fact, this kind of "hedge" can operate to the company's advantage in several ways. If one approach does not prove out, having the option of a second approach improves the odds of ultimate success. In the data compression example, the importance of success and the magnitude of the opportunity suggest that multiple paths may, in fact, be warranted. Yet, no matter how desirable, truly multiple paths may not be feasible due to constraints of time, money, or even human capital. Here, it may make sense to choose the optimal path to pursue in earnest, but to hedge, lay the groundwork with several early-stage innovations in one or several other technology approaches. Each of these might be initial forays into the approaches and not pursued to the depth of the principle approach. These forays and the ground they capture can provide a safe-harbor from which to begin again if the first path proves untenable, but may also provide blocking or valuable IP positions with respect to competitors. A blocking position can be used to hinder a competitor or gain financially from that competitor via licensing. If the competitor has its own blocking IP, yours may be used as a trading chip in a cross-license so that you won't be barred from working in that domain, or to comprise part of a "patent war chest" in the event that you are the target of an assertion. Anticipating all of these potential (beneficial) outcomes is a principal part of applying the IAP approach to risk management. Failing to do so can leave the company blocked from an important line of research or trammeled with the need to secure and pay for licenses to third parties.

Cost

Cost, of course, is equally familiar, but not as widely embraced as the profit objective. In the context of innovation, cost really needs to be looked at on two levels: the cost of innovation and the cost *implications* of innovation. Cost of innovation is fairly straightforward—the amount of money (and other resources) required in order to secure the innovations on my hit list. IAP has the potential to mitigate many of the costs associated with research and therefore increase its efficiency. It is not only the buck, but the "bang for the buck" that matters most. By obviating false starts in research areas that are fraught with technical or competitive stumbling blocks, a thorough IAP program has the potential to save a great deal of money and time. Innovation, however, can also have implications for cost savings. A good example of this is an innovation that eliminates a processing step in a semiconductor fabrication process for a company's products. There may be a cost associated with the innovation itself, but there is also a cost savings associated with the process improvement outcome. In a price-sensitive market, cost savings may be more important than new functionality or improved performance, so looking at your corporate cost objectives also provides a critical filter in terms of determining on the margin which innovations hold the most promise.

Risk

Strategic goals are perhaps the most varied and diffuse objectives to be served by innovation assets. They embrace a broad array of objectives, including the public relations advantage inuring to your benefit because of the sheer number of patents in your portfolio (e.g., IBM), the competitive advantage of being able to block/sue a competitor, or even enhancing an existing relationship. The unique IAP filters required to accomplish these objectives are a weighted combination of all of our measures of value. For example, where assertion is paramount because of its potential to hinder a rival, perhaps the legal patent principles of detectability and enforceability are weighted more heavily than they would be if the company simply wanted to enable its own products. If the corporate business model does not comprehend that kind of offensive assertion, then that vehicle and its attendant measures of value can be deemphasized in asset selection. Yet to create a truly serviceable IAP portfolio, even if you don't "do" assertion, you may want to protect against it. The advent of patent trolls and the increased competitive pressures in the marketplace have seen an attendant increase in assertion activity (spurious and legitimate). One might also argue that fierce competition over the same markets, the increasing complexity of many commercial products, and the resulting variegated IP landscape increase the risk of actual infringement. In that kind of environment, it is wise to have a few arrows in your quiver for defensive counterassertion even if you don't want to be the first to fire.

Again, the measures of value are cast broadly, and with an eye to secure equally broad corporate objectives. You may also get the sense that these objectives and the measures that support them operate in some fashion as overlays and/or inputs to one another. That is very true, and perhaps one of the more valuable benefits of an IAP approach is to help divine and anticipate the linkages and dependencies among these elements *and* all of the potential vehicles for realizing value from their output. With so many dependent variables, it's all too easy to optimize for one without realizing it has been done at the expense of another, perhaps more important, one. Cliché though it may be, here and elsewhere in developing an IAP portfolio, knowledge is most assuredly power.

Since we've now learned the various elements of "paint-by-numbers," let's put brush to canvas and examine how some of these IAP principles are realized in practice.

Selection of Research Targets

One of the first stops on the way to identifying and capturing the innovation leverage resident in an IAP portfolio is the actual selection of the research targets themselves. Using patents as shorthand for our innovation assets, there are myriad tools available for analysis and evaluation of the patent landscape. In general, though, most of these tools can be thought of as looking at patents in either the time domain or the application domain. Patent analysis of an application space across several related or even disparate domains can indicate which areas are densely populated and which are sparse. In short, it shows who is doing what and where they are doing it. Looking at the same data in the time domain can open a window into the activity in a specific field over time. It suggests growing or waning interest in an application area. Understanding how particular application areas evolve over time can help you predict opportunities to pursue and obstacles to avoid. From a competitive perspective, it can allow you to draw powerful inferences about the industry and its participants, and reveal how competitors are approaching the technology space. This is critical intelligence in determining whether to even enter that domain of inquiry, but also how you might gain advantage and avoid jeopardy. Looking at a competitor's patent landscape chronicles intensity of research activity over time, allowing inferences about both direction and speed of travel. That kind of information is invaluable if you want to "head them off at the pass" or simply avoid an IP collision in the marketplace. Perhaps equally important, it has the power to reveal the competency content of the competitor's products, their leverage points, and, to the careful eye, even their weaknesses.

When looking at the patent landscape for an industry or a technology domain, a common target on most people's radar is "white space." White space refers to a portion of the application space or technology domain only sparsely populated by IP. The potential allure here is that white space is a safe place to invest R&D efforts, since there are few blocking or competitive IP positions. One interpretation of the thinly populated space is that there is first-mover advantage to be gained, and a solid, enabling position in IP can be established. Of course, it might equally suggest that no one is there—and perhaps for good reason. They may have tried and failed because of insurmountable technical barriers, or concluded that there wasn't sufficient market advantage to merit the cost of the research in the first place. In reality, a white space really serves only to flag an opportunity potentially worth investigating. But white space opportunities have the potential to serve several broader corporate objectives. If they are truly an open field for creating a foundational IP position, having identified them early promises to increase research efficiency (lower its cost) and also increase its efficacy (secure an advantaged position in a market to increase revenue potential). Should the white space prove to be empty for good reason, IAP will have pointed to that fact before significant time and money was invested, also improving research efficiency.

In addition to the often coveted white space, there is also what I call "black space. These are areas of dense patent population, and general wisdom suggests that you avoid these; it is impossible to secure a meaningful position in such a crowded technology space. Well, I've never been accused of being conventional, so perhaps black space is really an opportunity in disguise. Although it may not be possible to enter a black space with the intention of building a stand-alone enabling position to bring to market, there are still potential opportunities to exploit. Since the assignee is part of the information contained in the patent, the patent has the power to illuminate the landscape of potential competitors to, and consumers of, your innovations. If these companies are active in the black space, they might be willing to license or otherwise acquire some of the IP you have generated. The transaction might take the form of an outright assignment in which you completely divest yourself of the asset. Or perhaps it would grant only rights in a field of use that is not invasive of your own commercial interests, enabling you to have your cake and eat it too (some of that "found" money that innovation commercialization promises to provide). Alternately, if the time-domain analysis suggests that a company is exiting the space (high-intensity waning to low-intensity patenting), you might be in a position to cost-effectively acquire some of their IP to use to your own advantage. And again, in the spirit of creating a strategic IAP portfolio, "advantage" is cast broadly. Assets of interest for acquisition would certainly include those to bolster or advance current internal research, but would also include assets that could provide a "hedge" alternative pathway in case the current line of research does not prove out. Acquisitions can also jump-start a new line of research or even be asserted against a competitor. So an area of research that might have initially been dismissed as too congested and contested to touch has the potential to yield competitive and financial advantage.

In today's research climate, both competitive and financial advantage are most welcome. We've seen how applying IAP principles can help identify advantaged positions in IP, but often advantage in a single position is not enough. That single point of advantage needs to be leveraged into multiple points of benefit. IAP has the potential to deliver leverage on those advantaged innovation assets in a number of different ways. In order to be attractive (and cost effective), research increasingly needs to have the potential to serve multiple masters simultaneously. These "masters" can include direct-to-product consumption of the innovation assets (designing them and using them with a specific product/service in mind as the end purpose), licensing, assignment, assertion, and even vehicles like spinouts or other equity plays. The pressure to find multiple vehicles for realizing value can arise from just the sheer cost of doing the R&D, its inherent risk, or the inability of the sponsoring company to provide sufficient "uptake" for the total utility of an innovation. To bring a little more clarity to the notion of uptake, look at the example of a semiconductor laser innovation that can be used for consumer electronics (e.g., CD/DVD players), medical therapeutics (e.g., photodynamic therapy), and telecom applications (e.g., optical switching). Companies in all three markets may want (or even need) the improvements that the innovation promises, but no one of them has sufficient market access across all of its potential uses to exploit all of its potential utility; perhaps no one market can really support the required research expense. None of these companies alone would invest in the research if it believed that it had no real prospect of realizing enough value in its own market to justify the expense and the attendant risk. Part of developing an IAP portfolio is to identify just exactly that kind of shortfall in revenue justification, saving the company from potential losses. Yet an even more powerful element of constructing an IAP portfolio is to identify how to make that innovation possible, *despite* the market realities of limited uptake. A licensing, or joint-venture, or cooperative R&D effort flowing from the IAP evaluation can make an untenable area of research suddenly possible or even very appealing. Here, a collaborative research endeavor between a company in each of two or even all three of these markets has the promise to make that laser innovation possible. Pooling resources and investments in the research reduces the distributed cost of the innovation (roughly by one third if all three participate) to the point where it becomes cost effective for each company. There is also no threat of competition from the fellow collaborators, since the reason for the collaboration in the first place was that none of the companies spanned more than one market space. So IPA can reveal and help execute against situations in which several companies have technology synergies but divergent markets. Doing so, and doing so effectively with minimal risk and optimal returns, however, requires that the IAP approach be a *formative* part of R&D strategy, not as a *reaction* to its output.

Multiple Commercialization Vehicles

Another key leverage element of an IAP portfolio approach is to identify, create, and exploit synergies in research efforts with an eye for downstream commercialization through multiple commercialization vehicles. These vehicles can represent the company's own products, as well as licensing of the asset to a third party, assertion of the asset against an infringer, spinouts in which there is sufficient critical mass of assets, or even new application areas in which to exploit the innovation assets. The creative foundation of many innovation assets is competencies. For example, in a semiconductor company, these might range from expertise in characterizing semiconductor materials to specific device architectures to data streaming on and off the chip. All of these can individually be thought of as competencies. Going beyond these individual competencies and leveraging them into IAP focuses can add a layer of value that is inaccessible in terms of individual competencies alone. An IAP focus is really a leveraged aggregation of complementary competencies in service of a particular application or objective.

In this semiconductor example, the obvious IAP focus might be their extant product—an input/output chip set. Ideally, a company should be operating within its IAP focus. This intersection of competencies is the innovation "sweet spot," where the company gets the most innovation leverage. However, a company can, and perhaps should, explore multiple IAP focuses. Looking at the native competencies in various ways, to see how they interact and how they can be recombined can reveal that they support a different purpose, an additional IAP focus. Let's look at an example of taking native competencies built around a specific product and extending them into a new IAP focus for realizing value. A company with a product line of ink-jet printers is likely to have core competencies in the ink-jet printing domain, for example, ejection, droplet control, precise fluid flow, droplet size, and so on. These competencies are uniquely suited to meeting the IAP focus of printing ink on paper—or are they? Might these native competencies be extended into new application domains, with new value potential? The answer is a resounding "yes." The same printing competencies can be extended into other application areas. For example, much of the same expertise in printing on paper lends itself to printing for semiconductor applications like printed organic electronics (POE). In POE, large feature-size elements of the device are in effect "printed" onto the substrate in accretive layers. A new IAP focus that makes this kind of new market domain accessible opens up vast potential for increasing revenues, and doing so with essentially the same innovation assets—leveraging them into a new application. Yet this potential can't be fully realized without the proper planning and anticipation that comes with an IAP portfolio approach. More than likely, if only the paper printing application was contemplated when the ink-jet patents were filed, the ability to extend this competency into the semiconductor application might be severely limited or even blocked by third-party IP. Without a protected position, the know-how alone might not be enough.

In developing an IAP focus, there are two principal leverage objectives at work. The primary objective speaks to identifying the innovations and/or competencies required to support the primary IAP focus of the company. Typically, this IAP focus is coincident with the company's core product line or service offerings. The IAP portfolio supporting this focus can be homegrown or also comprise innovations from other sources via licensing. As we've seen, the IAP process itself reveals information about the competitive landscape in the targeted application area. Based on the pathways and obstacles leading to the innovations in question, this intelligence can also be used in the make/buy decision for the research. In addition to serving the core product interests of the company, the IAP approach also attempts to leverage the native competencies and acquired complementary innovation assets into additional IAP focuses. These additional IAP focuses can be new applications in a new market space, as exemplified by the POE extension of the ink-jet IAP focus, but may instead comprehend different vehicles in the same market space. An example of this kind of leverage might be our printing company licensing or asserting its innovation assets in its principal market. The leverage point is still the same—the competencies that comprise the IAP focus—but the leverage derives from new vehicles in the same market here versus leverage from new markets in the POE example.

In each of these varied circumstances, there are layered goals of an IAP portfolio. Principally, the IAP portfolio is designed to serve stated corporate objectives, and then to divine which innovation assets can best serve those objectives. Operating in both domains creates a number of collateral benefits. Since the IAP process begins and ends with corporate objectives, it facilitates clarity around those objectives, their relative priorities, and the investment necessary to achieve them. This process anticipates the interactions, dependencies, and trade-offs inherent in the many potential options from which to choose. In fact, choice is one of the more powerful advantages of an IAP portfolio: It empowers proactive versus reactive decisions. It allows corporations to optimize among the options open to it. The attendant benefits to this kind of proactive approach include better risk management, resource planning, and product forecasting, and even helping obviate things like patent infringement.

The intent is not to suggest that the IAP approach should be the sole point of focus for realizing corporate objectives, nor that it is the panacea for any and all corporate weaknesses or missteps. Rather, our goal is to shed some light on and sharpen the edge of a powerful tool for rising to the challenges most corporations are now facing. Competition and the pressure to do more with less certainly calls IPA to our attention, and perhaps now, having seen some of its potential benefits, commands our attention.

PART 3

INNOVATION

6

Innovation Strategy: The Essential Ingredient

Michael Kayat

It's not the strongest of the species who survive, nor the most intelligent, but the ones most responsive to change.

—Charles Darwin

Introduction

. . . industrial mutation . . . that incessantly revolutionizes the economic structure from within, incessantly destroying the old one, incessantly creating a new one.

—Joseph Schumpeter

The world is becoming increasingly flat and populated with knowledge-based economies. The rules are changing; indeed, the game is changing. While we live in interesting times, we are all increasingly connected, our economies wired together. Markets in most industries are becoming more fragmented and segmented. Technologies are creating new markets. The difference between products and services is becoming blurred as the company *brand* becomes the all-important customer value proposition. Developed and developing countries are harnessing technology and process innovations in every type of industry. Low-cost providers are also becoming premium product innovators. Innovation involves inventing or finding new technologies and processes, product creation, strategy, and management, together with business models to capture revenues from subsequent product and service sales.

Innovation is inherently unstructured, unpredictable, and risky. Nearly 50% of enterprise research and development (R&D) budgets are wasted, and in the

United States this equates to approximately $100 billion a year invested in failed innovations (and enterprises with over 25,000 employees making up half this loss).[1] The biggest challenge in innovation is uncovering the right cost-effective technologies for identified customer or new market needs, together with the actual execution. Innovation can be both successful and profitable when combined with the proper commercialization strategy. But how can innovation be better managed?

Need for Innovation: The Strategy Review

Even during profitable times, enterprises must continue to review and reinvent their corporate strategy, especially in these high-speed times of change. Revenue and market share growth is again at the forefront with most Chief Executive Officers (CEOs) in many industries. Enterprises that have "right-sized" have generally reduced the "R" in R&D budgets and are now limited in internal resources. Even the largest global enterprises, with shareholder pressure on profitability, are struggling to maintain innovation and spot new markets. CEOs and their executive teams face many challenges.

An evolving, aware enterprise will take time and resources to organize strategy reviews and address a set of core questions:[2]

- Where do we put our priorities in allocating our resources in money and effort?
- What are the major policies that we choose to implement the strategy?
- What are the products and markets in which we choose to compete?
- What critical assumptions are we making about the competition and the environment?
- Exactly what do we expect to do differently or better than our competitors?

In many situations, executives lack clear information on how to answer these questions, even with input from customers, suppliers, and other advisers. It is vital that an enterprise understand the market forces and therefore the generic competitive strategies to adopt.[3]

---

[1]Organization for Economic Cooperation and Development. *OECD Economic Outlook*, vol. 2005, issue 1 (Paris: OECD, 2005).

[2]Henderson, Bruce D. *Henderson on Corporate Strategy* (New York: HarperCollins College Division, 1979).

[3]Porter, Michael E. *Competitive Strategy: Techniques for Analyzing Industries and Competitors* (New York: Free Press, 1998).

Fuel and Guidance for Innovation

Utilizing effective strategic intellectual property (IP) management can explicitly fuel, direct, and coordinate innovative activities to create successful market outcomes.

Indeed, IP assets comprising patents, trademarks, copyrights, technological know-how, designs, formulas, and trade secrets are the fastest-growing assets in many of the world's economies. The more visionary executives realize they can *quantitatively* answer some key questions on corporate strategy, competitive analysis, innovation opportunities (the product/market matrix) utilizing strategic IP management:

- Corporate strategy:
  - Is our IP aligned with our corporate strategy and business goals?
  - Who are our strategic IP partners?
  - Are we capturing all our IP?
  - How can we monetize our IP, which IP, and to whom?
  - How can we optimize the value of our IP portfolio?
  - Does our IP portfolio have high value with high protection?
  - Do we have any IP leakage?
  - Is our IP distributed over the whole value chain?
  - How can we get the best innovation return on investment?
- Competitive strategy:
  - Who are our *real* competitors, what do they have now, where are they going, and what are their IP landscapes and *innovation maps*?
  - Who will be our *surprise* competitors that we don't know in our IP universe?
  - Is our IP strong and complete enough for a product differentiation or low-cost leadership strategy?
  - What are the gaps in our competitors' IP portfolios?
  - What don't we know—what new IP and from whom?
- Product/market matrix:
  - Where are the new market space opportunities and how can we stake out and build IP in these white spaces?
  - How can we identify the new technologies, IP, and inventors we need to build new products?
  - What external IP can we use in our products?
  - How can we map IP to technology platforms and products to build *dominant position/pacing products*?

- How can we build a strong IP position and fill any gaps?
- How can we lock in these new technologies and build high-value IP portfolios?
- Do we have a *balanced* product portfolio?

Nature of Innovation

"Innovation is organized, systematic, rational work."

—Peter Drucker

". . . the bigger a business gets, the less and less interest it has in small opportunities. And all the big growth markets of tomorrow are small today."

—Clayton Christensen

Only about one in ten enterprises is somewhat successful at innovation and can maintain long-term growth levels acceptable to shareholders.[4] While there are occasional spectacular successes of innovation, very few can sustain innovation on a consistent basis. This section discusses the sources of innovation along with a review of a strategic approach to innovation, *disruptive innovation*, and a tactical approach, *open innovation*.

Sources of Innovation

Innovation can and should be systematized, much like invention and R&D. Enterprises generally have difficulty and delays in identifying opportunities for innovation in their industries. As noted, innovations exploit change, and Drucker[5] has provided a hierarchical list of *seven sources* of innovation that identifies areas to look and helps prioritize the innovation efforts within an enterprise. These sources are listed in the following table, in order of importance.

---

[4]Christensen, Clayton. *The Innovator's Dilemma: When New Technologies Cause Great Firms to Fail* (Boston: Harvard Business School Press, 1997).

[5]Drucker, Peter F. *Innovation and Entrepreneurship* (New York: Harper & Row, 1985).

Sources of Innovation

Within the Company	*Outside the Company*
1. Unexpected events or results	5. Population changes
2. Incongruities	6. Perception changes
3. Process needs	7. New knowledge
4. Unexpected changes in the industry and market structure	

The idea is to assign responsibility of monitoring and reporting on each of these areas to individuals or groups. Most R&D centers focus on *new knowledge* and *process needs*.

The most important area is *unexpected events or results*, indicating a shift or trend that opens up a new or larger market for the enterprise. After identifying the causes, new products or services can be developed if these are within the core competencies of the enterprise.

Then the area of *incongruities* ("things are not as they ought to be; something is screwy") usually indicates an important change that has yet to be recognized. Symptoms include high growth in an industry with no profits, or "offsets" between facts and assumptions or products and customer expectations. These are often ignored by the enterprise but are ripe opportunities for smaller, agile companies who build disruptive but simple, straightforward technologies and completely new markets. The area of *unexpected changes in the industry or market structure* also provides opportunities for disruptive innovation.

Innovation Models

The *disruptive innovation* paradigm was developed by Christensen[6] and is defined as: "An innovation that cannot be used by customers in mainstream markets. It defines a new performance trajectory by introducing new dimensions of performance compared to existing innovations. Disruptive innovations either create new markets by bringing new features to non-consumers or offer more convenience or lower prices to customers at the low end of the market."

---

[6]Christensen, Clayton M., and Raynor, Michael E. *The Innovators Solution: Creating and Sustaining Successful Growth* (Boston: Harvard Business School Press, 2003), and Christensen, *Seeing What's Next.* Harvard Business Press, Boston. (2005).

Enterprises and smaller companies need to integrate corporate strategy, market knowledge, technology, and IP management to develop a repeatable process for disruptive innovation. Disruptive innovations offer diminished performance in exchange for simplicity, convenience, and low price. Disruptive changes in an industry take advantage of the incumbent enterprise's weaknesses and blind spots.

In contrast, the more conservative approach of *sustaining innovation* aims to provide better, improved products and services usually at higher unit prices with next-generation performance. While the technology is a great leap forward ("breakthrough innovation"), it is usually more complicated and overshoots the capabilities (as well as the pocketbook) of a large number of potential customers.

The following table shows the strategy and tactics for developing and implementing disruptive innovation.

Disruptive Innovation Strategy and Tactics

Strategy	*Tactics*
Find markets that are not being addressed by established competitors	Target markets that are too small to meet the growth needs of large enterprises
Target the low end of the market or non-consumers ("great leap downward")	Create separate marketing and sales channels with new strategic partners, to focus on these new markets
Provide simpler, more cost-effective solutions	Develop stripped-down products and services for "overshot" customers who will accept "just good enough" performance trade-offs
	Avoid large R&D investments, be agile and able to turn in different directions as things become more certain

The strategy for disruptive innovation follows the classic maxim on corporate strategy:[7] "Induce your competitors *not* to invest in those products, markets, and services where you expect to invest the most. This is the fundamental rule of strategy."

[7]See note 2.

The *open innovation* paradigm developed by Chesbrough[8] describes how the more visionary, innovation-driven enterprises are now moving to cooperate with others in similar or completely different industries, to gain access to and share IP and technologies. To increase return on R&D expenditures, organizations are complementing in-house R&D with technologies from the outside. There are several driving forces:

- Reduced research budgets.
- IP/technologies remain unused.
- Product cycle times are shorter.
- Enterprises do not have all the best technologies that they need for sustaining innovation.
- A smart and mobile workforce.
- Venture capital will fund promising start-ups staffed by disillusioned "intrapreneurs" who leave innovation-resistant enterprises.
- Generally, technology has value only with business models, and enterprises should take advantage of all the IP that is available from other companies, universities, and federal laboratories.

A network of *IP suppliers and consumers* is established, including competitors. An enterprise that is utilizing R&D processes to create and develop new inventions from both internal and external sources will also make IP available for licensing and other commercialization. The boundaries are open between strategic, synergistic partners in different markets. The open innovation concept is shown in Exhibit 6.1.

The business model for the open innovation IP paradigm comprises three components: (1) using technology in existing businesses and markets; (2) licensing technology to other companies; and (3) launching new ventures (spin-offs) that use core technology. The pharmaceutical industry has been particularly successful at utilizing the open innovation approach.

Big pharmaceuticals have core competencies in sales and marketing and managing expensive and time-consuming clinical trials but lack the high degree of R&D inventiveness needed to keep their drug discovery pipelines filled. Highly inventive biotechnology companies are the IP suppliers to the pharmaceuticals, utilizing a range of licensing models with multiple partners for specific therapies in different markets. The pharmaceuticals acquire and codevelop the IP they need at relatively low cost and little time.

---

[8]Chesbrough, Henry. *Open Innovation: The New Imperative for Creating and Profiting from Technology* (Boston: Harvard Business School Press, 2003).

EXHIBIT 6.1 Open Innovation Model

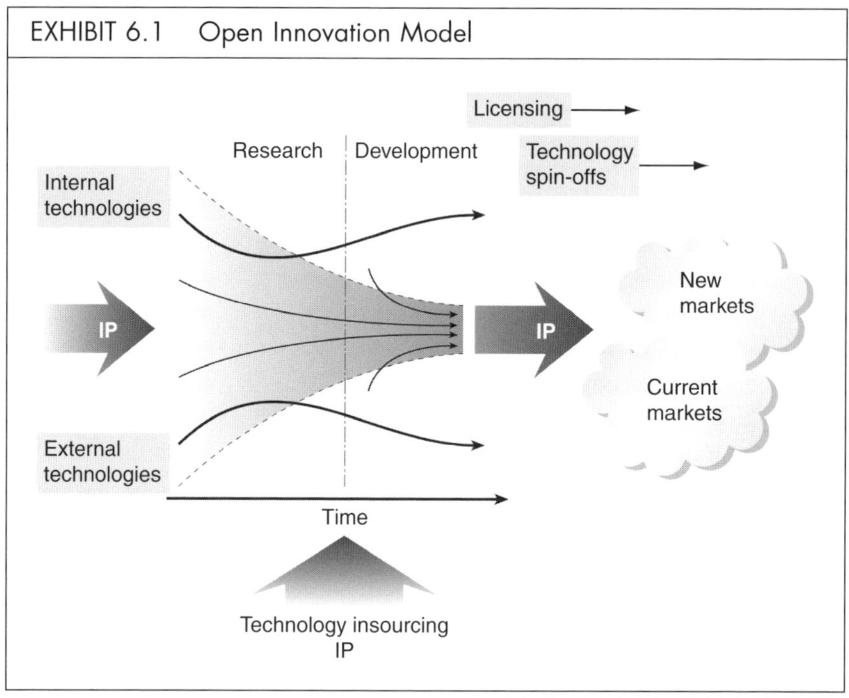

Similarly, the chemical, consumer product, semiconductor, and telecommunication industries are utilizing forms of open innovation. While the open innovation model can be applied to the leading high-technology U.S. enterprises such as Abbott Labs, Air Products, AstraZeneca, DuPont, Hewlett-Packard, Kraft, Procter & Gamble (P&G), Pfizer, and 3M in the industries we have just mentioned, the currently more "IP defensive" nature of European and Asian enterprises may inhibit the full adoption of open innovation, although this remains to be seen. However, multinational enterprises like P&G, for example, have publicly stated a goal of having 50% of innovations coming from outside P&G.[9]

Current Issues with Innovation

> *". . . Because its purpose is to create a customer, business has two, and only two functions: marketing and innovation. Marketing and innovation produce results, all the rest are costs."*
>
> —Peter Drucker

[9] *BusinessWeek*, July 2003.

Technological innovation creates substantial intangible asset valuation within global enterprises. Today, about 80% of the Standard and Poor's (S&P) 500 market capitalization is mainly due to intangible assets (a large portion coming from IP), up from less than 20% in 1975.[10] However, between enterprises there is a large variability of *innovation return of investment (ROI)*, defined as the ratio of net income to R&D expenditure. Companies with high R&D budgets and large numbers of patents do not necessarily have high revenues from products, services, and technology license agreements. While there are no absolute measures of *innovation success*, some gauges include revenues and profitability, increases in market share, number of new markets entered, number of new products launched, frequency of technological breakthroughs, and the ultimate—creation of completely new markets with new products.

The three key issues impacting innovation effectiveness are the existence of innovation value gaps, the difficulty in finding new ideas and opportunities, and the patent portfolio paradox.

Innovation Value Gap

Among the leaders in the innovation-dependent industries—biotechnology, chemicals, computers, consumer products, electronics and semiconductors, industrial machinery, health care and medical devices, and software—there are large variations in shareholder valuations, profits, and returns on R&D investments. The *innovation value gap* can be defined as the differences between the amounts of R&D invested and market values created. An analysis by Computer Patent Annuities[11] found that while companies within the same industry have similar *R&D intensities* (percentage of company's annual revenues invested in R&D), there are wide variations in innovation ROI. The industrial machinery industry with average R&D intensity of 3% and exhibiting the overall highest innovation ROI had variations between approximately 100% and 700%. The chemical industry with average R&D intensity of 3% yielded innovation ROI variations between 100% and 500%, while the medical devices industry with average 8% R&D intensity showed ROIs between 80% and 500%. The biopharmaceutical industry with high average R&D intensity of 17% produced innovation ROIs between 50% and over 200%. The market values of companies above and below the average innovation ROIs reveals the innovation value gaps in each industry.

---

[10]*The Brookings Institution*, 2004.

[11]Maddox, Jeff. "Innovation Gap," *IAM*, December/January 2006.

A recent Boston Consulting Group survey[12] on innovation and the innovation-to-cash process (or cash curve) involving nearly 1,000 senior company executives in 68 countries, found that 50% of executives were not satisfied with the financial return on their innovation investments. Some industries were worse than others, for example, 60% of executives in industrial goods (even with the top R&D spenders), 64% in energy, and 56% in health care. In contrast, 66% said that innovation is one of their company's top three strategic priorities, including 19% who said it was their company's single most important initiative. Other key findings include: 74% of the executives surveyed said that their companies will increase spending on innovation in 2005; almost 90% of the executives surveyed said that generating organic growth through innovation has become essential for success in their industry. The statistics reveal a definite gap between expectations from corporate stakeholders and their execution of innovation to generate competitive advantage, market share, and profits.

Companies across all industries are investing in innovation (with unnecessarily uncertain outcomes and probable failures) to develop new sources of business growth, made more difficult due to increasing global competition and commoditization. The need for breakthrough innovation is particularly high in the consumer products, technology/IT, and health care industries, due to a number of factors, including short product life cycles, frequent disruptive innovations, and global competition.

Uncovering New Ideas and Opportunities

Enterprises typically focus R&D time, resources, and activities in the following two areas: 80% on product improvements and 20% on new groundbreaking technologies (striving for disruptive innovation but usually missing!). Boston Consulting Group found that over 50% of senior executives realized they were weak on discovering new ideas and quickly moving from idea generation to product sales. They tend to get blindsided by new innovations that "come out of left field."

Barriers to creativity and innovation within enterprises can arise from management, process, and culture issues. There are several symptoms, including the following:

[12]Boston Consulting Group. *2004–2005 Senior Management Survey on Innovation.*

- *Management:* No senior management support or sense of urgency, management exclusion from the innovation process, excessive bureaucracy and rationalization, no specific projects tied to corporate strategy, no training/coaching of innovation teams, short time horizons for payback, lack of diversity among teams.
- *Process:* Lack of enterprise-wide innovation process; isolated silos of technical centers and business units; lack of resource and time allocations; lack of tools, criteria, and metrics; no documentation or idea management system.
- *Culture:* No culture that supports innovation, fear of failure and intolerance of out-of-the-box thinkers, no recognition and lack of appropriate rewards that value disruptive thinking.

A usual approach taken by enterprises interested in adopting a more formal innovation process is to establish *new technology committees* staffed by representatives from several business units such as engineering, R&D, marketing, and business development. Meeting once a month or even less frequently, they strive to discover new ideas and opportunities for new products and services. Focus groups held with customers and suppliers are also used to elicit suggestions for new product and market directions. Usually, the results are recommendations for incremental product features with little or no "out-of-the-box-thinking" or "connecting the dots" from other industries and markets.

Patent Portfolio Paradox

A measure of proactive invention (not necessarily innovation) within an enterprise is the number of patents and patent applications filed. However, typically between 2% and 5% of patents in an enterprise portfolio are utilized in products. Fewer than 10% will have potentially significant valuations.[13] There is growing empirical evidence that larger enterprises are building bigger patent portfolios, irrespective of the quality and values of the individual patents, to achieve a situation where *the whole is greater than the sum of its part*. The true value of patents lies not in their individual worth, but in their aggregation into a collection of related patents. This leads to the *patent paradox*: In recent years, patent intensity—patents obtained per research and development dollar—has

[13]*Knowledge Management*, April 2001.

risen dramatically even as the expected value of individual patents has diminished.[14] The benefits of patent portfolios are so significant that a proactive company's patenting decisions are essentially unrelated to the expected value of individual patents because patent portfolios simultaneously increase both the scale and the diversity of available marketplace protections for innovations.

A patent portfolio is superior to a single patent: It is more difficult to design around, has multiple areas of protection, and covers technology improvements over time. Companies typically seek to obtain a large quantity of related patents, rather than evaluating their actual worth. The result is that the current patenting environment exhibits a high-volume, portfolio-based approach, giving rise to *patent thickets* with questionable patent quality and strength, creating a market for service companies offering invention on demand for *theoretical* utility patents that have no physical basis. We see examples in new emerging areas such as nanotechnology and genetics, as well as more mature but rapidly innovating industries like medical devices and semiconductors.

With patent filing and maintenance expenses of typically $20,000 to $25,000 over the 20 years (or less) exploitable lifetime of a patent in the United States, or over $200,000 for each patent in multiple international jurisdictions in addition to the United States, the strategy of managing large patent portfolios creates substantial costs. For a portfolio with 1,000 patents, the lifetime costs would be on the order of $20 million for U.S. patents and $200 million if all the patents were filed in foreign jurisdictions. In practice, about 30% on average would be foreign patents, reducing the associated lifetime costs to about $80 million.

In addition, recent studies show that the average number of lawsuits filed over the life of a patent is increasing. The more patents a company has, the more risk there is of a patent infringement lawsuit, which may arise from a totally different industry. The U.S. Patent and Trademark Office (USPTO) currently approves over 95% of all original patent applications (compared to 65% in Europe and Japan), giving rise to a relatively large number of patents with broad claims and suspect validity that are spurring an increasing number of patent lawsuits (currently three times the number in the 1980s) and the rise of the troll phenomenon.

With the high costs of patent litigation and the threat of product injunctions, owning a sizable patent portfolio can be costly. Another side effect is that shareholder value can significantly decrease for defendant public companies mired in litigation. This negative shareholder value effect is typically tens of millions of dollars for mid-size enterprises.

[14]Parchomovsky, Gideon, and Wagner, R. Polk. University of Pennsylvania Law School Paper 51 (2004).

Best Practices for Strategic IP Management

> *"The way companies define, measure and reward excellent research has to change. Accessing a valuable external technology is a useful research activity. Companies today seldom reward this activity, though, in the same way that they recognize someone who discovered a valuable technology on the inside."*
>
> —Henry Chesbrough

An IP-intelligent enterprise gains increased shareholder value, enhanced transaction leverage, competitive advantage, and defensible market positions in existing and new market segments. The management, process, and cultural barriers to innovation are removed. Utilizing IP analysis and strategy can give a clearer purpose and insight for corporate development and growth through sustained and disruptive innovations. Strategic IP management can reduce the risks involved in executing disruptive innovation.

Industry-leading enterprises can utilize the real benefits of the open innovation paradigm to in-license new IP and build high-value portfolios. They can find new inventions for developing and commercializing disruptive or breakthrough technologies from smaller companies, universities, federal laboratories, and individual inventors. They can lock in the new technologies and construct strong patent portfolios with blocking patents around core IP and picket-fence patents for new IP needed in new market spaces. And they can out-license noncore and core IP to a network of strategic IP partners in multiple industries, spin out new IP-rich entities, or form joint ventures.

IP Strategies for Disruptive Innovation

To support a disruptive innovation approach, strategic IP analysis can be deployed to perform quantitative research into evolving markets, technologies, and competitors.

Exhibit 6.2 shows the typical product/market matrix of corporate growth options[15] together with IP strategies to support disruptive innovation for a diversification strategy.

[15]Ansoff, H. Igor. *Corporate Strategy* (New York: McGraw-Hill, 1965).

EXHIBIT 6.2 IP Strategy and Analysis for Disruptive Innovation

	Current Products	New Products
New Markets	Market Development • New market segments • New market geographies • New channels • Cross-licensing, joint ventures • Licensing (noncore IP)	**Diversification** ***Disruptive innovation*** • New products and new markets • New business models • In-licensing emerging technology/IP • Build IP portfolio
Existing Markets	Market penetration *Sustaining innovation* • Increase customer loyalty • Increase price points • Attract new customers • Incremental new products and services • In-licensing complementary IP	**Product development** *Sustaining innovation* • New products and services • Services around products • Faster, better, cheaper products • Blocking and picket-fence patents • Maintain exclusive position

The objective is to spot new, emerging markets or gaps (*white spaces*) in current markets that are maturing, together with new IP that is becoming available, perhaps in adjacent industries, that can be converted into lower-cost products and services that achieve adequate levels of performance and accessibility.

IP Strategies for Open Innovation

An enterprise that is adapting the open innovation process needs to formulate a strategy about which research to perform in-house versus acquiring from outside organizations. It also needs to determine what IP it will out-license to others, including competitors, and what IP it will spin out into separate operations.

The open innovation approach places increased emphasis on effective, efficient, and timely strategic IP management. With potentially high levels of in-

EXHIBIT 6.3 IP Strategy for Open Innovation

	Cost Centered *Value extraction*	**Revenue Centered** *Value creation*
Proactive	Limit competitors • Blocking patents • Picket-fence patents (design freedom) • Create standards • Maintain exclusive position	**Leverage full potential of IP** • Licensing (core and noncore IP) • Spin-outs • Joint ventures • Strategic alliances
Reactive	Protect intangibles • Blocking patents (avoid litigation) • In-license complementary IP	Establish income revenue stream • Licensing (noncore IP)

licensing of external IP and associated payments, out-licensing and associated commercialization, spinouts, joint ventures, and other activities, the demands increase for regular portfolio analysis (mining), restructuring and optimization, valuation, IP landscape analysis, and continuous refinement of overall IP strategy.

A unique, streamlined process for finding, evaluating, and expediting the acquisition of IP and technologies from universities and federal laboratories utilizes the U2B™ model.[16] This market-driven technology transfer model is a perfect fit with the open innovation process and objectives.

Exhibit 6.3 shows the IP strategy for the open innovation that leverages the full potential of the portfolio.

An additional challenge for adopting the open innovation paradigm is to manage IP outsourcing holistically by establishing carefully selected, consistently available channels, which are chosen to match corporate strategy requirements.

[16]Gross, Clifford M., and Allen, Joseph P. *Technology Transfer for Entrepreneurs: A Guide to Commercializing Federal Laboratory Innovations* (Westport, CT: Praeger Publishers, 2003).

IP as a Core Strategic Element

The connection of IP to business strategy is at the center of a company's success. Patents and IP can provide a strategic purpose, beyond the protection of core product lines. Articulating a clear business strategy, with IP at the hub, is key to remaining competitive and closing any innovation value gaps.

An integrated strategic IP management process[17] is shown in Exhibit 6.4, which utilizes a *total quality management* (TQM) model for strategic IP management. A TQM approach is critical for enterprises to achieve business growth goals, including creating an entirely new category and market for a disruptive product. IP management focuses on value creation and value extraction. IP strategy is either offensive or defensive, or a mix of both (including negotiation) and should be aligned with a corporate strategy, which can be broadly or narrowly focused.[18] For a broadly focused strategy, portfolios tend to include

EXHIBIT 6.4 TQM Approach to Strategic IP Management

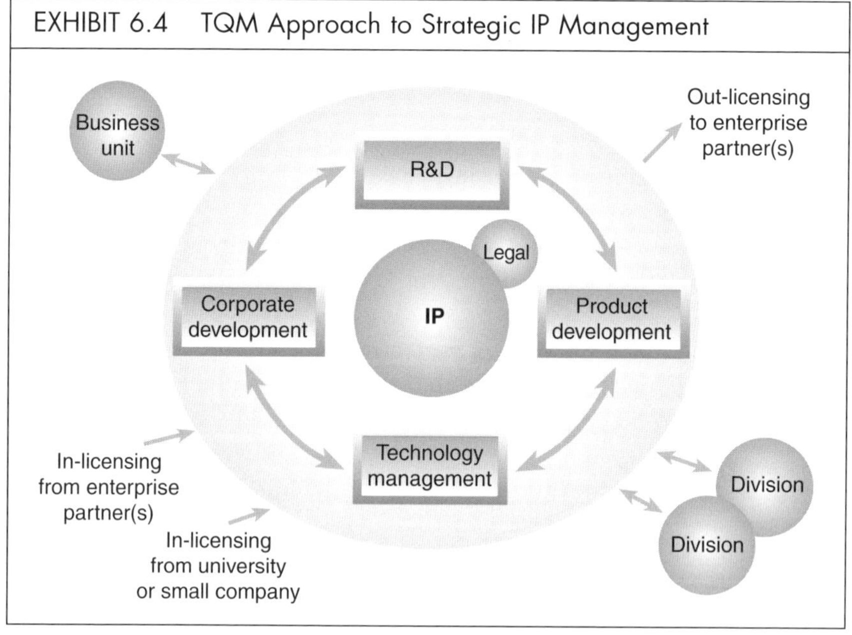

[17]Kahn, Edward. "TQM for IPM in Technology Licensing." In Parr, Russell L., and Sullivan, Patrick H. (eds.). *Technology Licensing: Corporate Strategies for Maximizing Value* (New York: John Wiley & Sons, 1996).

[18]See note 3 above.

picket-fence patents that are invented around new market spaces and applications to gain design freedom. For narrowly focused strategy, we see specific patents addressing shorter-term market segments with blocking patents around core technologies.

Within enterprises, the patenting process is usually administered by the *patent committee*, with representatives from R&D, engineering, legal, and business development groups.

The IP strategy has to address several issues for corporate strategy, invention strategy, and product-line strategy, as summarized below:

- Corporate strategy areas:
  - Technology focus and product platforms
  - IP objective
  - Protection of unpatented technology
  - Principles and procedures for managing and protecting IP
  - Response to competitive threats
- Invention strategy areas:
  - Objectives for patent(s)
  - Technical information needed
  - Extend of patent claims: narrow or broad
  - Need for trademark
  - When and where to file the patent application(s)
  - International jurisdictions for patent(s)
- Product-line strategy areas:
  - Maintaining continuity of patent grant(s)
  - Coordinating patent application filings
  - Gap analysis and new IP requirements
  - Improving competitive strengths
  - Sustaining and disruptive technology opportunities
  - Where, how, when to compete and against whom?

A generic IP management system is shown in Exhibit 6.5, which summarizes the major activities and decision processes.[19,20] The five core elements include: (1) converting appropriate inventions to patents, (2) portfolio management and

[19]Davis, Julie L., and Harrison, Suzanne S. *Edison in the Boardroom: How Leading Companies Realize Value from Their Intellectual Assets* (New York: John Wiley & Sons, 2001).

[20]Sullivan, Patick H. *Profiting from Intellectual Capital: Extracting Value from Innovation* (New York: John Wiley & Sons, 1998).

EXHIBIT 6.5 IP Management System

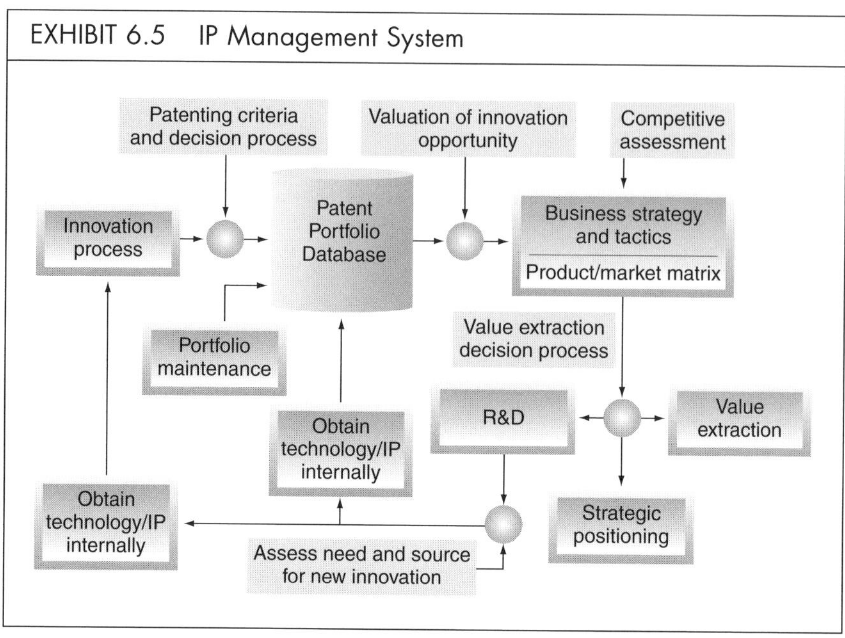

maintenance, (3) valuations of patents and technology platforms, (4) competitive assessment, and (5) strategic actions (commercialization or defining the need for additional technologies to be developed internally or acquired from outside the enterprise).

Exhibit 6.6 shows the key *holistic* strategic IP management process, from IP invention and strategy through analytics to commercialization, along with an underlying portfolio optimization approach to maximizing value and other characteristics. The IP analysis includes both comprehensive patent analysis tools and teams of industry/technology experts who can interpret data visualizations in context and make valuable recommendations to enterprise executives.

IP Portfolio Optimization

An IP portfolio must be continually reviewed and optimized for maximum patent valuations, high patent (invention) quality, and broad coverage over exclusive space, with high patent-to-product mapping, together with expedited patent to product conversion.

Enterprises can establish a foundation for strategy development to obtain the highest and best use of the IP portfolio:

EXHIBIT 6.6 Integrated Strategic IP Management Elements

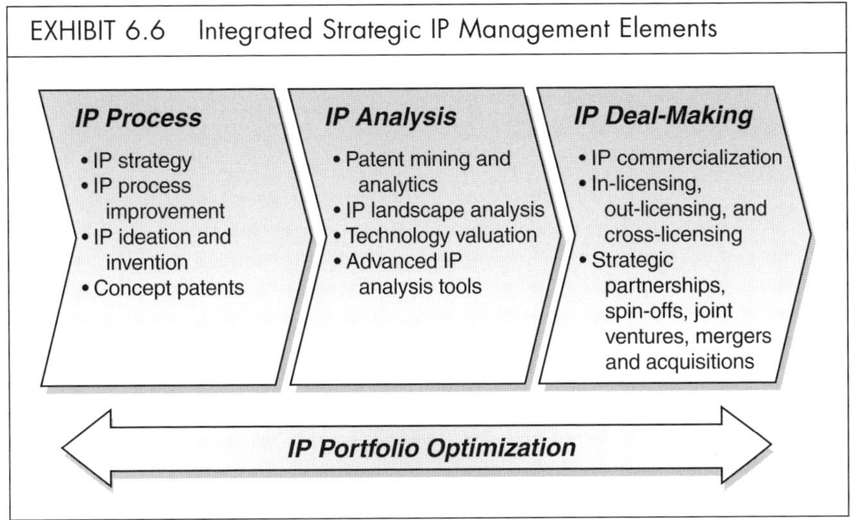

- Identify estimated optimal value of the existing IP portfolio.
- Evaluate optimal combinations and deal structures to obtain the highest value.
- Ability to rapidly evaluate licensing, partnering and joint venture options on an integrated basis.
- Ability to evaluate effect on remaining portfolio as deals occur.
- Immediate integration of new IP value into the existing portfolio.
- Identification of gaps in IP by product category.
- "What if" scenarios, optimize risk and return trade-offs.
- Identify resources needed to meet licensing objectives.
- Direct product development and R&D investments to fill technology gaps.

IP metrics and innovation ROI. Enterprises need to develop a standard set of IP metrics to measure IP strategy. In the open innovation model, IP produces income, cash flow, and profits. Useful metrics for any reporting period include the following:

- Inputs:
  - Number and frequency of brainstorming (ideation) sessions
  - Number of invention disclosures
  - Patent activity
  - Budgets allocated by management to innovation systems
  - Number of external IP searches

- Outputs:
  - Revenues and income from new products/services
  - Percentage of revenues from new products/services
  - Percentage of income from product revenue utilizing patented technology
  - Percentage of income from out-licensing IP generally
  - Percentage of revenue expended on out-licensing IP
  - Percentage of income from patent licensing
  - Percentage of revenue expended on in-licensing IP from outside
  - Percentage of revenue expended on registering IP
  - Percentage of revenue expended on enforcing IP
  - IP expenditures to produce new products compared with in-sourcing IP
  - Number of in-licensing deals
  - Number of out-licensing deals
  - Number of patents filed
  - Number of new products/services
  - Number of new ideas being developed
  - Innovation ROI in each market/product area

As discussed earlier, the innovation ROI is defined as the ratio of net income to R&D expenditure and can be applied to individual patents, patent clusters, and patent portfolios.

Structure and strength. The structure and strength of individual patents, clusters of patents (technology platforms), and the portfolio as a whole should be assessed regularly. The important elements are as follows:

- Technologies (breadth, range of technology types, depth—number of patents and clusters in each type)
- Range of patent-independent and -dependent claim strength (broad to narrow)
- Patent filing dates
- Prior art and search classification sections

Value and costs. The financial valuation of a portfolio is measured in terms of income and cost. The key elements are as follows:

- Income:
  - Number and value of ongoing royalty streams from out-licensing and cross-licensing
  - Number and value of up-front fees
  - Number and value of patent sales

- Costs:
  - Number and value of in-licensing fees and royalties
  - Number and value of patent registrations
  - Number and value of patent maintenance fees
  - Legal costs, taxes, insurance, etc.

Patent-to-product mapping: Based on a product life cycle approach, the IP portfolio should facilitate the mapping of patent-to-product categories. The ADL portfolio management method[21] is used by many enterprises and is based on industry/product life cycle and a measure of product competitive positioning. Using this approach, an enterprise can determine which products (and IP) are placed in the current markets and determine the need to invent (or acquire) new technologies (and IP) to create pacing products in emerging, high-growth markets. Exhibit 6.7 illustrates the ADL product life cycle matrix.

The following definitions explain the ADL product life cycle methodology and how we can integrate this into strategic IP management to guide product development strategy by accomplishing the patent to technology platform/product mapping.

- Market position characteristics:
  - Dominant: Sets the pace of technological development
  - Strong: Can express independent technical actions and set new directions
  - Favorable: Can sustain technology competitiveness in general and/or in niches
  - Tenable: Unable to set independent course, continually in catch-up mode
  - Weak: Unable to sustain technology quality versus competitors, in fire-fighting mode

- Technology characteristics:
  - Base: Essential to the company, widely used by competitors, not differentiating
  - Key: High and differentiating competitive impact, well integrated in products
  - Pacing: Competitive impact may be high, under development by competitors

[21]Roussel, Philip A., Saad, Kamal N., and Erickson, Tamara J. *Third Generation R&D: Managing the Link to Corporate Strategy* (Boston: Harvard Business School Press, 1991).

EXHIBIT 6.7 Product Life Cycle/Market Matrix Combined with Product Strategy

Competitive Position	*Industry life cycle stage*			
	Embryonic	*Growth*	*Mature*	*Aging*
Dominant	All out push for share. Hold position.	Hold position. Hold share.	Hold position. Growth with industry.	Hold position.
Strong	Attempt to improve position.	Attempt to improve position.	Hold position. Growth with industry. All out push for share.	Hold position or harvest. Push for share.
Favorable	Selective or all out push for share. Selectively attempt to improve position.	Attempt to improve position. Selective push for share.	Custodial or maintenance. Find niche and attempt to protect it.	Harvest or phased-out withdrawal.
Tenable	Selectively push for position.	Find niche and protect it.	Find niche and hang on or phased-out withdrawal.	Phased-out withdrawal or abandon.
Weak	Up or out.	Turn around or abandon.	Turn around, orphaned-out withdrawal.	Abandon.

- Emerging: Early research stage (or emerging in other industries), unknown competitive impact

Exhibit 6.8 shows typical results of the patent/product/market position mapping that reveals a need for new competitive technologies and identifies emerging markets along with sustaining innovation.

EXHIBIT 6.8 Technology/Platform Portfolio Mapping

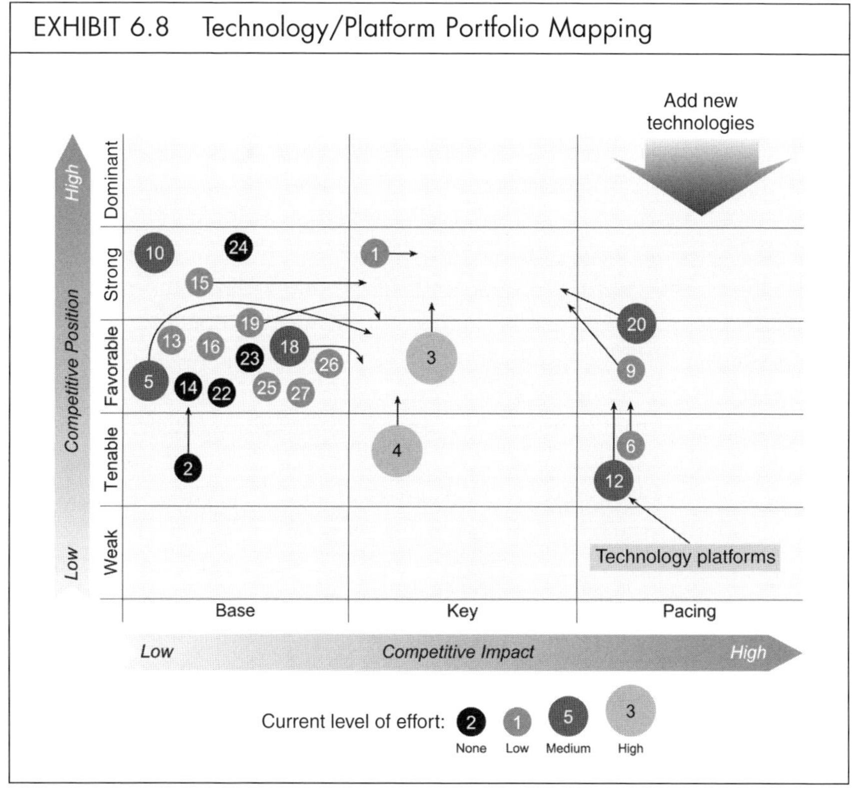

Executive and Board Support

Any business initiative is likely to fail unless it is supported by executive management. Corporate executives and their boards of directors are beginning to see the value of proactively managing IP as a core strategy element in staying ahead of the innovation curve. Budgets are created to provide the resources necessary for IP managers to scan the patent landscape, identify patents and technologies of interest, and in-license or acquire them. In addition, companies continue to regularly perform portfolio optimization, patent mining, and technology clustering to generate revenues from out-licensing IP to strategic partners.

Senior executives, business unit managers, and product managers must be IP aware. With increased reporting and corporate accountability, particularly Sarbanes-Oxley and the Financial Accounting Standards Board (FASB) (corporate responsibility for financial reports, real-time issuer disclosures, separate naming of intangible assets, intangible asset value measurement), board members must also be involved in strategic IP issues, which directly affect corporate growth and shareholder valuation.

Conclusions

Strategic IP management is an essential ingredient in guiding the process of innovation to a successful execution and closing innovation value gaps. A total quality management approach to IP must be developed by organizations, which will facilitate portfolio optimization in terms of value, structure, revenue, income, and other parameters. IP analysis can provide early market and technology insights for disruptive innovation programs. In addition, IP strategy, analysis, and commercialization builds high-value and high-protection portfolios.

The open innovation paradigm places even more importance on effective, efficient, holistic strategic IP management. In addition, the open innovation approach encourages the generation of high-quality patents and high-value, high-leverage portfolios, and not necessarily large portfolios. This leads to a portfolio strategy of *patent more carefully*, not *patent more*, and overcomes the patent portfolio paradox. The innovation ROI will be stronger with high-strength patents and flexible, proactive IP-based business models.

7

Maximizing Innovation Teams: The Internal and External Connection Network

Carsten Wittrup

Every corporate leader understands that the greatest company asset is the people that form the company and populate its structure. Most business leaders are in pursuit of a formula for unlocking and realizing the full value of the people they lead, mentor, or hire into their organization.

The combination of diverse competencies, skill sets, interests, and personal networks that people bring to the business form the greatest potential for growth, success, and continued innovation.

The source of innovation is changing. Previously, innovation was primarily a deliverable through internal corporate research and development (R&D) departments comprised of subject matter experts with few external links or networks. Such teams were in many cases working on specialized projects or topics with little or no awareness of other internal team activities. This isolation was even more pronounced when teams resided in different departments, sister companies, or business units within the corporation.

How to effectively connect projects and efficiently leverage utilization of expert resources into an efficient network of free-flowing information has been a central topic within R&D management and innovation for the last 25 to 30 years. Innovation and R&D networks have been gaining focus within the discussion, and the concept of the networked organization has been at the center of research papers and management workshops for the last three to five years.

This chapter shares some of the insights gained from working with cross-functional innovation teams and will discuss how to assemble effective innovation teams from a multidisciplinary base with a special focus on team internal/external networking capabilities. The chapter also offers a selection of important papers and resources for further insight into network theory and practices.

Case Story

The BOC Group is the world's second largest producer and supplier of industrial gases on a global scale. Gases such as nitrogen, oxygen, and argon are produced by a cryogenic distillation process invented at the beginning of the century and constantly refined and optimized by incremental improvements by the six to eight major companies in this specialized industry. Industrial gases play an important role in most industrial processes. Whereas quality and purity of the delivered gases was a competitive factor early on, the battlefield among competing companies today is in manufacturing cost, distribution cost, and in the knowledge about the optimal use of the gases within the customer process or application.

In late 2000, the company was putting the final pieces in place to launch two new step-changing technologies. Each technology had been developed by highly specialized teams of material experts that had worked focused side by side for the prior five years. One team worked on a glass-melting technology for industrial glass furnaces, utilizing crown-fired oxygen combustion burners to increase the melting rate. Another team worked on a highly efficient liquid nitrogen freezer capable of freezing a hamburger patty within 42 seconds as compared to the current three to five minutes. The two teams worked at the same location, had their lunch at the same company cafeteria, and exchanged polite greetings when their paths crossed in the corporate corridors. They had no real incentives or reasons to discuss their projects with each other.

What do glass melting and food freezing have in common? Well actually, more than meets the eye! Both technologies were based on the same physical principle of impingement heat transfer, and the projects had faced very similar challenges and had achieved similar advantages (see Exhibit 7.1)—the glass team for a process occurring at 1,000°C and the food team for a process occurring at –196°C. The high degree of specialization had made it difficult for the teams and the organization to identify the similarity of the challenges and the potential synergies in the two projects (see Exhibit 7.2).

EXHIBIT 7.1 Impingement Heat Transfer

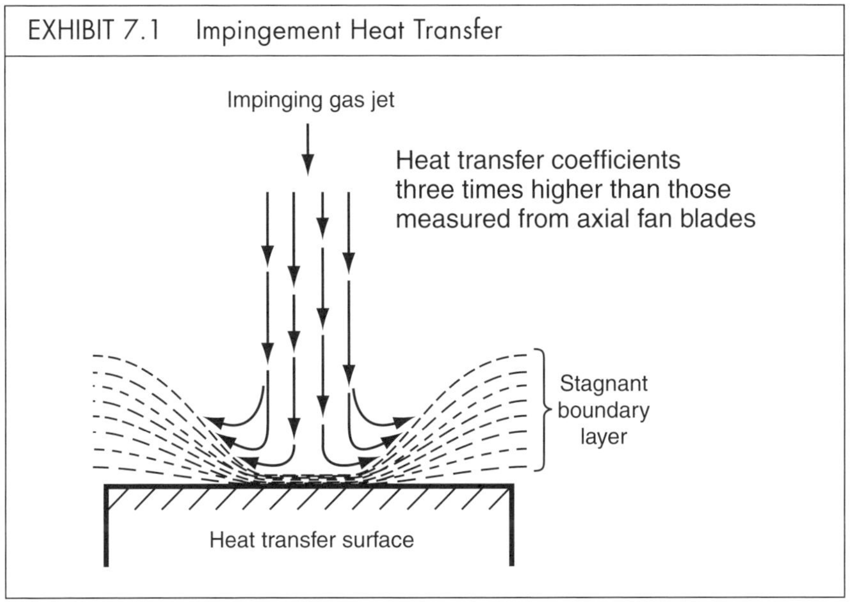

EXHIBIT 7.2 Evaporative Heat Transfer

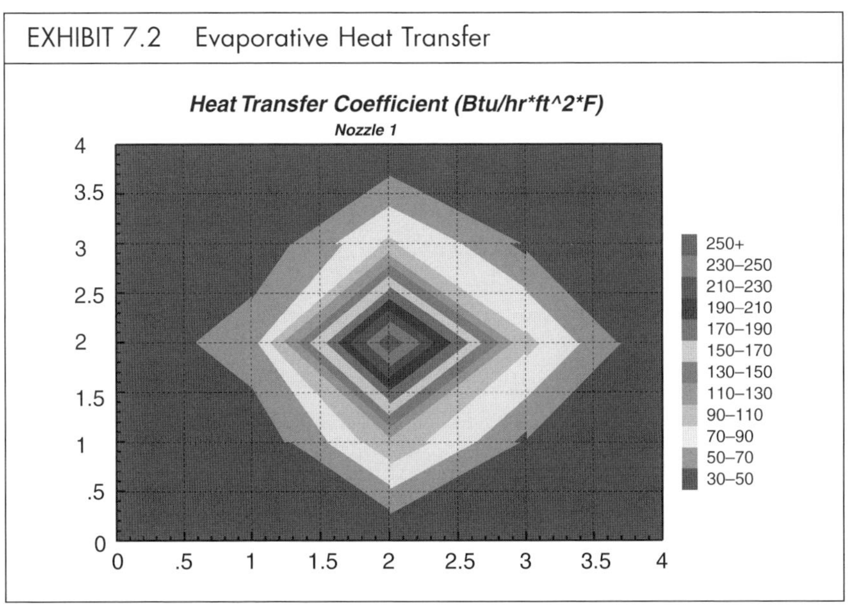

During a subsequent evaluation of the development efforts and environment, several key issues were identified:

- Cost of finding and development (F&D) is skyrocketing.
- Overflow of information, opportunities, and new technologies:
- Screening and selecting technologies becomes major bottlenecks.
- Parallel or no development efforts caused by high specialization and silo behind cut.
- Diversity of knowledge residing within different disciplines.
- How to tap into the corporate bank of knowledge.
- Global access to knowledge experts.
- Communication across disciplines.
- Teams to support organizational strategies.

For the two specific projects, the key issues were identified as:

- Communication.
- No links between projects.
- No sharing of team members.
- No diversity.
- All team members were subject-matter experts (glass and food).
- Engrained innovation culture (engineer around/through obstacles).

Both technologies were successfully launched in 2001 and 2002 and have since established themselves as benchmarks within their respective industries; they are currently licensed to several of the BOC industrial gas competitors. It was estimated that the development time could have been reduced by 12 to 18 months for each of the projects, thus preserving valuable R&D resources ($1–2 billion) and increase market timing (and revenues) by an additional 1 to 1.5 years.

New Approach

The innovation and R&D island needs internal and external bridges to extend its scope of interaction and to build an effective network where ideas, feedback, and information flow and assemble into new products and solutions. Eric von Hippel studied the sources of innovation in 1988 and identified an emerging trend of user/manufacturer/supplier interdependence in bringing forward innovations within different key industries.

For the BOC business of innovation in the use of industrial gases, the source of such innovation was:

- 42% user
- 17% manufacturer
- 32% supplier
- 8% other

Which requires a solid external network to link the innovation and stay in the front of this demanding industry.

For engineering plastics, the source of innovation was:

- 10% user
- 90% manufacturer

Which requires a solid internal network for the manufacturer to assure diversity and coordinate among innovation teams.

So how to rethink the innovation process so that corporations can:

- Do the right innovation better, quicker, and easier, using less resources.
- Cross-pollinate the corporate core competencies.
- Create cross-functional and virtual project teams.
- Link the innovation process to team member covering development.
- Quickly commercialize and deliver innovations to the customer.

While at the same time building and reinforcing the following knowledge competencies within the organization and the team:

- *Learning:* The ability to acquire knowledge and to transform it into value-adding activities
- *Changes:* Ability and willingness to change mentally, physically, and in terms of role ability to carry ideas into effect
- *Relationship:* Building networks and the ability to handle diversity for individuals, organizations, companies, and society
- *Meaning:* The ability to individually and collectively identify, create, and share a context for meaning

Innovation Teams and Networks

The increased understanding of network theory and the analogies among electronic, social, and physiological models has stimulated interest into the internal interaction of innovation teams and the team interface with the surrounding world.

Team member function, roles, and connectivity has been described, analyzed, and evaluated. Focus has been on team communication, culture and values, and the team's connectivity and networking capabilities.

Innovation team members all bring different internal and external relationships in the form of networks into the team (see Exhibit 7.3). By mapping out the combined network, it is possible to explore relationships based on different criteria (see Exhibit 7.4). However, most information can be extracted from analyzing the simple set of immediate relationships for a person and identifying the "ego" network of different individuals and different factions or groups within the network (see Exhibit 7.5).

It quickly becomes apparent that certain individuals in the network function as *connectors* between the different factions or groups in the network, and these individuals have a vast internal and external personal network.

EXHIBIT 7.3 A Network of Relationships Exists Between Various Entities

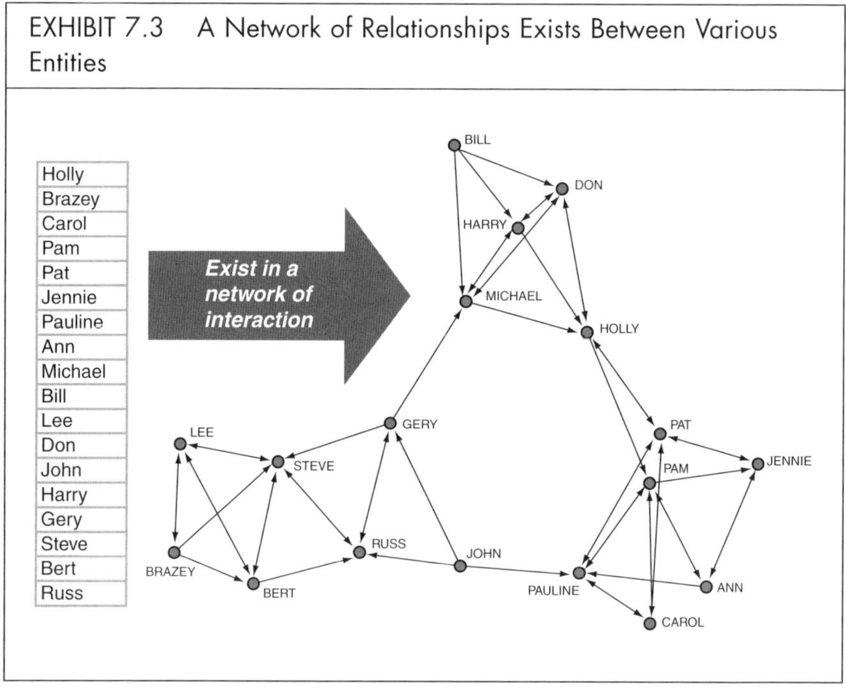

EXHIBIT 7.4 Network Analysis Enables Exploration of the Relationships within a Network

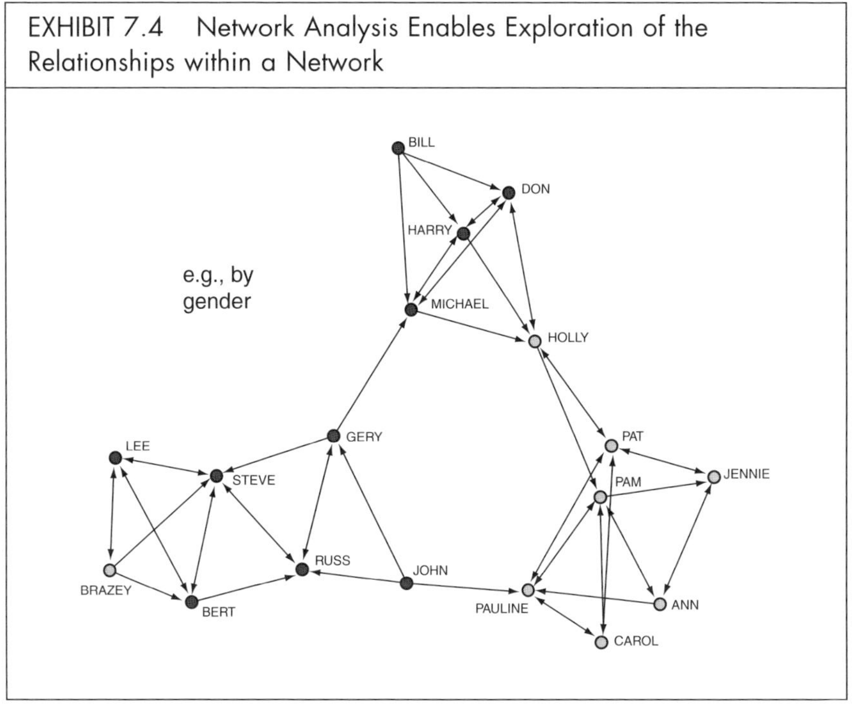

Malcolm Gladwell described in 2002 such "connectors" in his excellent book *The Tipping Point*,[1] and Brian Uzzi and Shannon Dunlap use the term "information brokers" in their *Harvard Business Review* article from December 2005.[2] Connectors are found within every organization, on all levels, however one would have to tab into the "real" organizational chart for the functioning of the corporation, not the official organizational charts, to be able to identify the connectors.

[1]Gladwell, Malcolm. *The Tipping Point: How Little Things Can Make a Big Difference* (New York: Little, Brown, 2000).

[2]Uzzi, Brian, and Dunlap, Shannon. "How to Build Your Network," *Harvard Business Review*, December 2005.

EXHIBIT 7.5 More Information Can Be Extracted from Analyzing the "Simple" Set of Relationships

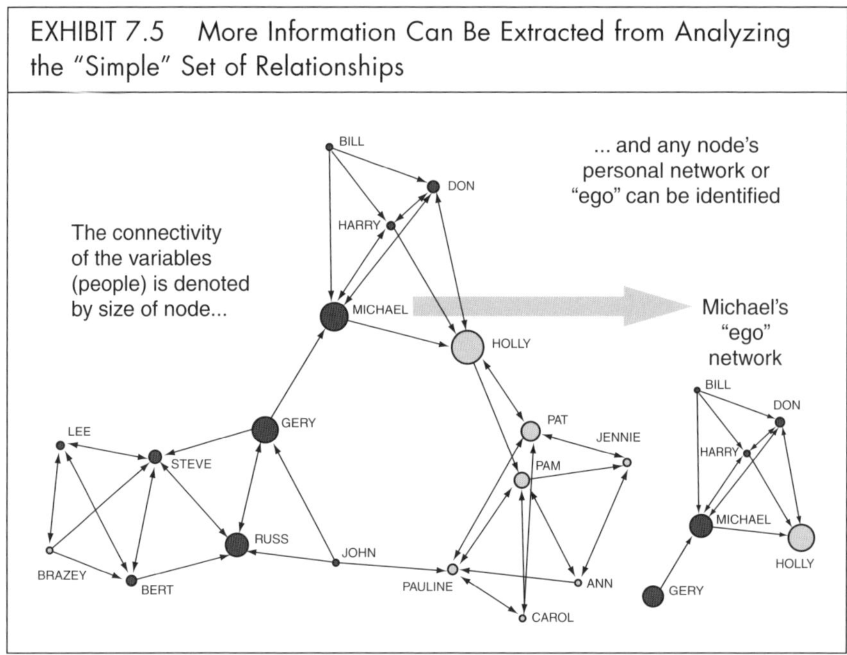

These people are not always as visible as their network would suggest, but they can often be found among "go-to" persons within the organization (see Exhibit 7.6). Holly would be an important member of your innovation team if you needed to utilize input or resources from Michael's, Gery's, or Pat's networks.

Innovation Team Member Selection Criteria

The current state of research clearly indicates that an effective innovation team should be created while observing the following criteria:

- Team should have an adequate size (five to eight core members are considered optimum depending on assignment).
- Members should have different expertise.
- Members should have different team roles (and more than one role during the project).

EXHIBIT 7.6 "Factions" Can Be Identified

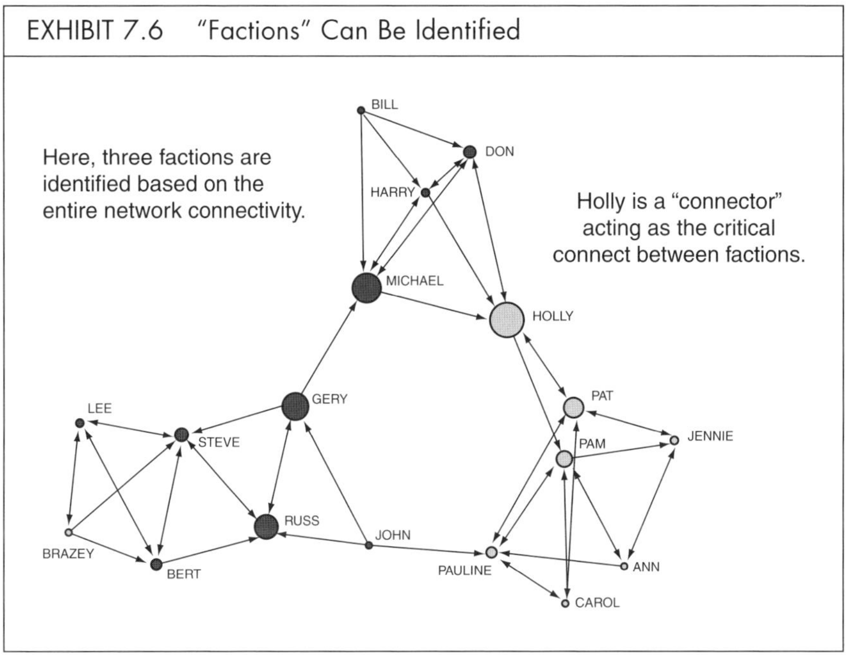

- Members should have different personalities.
- Members should have different experience (tenure and professional).
- Members should have different thinking styles.

The research also indicates that team culture and values have a significant impact on a successful innovation process for the team. The attitudes that team members bring into the team deeply influence the team culture and values, and it may be necessary to review these attitudes as a team in an initial session and team-building exercise.

David J. Skyrmer has indicated a list of healthy team member attitudes to observe:

- Every individual must have a sense of self-value and must value every other team member for their contribution.
- There must be a high level of trust in a working team; this may take time to build.
- Individuals must be mutually supportive—commitments made should be met.

- Reciprocity must reign—give as much as you get in terms of support, transfer of information, and knowledge.
- Individual feelings must be recognized and expressed.

The climate for innovation is strongly affected by the corporate climate and individual past experience and affects the team culture and formation of team values. Charles W. Prather has identified the following five important dimensions to observe:

1. *Challenge:* To what degree are people challenged by their work, as well as emotionally involved and committed to it?
2. *Risk-taking:* To what degree is it okay for a well-reasoned attempt to not meet expectations when trying something new?
3. *Trust and openness:* To what degree do people feel safe speaking their minds and offering different points of view?
4. *Idea time:* To what degree do people have time to think things through before having to act?
5. *Idea support:* To what degree are resources made available to give new ideas a try?

Other important dimensions to observe are:

- *Valuing diversity in thinking style:* To what degree do we demonstrate value for others who think differently from ourselves by including them in the business process?
- *Freedom:* To what degree are people free to decide how to do their job?
- *Playfulness and humor:* How relaxed is the workplace? Is it okay to have fun?
- *Absence of interpersonal conflicts:* To what degree do people refrain from engaging in interpersonal conflict or warfare?
- *Debates:* To what degree do people engage in lively debates about the issues?

With a clear understanding of the team values and culture to be fostered, the team members have a good foundation to carry on their team roles and team functions.

Team Function and Roles

The research into effective innovation teams published by Allan Fahden in 1993 in the book *Innovation on Demand*[3] and the work done subsequently by Gene

[3]Fahden, Allan. *Innovation on Demand* (Minneapolis: The Illiterati, 1993).

C. Mage of Soaring Oaks Consulting Inc., identifies the four basic approaches to innovation expressed by team members:

1. *The conceptual approach:* Individuals who use a conceptual approach tend to generate lots of fresh ideas. These are the people who see things from a different angle. They are bubbling over with alternatives and want to explore the many avenues available before landing on a way to proceed.
2. *The spontaneous approach:* The spontaneous teammate may appear to be flighty and inconsistent, bouncing from topic to topic. He might keep three or four conversational balls in the air at the same time. He enjoys doing many things at once, and doesn't feel wedded to a straight-line approach to reaching the objective. He has great energy and enthusiasm.
3. *The normative approach:* The normative team member talks about the impact of the project on others, how the new ideas fit into the history and values of the broader organization, and ways to integrate the future with the past. She is sensitive to doing things the right way and following the appropriate protocol.
4. *The methodical approach:* The methodical participant likes to have things organized into a neat, logical flow. Each step should follow a rational pathway. This person will have the Gantt charts and task lists and keep them up to date.

Each of these approaches will be present at any given time in the project. Depending on the stage of the project, one of the approaches will have a more constructive contribution than the others, so when team projects tend to evolve over time the strength of each approach can be leveraged. When teammates are aware of their natural patterns and value those of their coworkers, they can agree to choose individuals and roles that will fit well with the work to be done in each phase.

The different roles have different relevance as the project progresses:

- *The creator:* Early on in the project, the team needs somebody to stimulate the team to develop new ideas. Your coworkers with the conceptual approach and their spontaneous colleagues are ideally suited for this role. If the methodical and normative teammates can bite their tongue during the early stages, the team will reap rewards of new solutions that may be superior to the present set of alternatives.
- *The advancer:* As the project moves forward, certain ideas will begin to emerge as winners. The advancer will put these ideas forward in a way that will be accepted. Your normative partner is ideal for this role, since she

will have a great sixth sense about what it takes to get things to work based on her experience and sensitivity to organizational norms. Your spontaneous coworker can chip in to this role with his infectious enthusiasm and energy.

- *The refiner:* Once some straw-man ideas are on the table, it's time to examine them in the cold light of day. Our methodical and normative friends are ideal for this role, examining the proposal logically and evaluating the potential for acceptance in the organization. Now is the time to engage in constructive criticism and potential problem identification, so that you can plan ahead to avoid problems. If you do this step too early, however, no baby ideas will survive.
- *The executor:* Once a winning proposal has been agreed upon, the spontaneous approach combined with methodical planning will ensure error-free execution of the project. The energy of the spontaneous person will be needed to stay the course and overcome the inevitable obstacles and setbacks along the way. The methodical team member will be able to keep everything on a detailed schedule so that critical tasks do not fall through the cracks, budget overruns are avoided, and delays are prevented.
- *The facilitator:* This role doesn't really come in sequence as the other roles do, but is needed from beginning to end. Here, you need the objective, well-balanced perspective of a team member who can step outside of the process and make sure the team is functioning. This is a tough role, because the facilitator must put her own ego aside, at least temporarily, and focus strictly on how well the team is working together.

Team Leader

The team leader needs to manage the innovation process from the thinkers generating ideas through the end with operators managing the business adoption and benefit realization. He or she must be the facilitator for excellent communication and team member transition between team roles. The leader must lead the team toward the most appropriate approach, depending on project state and issues that have arisen.

The team leader must be a true connector to project sponsors and key stakeholders, preferably with a broad internal and external network. He or she must be able to manage team member turnover, which, according to Innovation BBL, can be as high as 20% per year and 65% for a team over a three-year period. They must be willing and able to stay in the role until the project has reached the execution phase, as it is especially unfortunate that 25% of innovation managers tend to switch jobs within a 12-month period.

The Connectors

An innovation team of five to eight innovators would not need more than two well-chosen independent connectors to be successfully networked into the organization and with a sufficient external network to identify solutions through other external connectors. Other team members should be evaluated and chosen while observing their level of connectivity.

Team Communication

Communication is an actor of impact in the successful innovation process. Both quantity and quality appear to have significant impact on creative output. Jan Kratzer reported in his PhD thesis "Communication and Performance—An Empirical Study in Innovation Teams" in 2001 that three underlying performance dimensions determine team performance as critical success factors (CSFs): team dissensus, individual creativity, and individual commitment, all strongly influenced by structures of communication. Kratzer investigated the CSFs as related to three types of team communication—problem solving, managerial, and friendly communication—and he shows how it is possible to use network theory and simulation to analyze team performance and the importance of managing the quality of the three communication streams.

In March 2004, Kratzer published another paper together with his thesis professors Roger Leenders and Jo van Engelen in the publication *Creativity and Innovation Management*,[4] in which they reported that the frequency of communication was found to be a significant factor in creative output. It was also found that if teams overcommunicated and became "ingrown," it could lead to group-think mentality, which stifles originality.

The team leader has an important role as communications facilitator and guardian for diversity in thinking and team discussions. The connectors play a

---

[4]Kratzer, Jan, Leenders, Roger Th.A.J., and van Engelen, Jo M.L. "Stimulating the Potential: Creative Performance and Communication in Innovation Teams," *Creativity and Innovation Management,* March 2004.

vital role in facilitating the flow of information into the team and also in seeking new and different solutions to project problems within their network of contacts. Another important role for the connector is to update the network on project progress and help manage corporate expectations by using the network as a communication channel.

The Innovation Team Test Drive

The BOC Group decided to run several experiments with innovation teams that were established based on previously untested parameters. The teams would be:

- Smaller teams with five to eight team members led by a team leader
- Virtual teams selected for their complementary professional and personal skill sets
- Cross-pollination of core competencies
- Selected for diversity, connectivity, and internal and external networks
- Tasked with specific goals and objectives
- Challenged to operate differently

For one six-member team, the core competencies could be listed as shown in Exhibit 7.7. These are specific competencies in addition to the base competencies that BOC employees would generally have. These first-level competencies are being complemented by the second-level competencies available through the combined network of contacts, in this case defined as "excellent rela-

EXHIBIT 7.7 The Team Competencies

- Competencies
  - — Heat and mass transfer
  - — Modeling and vacuum
  - — Food science
  - — R&D
  - — Project management
  - — Licensing
  - — Technology assessment
  - — Waste treatment
  - — Crystalization
  - — CO_2, O_3, H_2
  - — Gas and liquid mixing
  - — Cryogenics
  - — Combustion
  - — Freezing and cooling
  - — Marketing
  - — Business development
  - — Commercialization
  - — Emissions control

EXHIBIT 7.8 The Innovation Team Connectors

- Directly connected to:
  - — Fiber-optics
  - — Food
  - — H_2 energy and fuel cells
  - — Chemicals
  - — Petroleum
  - — Pulp and paper
  - — Glass
  - — Metal
  - — Electronics packaging
  - — Key customers
  - — Edwards vacuum division
  - — Global engineering team
  - — Global product management
  - — ISP division
  - — New products and services
  - — Venture group
  - — Licensing and IAM group
  - — Legal and IP department
  - — Technology functional support

tionships" (whom you can reach out to on a Saturday and get the intended response or help).

In many cases, the contacts can become virtual members of the innovation team, depending on the challenge and personal commitment. The team was found to have the internal connecting points to other functional teams or departments as shown in Exhibit 7.8. The team has excellent relationships with all project sponsors and key functional departments for ensuring progress across the continuum of the project.

Communication continues to be an issue for the team, and after trying many different forms and formats of team communication, frequent team meetings (or conference calls) three to five times per week seems to be the most effective way to keep all team members creatively engaged, aligned, and focused without creating smaller cliques.

The tools that the team is currently using support lateral thinking and drive awareness at the individual and group levels. They include:

- Six Thinking Hats by Edward de Bono
- Adaptations of the Johari window by J. Luft and H. Ingham

These tools are combined with lightly facilitated team brainstorming sessions with or without "invitees" from the team network. It seems appropriate to end the chapter with a relevant quote from Marcel Proust:

> "The real voyage of discovery consists not in seeing new landscapes, but in having new eyes."

8

Road-Mapping Disruptive Technical Threats and Opportunities in Complex, Technology-Based Subsystems: The SAILS Methodology

Bruce A. Vojak and Frank A. Chambers

Background

Technology road-mapping[1,2,3,4,5,6] has generated significant and growing interest both within corporations[7,8] and across industries.[9] As a result, much energy is expended developing technology road maps in support of technology planning efforts.

---

[1]Kostoff, R.N., and Schaller, R.R. Science and Technology Roadmaps, *IEEE Transactions on Engineering Management* 48(2), 132–143, 2001.

[2]Schaller, R.R. *Master Roadmap Bibliography*. http://mason.gmu.edu/~rschalle/master.html. Accessed January 2003.

[3]Garcia, M.L., and Bray, O.H. *Fundamentals of Technology Roadmapping*. http://www.sandia.gov/Roadmap/home.htm. Accessed January 2003.

[4]Kappel, T.A. "Technology Roadmapping: An Evaluation." PhD thesis, Northwestern University, Evanston, IL, 1998

[5]Peet, C.S. "Technology Road Mapping: A Tool for the Formulation of Technology Strategy." MS thesis, University of Manchester Institute of Science and Technology, Manchester, U.K., 1998.

[6]Phaal, R., Farrukh, C.J.P., and Probert, D.R. "Characterization of Technology Roadmaps: Purpose and Format," *Proceedings of the Portland International Conference on the Management of Technology (PICMET)*, 367–374, 2001.

[7]Willyard, C.H., and McClees, C.W. "Motorola's Technology Roadmap Process," *Research-Technology Management*, September–October 1987, pp. 13–19.

[8]Groenveld, P. "Roadmapping Integrates Business and Technology," *Research-Technology Management*, September–October 1997, pp. 48–55.

[9]*International Technology Roadmap for Semiconductors*. http://pubic.itrs.net. Accessed January 2003.

In spite of the relatively wide use of this tool, some variation exists among users regarding exactly what road maps and road-mapping entail. For example, former Motorola chairman Robert Galvin has suggested that "A 'roadmap' is an extended look at the future of a chosen field of inquiry composed from the collective knowledge of the brightest drivers of change in that field . . .".[10] Further, Groenveld, in his discussion of road-mapping at Philips Electronics, describes road-mapping as ". . . a process that contributes to the integration of business and technology and to the definition of technology strategy by displaying the interaction between products and technologies over time . . ."[11] Additionally, in their review of science and technology road maps, Kostoff and Schaller indicate that ". . . the single word 'roadmap' has surfaced as a popular metaphor for planning S&T (science and technology) resources."

Based on these definitions, it is reasonable to assert that road maps and road-mapping can be divided into two activities. First, the selection of a type of road map to properly display trends and interactions is required. Options for the type of road map are many, including market, product, and core technology road maps. Second, a means for the identification of entries for incorporation in the road map is required. The tools of technology forecasting are employed to establish what technology trends will actually occur and when they will occur. This division is shown schematically in Exhibit 8.1. Based on this division, it is interesting to note that, in many respects, technology road-mapping is similar to geographic mapping, where decisions regarding the nature of the map (ranging from political to topographic to weather) and the imaging technique employed to generate entries in the map (ranging from census taking to traditional surveying to satellite imaging) are required.

In stable areas of technology development, the more traditional tools of technology forecasting,[12,13,14,15,16] a field with a rich heritage of methodologies

---

[10]Galvin, R. "Science Roadmaps," *Science*, 280 (1998), p. 803.

[11]See note 10.

[12]Cetron, M.J. *Technological Forecasting* (New York: Gordon and Breach, 1969).

[13]Bright, J.R., and Schoeman, M.E.F. (eds.). *A Guide to Practical Technological Forecasting* (Englewood Cliffs, NJ: Prentice-Hall, 1973).

[14]Millett, S.M., and Honton, E.J. *A Manager's Guide to Technology Forecasting and Strategy Analysis Methods* (Columbus, OH: Battelle Press, 1991).

[15]Porter, A.L., Roper, A.T., Mason, T.W., Rossini, F.A., Banks, J., and Wiederholt, B.J. *Forecasting and Management of Technology* (New York, John Wiley and Sons, 1991).

[16]Martino, J.P. *Technological Forecasting for Decision Making* (New York: McGraw-Hill, 1993).

EXHIBIT 8.1 Hierarchy of Technology Road-Mapping

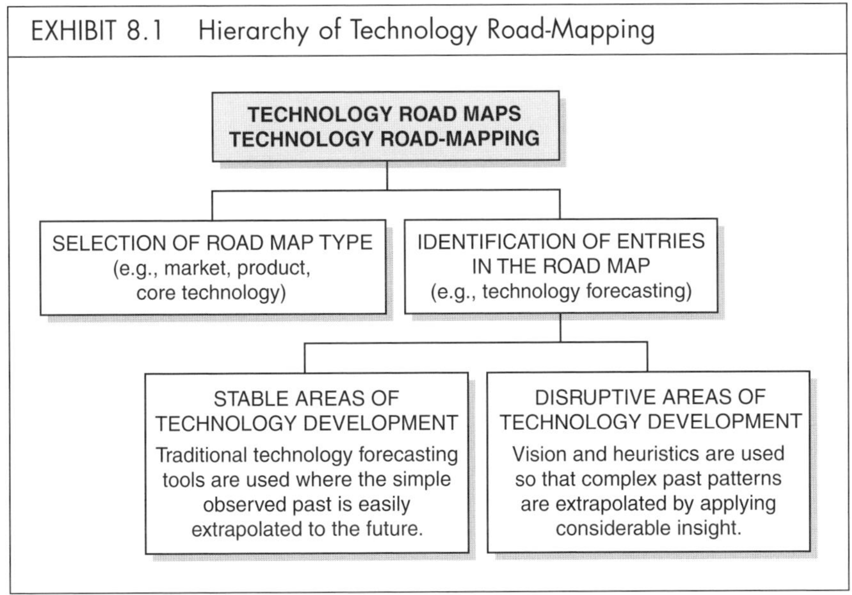

used to gain insight into future possibilities, can be reasonably applied to the task of road-mapping (see branch for "Stable Areas of Technology Development" in Exhibit 8.1). The techniques of this field are numerous and include trend extrapolation, trend correlation, and the use of growth analogies. The traditional technology forecasting techniques generally are based on the notion that past or related performance and trends are indicators of future performance and performance trends, a rational extrapolation of the past and present. The literature of technology road-mapping also indicates that predicting what will happen and when it will occur can be accomplished by using an extrapolation of past trends, with computer-based approaches to road map construction being such a technique. These extrapolation methodologies typically lead to the identification of monotonic trends in performance characteristics. Further, these methodologies allow a firm to defend itself against the threats that arise from the incremental progress of its competition and new entrants in its field.

Fortunately for those who seek to gain competitive advantage, the future is often anything but stable and deterministic. Thus, in addition to technology improvements that are evolutionary, sustaining, and incremental, another, more competitively powerful, set of disruptive, radical, and emergent improvements can be expected.[17,18,19,20] The real challenge for technology road-mapping and forecasting, then, is identifying when the discontinuous, the unexpected, and the disruptive will occur[21,22,23,24]—the type of innovation that is at the heart of significant economic development.[25]

While consideration has been given to the strategic response options that firms have to technological threats,[26,27] the more conventional tools of technology road-mapping and forecasting described above do not predict the emergence of radically disruptive technologies and approaches. As a result, when unanticipated threats arise, the response may come too late. This difficulty is compounded by the severity of this type of threat. A poor, or erroneous, road map of a monotonic trend can place a business at a competitive disadvantage, at least for a while. Generally, the disadvantage is not fatal to the business as there is usually time to recognize the problem and respond. The issue with disruptive technologies is that they, in fact, can change the competitive environment so much that the very survival of the business is at stake.

---

[17]Bitindo, D., and Frohman, A. "Linking Technological and Business Planning," *Research Management*, November 1981, pp. 19–23.

[18]Bower, J.L., and Christensen, C.M. "Disruptive Technologies: Catching the Wave," *Harvard Business Review*, January–February 1995, pp. 43–53.

[19]Morone, J. *Winning in High Tech Markets* (Boston: Harvard Business School Press, 1993).

[20]Kirchhoff, B.A., and Walsh, S.T. "Entrepreneurship's Role in Commercialization of Disruptive Technologies," in Brauchlin, E., and Pichler, J.H. (eds.). *Unternehmer und Unternehmensperspektive für Klein- und Mittelunternehmen* (Berlin: Dunker & Humbolt, 2000).

[21]Foster, R.N. "Timing Technological Transitions," in Tushman, M.L., and Moore, W.L. (eds.). *Readings in the Management of Innovation* (Cambridge, MA: Ballinger, 1988).

[22]Tushman, M.L., Anderson, P.C., and O'Reilly, C. "Technology Cycles, Innovation Streams, and Ambidextrous Organizations: Organization Renewal Through Innovation Streams and Strategic Change," in Tushman, M.L., and Anderson, P. (eds.). *Managing Strategic Innovation and Change* (New York: Oxford University Press, 1997).

[23]Veryzer, R.W. "Discontinuous Innovation and the New Product Development Process," *The Journal of Product Innovation Management* 15 (1998), pp. 304–321.

[24]Walsh, S.T., and Linton, J.D. "Infrastructure for Emergent Industries Based on Discontinuous Innovations," *Engineering Management Journal* 12(2) (2000), pp. 23–31.

[25]Schumpeter, J.A. *The Theory of Economic Development* (Cambridge, MA: Harvard University Press, 1934).

[26]Cooper, A.C., and Schendel, D. "Strategic Responses to Technological Threats," in Tushman, M.L., and Moore, W.L. (eds.). *Readings in the Management of Innovation.* (Cambridge, MA: Ballinger, 1988).

[27]Cooper, A.C., and Smith, C.G. "How Established Firms Respond to Threatening Technologies," in Tushman, M.L., and Anderson, P. (eds.). *Managing Strategic Innovation and Change.* (New York: Oxford University Press, 1997).

To begin to address the problem of anticipating the unexpectedly disruptive innovation, the literatures of both technology road-mapping and forecasting also indicate that predicting what will happen and when it will occur can be performed based on the intuitive insight of visionaries or experts (see branch for "Disruptive Areas of Technology Development" in Exhibit 8.1).[28,29] Within the technology forecasting literature, the Delphi method[30] stands as a classic example of such an approach. Further, expert-based road map development is identified as a key road-mapping approach. Thus, in spite of corporate efforts to mechanize road-mapping, this process proceeds largely through the interpersonal insights and dynamics of those who construct the road maps.[31]

Unfortunately, however, all too often the expert's vision is limited by the very experience they rely on to form their forecasts and they cannot see the truly disruptive. Even when they do, there often are tremendous barriers to belief within the organizations that they are a part of. The present is a very comfortable place to be, no matter how uncomfortable, compared to the uncertainty of a disrupted future. Prediction of disruption is often discounted as wild speculation or guesswork that is too unreliable to invest in.

Yet another approach to predicting future disruptive technical opportunities and threats is to identify more complex patterns of change (see branch for "Disruptive Areas of Technology Development" in Exhibit 8.1). Christensen's work, for example, as summarized in *The Innovator's Dilemma*,[32] represents such an approach in that he identifies changes in terms of the disruption to the underlying business or industry. Christensen does not, however, present a methodology for identifying disruptors, although he does identify warning signs. Recurrences of these patterns of change are used to offer insight into how future change might occur. Only this last approach, that of identifying patterns of change, addresses disruption directly. However, it has little established methodology.

---

[28]O'Connor, G.C., and Veryzer, R.W. "The Nature of Market Visioning for Technology-Based Radical Innovation," *Journal of Product Innovation Management* 18 (2001), pp. 231–246.

[29]Linton, J.D., and Walsh, S.T. "Forecasting Micro Electro Mechanical Systems: A Disruptive Innovation," *Proceedings of the Portland International Conference on the Management of Technology (PICMET)* (2001), pp. 391–399.

[30]Linstone, H.A., and Turoff, M. *The Delphi Method: Techniques and Applications* (Reading, MA: Addison-Wesley, 1975).

[31]Radnor, M. "Roadmapping: How Does It Work in Practice?" *Proceedings of the National Center for Manufacturing Sciences Conference and Exposition* 14 (1998).

[32]Christensen, C.M. *The Innovator's Dilemma.* (Boston: Harvard Business School Press, 1997).

One of the key opportunities for improving the forecasting and evaluation of disruptive technical events for road map development is to establish methodologies or heuristics[33,34] to guide the intuition of the visionary or expert. A well-thought-out methodology can bring credibility to the predictions and reduce guesswork and speculation dramatically. An additional advantage is that a good methodology may also indicate proactive opportunities for disruption. Further, such tools will also be useful in the formation of the intuition of the more junior technologist as he or she develops the insight required to predict the future of technology.

For the present work, we have developed a heuristic methodology, based on observations of past patterns of change across several complex, technology-based, subsystem-level industries, for the identification of the emergence of potentially disruptive technologies and opportunities for development of disruptive technologies. The identification of potential disruption can indicate portions of a road map that need to be more carefully evaluated and monitored in order to better respond to the disruptive elements that may appear or gain competitive advantage through a planned disruption. The present work fits structurally in the "Disruptive Areas of Technology" branch in Exhibit 8.1.

An important source of innovation in many instances is the interaction between the firm and the customer.[35,36,37,38] Further, the magnitude and timing of customer acceptance of innovation often drives the timing of innovation. Note, however, that we have intentionally focused our attention on the identification of disruptive opportunities within the firm or those for which existing customers do not exist.[39] Thus, insights on the relationship between the firm and its customers can be applied after the technique described here in order to gain insight into the timing and magnitude of customer acceptance.

---

[33]White, G.R. "Management Criteria for Effective Innovation," in Burgelman, R.A., Maidique, M.A., and Wheelwright, S.C. *Strategic Management of Technology and Innovation* (New York: McGraw-Hill/Irwin, 2001).

[34]Teece, D.J. "Profiting from Technological Innovation: Implications for Integration, Collaboration, Licensing, and Public Policy," in Burgelman, R.A., Maidique, M.A., and Wheelwright, S.C. *Strategic Management of Technology and Innovation* (New York: McGraw-Hill/Irwin, 2001).

[35]Mansfield, E. *The Economics of Technological Change* (New York: W.W. Norton, 1968).

[36]Von Hippel, E. "Lead Users: A Source of Novel Product Concepts," in Tushman, M.L., and Moore, W.L. (eds.). *Readings in the Management of Innovation* (Cambridge, MA: Ballinger, 1988).

[37]Von Hippel, E. *The Sources of Innovation* (New York: Oxford University Press, 1988).

[38]Moore, G.A. *Crossing the Chasm* (New York: HarperCollins, 1991).

[39]Walsh, S., and Kirchhoff, B. "Entrepreneurs' Opportunities in Technology-Based Markets," in Phan, P.H. (ed.). *Technological Entrepreneurship* (Greenwich, CT: Information Age Publishing, 2002).

The subsystem level of the value chain was deliberately selected for this study. Some important differences exist between road-mapping and forecasting techniques used at different levels of the value chain. For example, system-level suppliers have relatively free access to customer information, used for technology planning, by probing end-user demand directly (e.g. reviewing actual customer orders for existing products). Thus, road-mapping and forecasting at the system level often is an exercise in understanding end-user customer acceptance of a new product or technology.

While information sharing throughout the value chain is critical to successful road-mapping,[40] material-, component- and subsystem-level suppliers often face relatively more difficulty than systems-level suppliers in their pursuit of information for their road maps and forecasts.[41] This occurs for at least two reasons. First, system-level suppliers typically are not entirely transparent regarding the details of their future needs. This is often due to a desire to not divulge the complete details of sensitive tactical and strategic competitive information in the form of road maps to their suppliers. Second, since material-, component- and subsystem-level suppliers are removed from regular, direct interaction with end users, miscommunication and substantial delay is to be expected as information makes its way through the higher levels of the value chain to these lower levels.[42] As a result, material-, component- and subsystem-level suppliers are especially in need of effective tools for the road-mapping and forecasting of disruption that do not rely entirely on ultimate end-user information.

Note that, while our focus is on predicting disruption in technical subsystems, we realize that it is likely that much of the methodology presented will be able to be generalized to other situations, throughout the value-added chain, from basic materials to the super-system level of architecture.[43]

---

[40]Petrick, I.J., and Echols, A.E. "Technology Choice and Pooled Investment Among Networks: Supply Chain Roadmaps," *Proceedings of the IEEE International Engineering Management Conference* (2002), pp. 894–899.

[41]Vojak, B.A., and Suarez, C.A. "Sources of Information Used in New Product and Process Technology Planning within the Electron Device Industry," *Proceedings of the IEEE International Engineering Management Conference* (2002), pp. 623–628.

[42]Lee, H.L., Padmanabhan, V., and Whang, S. "The Bullwhip Effect in Supply Chains," *Sloan Management Review* 38(3) (1997), pp. 93–102.

[43]For the purpose of this paper, we define levels of the value-added chain as materials, components, subsystems, systems, and super-systems. The super-system level is used to define collections of systems that comprise a still larger entity. For example, a wireless communication super-system is comprised of a number of cellular handset systems (cell phones) and base station systems, and, in turn, is connected to the land-based wire-line telecommunication super-system, which is comprised of switching systems, transmission network systems, and conventional wire-line telephone systems. Further, for the purpose of this paper, the term *element* is used to identify any portion of the value-added chain below the system level. Thus, a material, a component, or a subsystem may all be identified as elements of the system.

Finally, while the methodology is presented using both retrospective and prospective examples in a competitive industrial environment it could also be applied to industry-wide, precompetitive road-mapping processes.

The SAILS Methodology

The proposed methodology identifies five different types of disruptive contributors commonly observed at the subsystem level, those due to:

- Changes in industry ***S****tandards*
- Changes in ***A****rchitectures*
- Various forms of ***I****ntegration* and disintegration of elements
- ***L****inkages* between various elements across the super-system
- ***S****ubstitutions* within the subsystem

The contributors are summarized schematically in Exhibit 8.2 and developed more fully below. Needless to say, there can be strong interactions among the various elements. Activity in any of these areas can provide an early indicator of a potential disruption.

Industry standards set a specification for the performance of an element of a super-system at some level in the hierarchy. As such, standards provide a set of performance definitions without necessarily specifying how the performance is to be obtained. Additionally, the internal changes brought about by changes in standards often lead to further opportunity for disruptive changes at the subsystem level. Widely adopted standards provide a consistent framework within which to innovate and potentially disrupt. This is especially true in standards-driven industry segments, for example, data communications and telecommunications, or the automotive industry, where commercial success requires adherence to standards, often to ensure interoperability among equipment offered by different vendors. The standards for the output of modems, for example, allowed the substitution of sound/modem integrated circuits, such as Rockwell's, or even the use of the processor itself in personal computers, Winmodems, for the generation of the correct signals. This was disruptive to the dedicated modem products and provided significant cost savings to the end user. Close monitoring of standards activities can provide an early warning of a potential disruption.

Architectural changes occur when a subsystem, system, or super-system performs the same function with different elemental technology. Inputs, outputs, and key functionality are essentially maintained, but a new arrangement or combination of the internal elements is used to accomplish this end goal. This

EXHIBIT 8.2 Five Components of the SAILS Methodology

SAILS CONTRIBUTOR	BEFORE	WHAT OCCURS	AFTER
STANDARDS	A	New performance within, but outside performance still essentially the same	A′
ARCHITECTURES	A B C	New arrangement of elements, with possibly some of the same elements	D E F
INTEGRATION	A B	A and B integrated into new product, C	C A B
	C A B	C divided into two products, A and B	A B
LINKAGES	A B	Change in B requires more or less of, or from, A	A′ B′
SUBSTITUTIONS	A	B replaces A	B

area can be strongly influenced by the existence of standards at some level in the systems hierarchy. Per Exhibit 8.2, a new arrangement of elements, with possibly some of the same elements as before, is used to accomplish the same end goal.

Integration broadly covers a wide range of activity, including:

- Integration—combining several constituent elements to form a new subsystem
- Disintegration—separating a subsystem into its constituent elements
- Reintegration—combining a new subset of constituent elements after disintegration

To accomplish integration, the designer must look for commonality of technology and function in all elements, for example, the integration of multimedia and modem functionality mentioned above. Note that this threat or opportunity can be used against suppliers (backward integration), customers (forward integration), and makers of other elements in a subsystem (lateral integration). Further, it is important to note that this threat or opportunity can come from more than one level of the value chain away from the element under consideration. Integration can also be used to take advantage of process technologies, for example, the integration of the serializer/deserializer function with the drivers for optical communications on the same chip.

In his seminal work on competitive advantage, Porter[44] discusses the concept of linkages both within the value chain and with other levels of the value chain. Linkages are defined as "relationships between the way one value activity is performed and the cost or performance of another." Porter illustrates this concept with the example of moving from metal to sintered, net-shaped ceramic engine parts. The process of doing so eliminates the need for machining of parts and, as such, serves to compete with suppliers of machined metal parts. Linkages can result from increases in the functionality of an element in one part of a super-system, causing either increases or decreases in the functionality or requirement for other elements in the super-system. Similarly, decreases in the functionality of an element in one part of a super-system can cause either increases or decreases in the functionality or requirement for other elements.

Porter has identified linkages within the value chain and with other levels of the value chain as crucial, but often subtle and unrecognized. Further, he goes on to point out that "managing linkages is a more complex organizational task than managing value activities themselves" and that "given the difficulty of recognizing and managing linkages, the ability to do so often yields a sustainable source of competitive advantage." This concept of linkages can be adapted from its application in business systems to complex, technology-based subsystems. The identification of linkages in complex, technology-based subsystems is as challenging a task as Porter suggests it is in a business system and offers similar potential disruptive competitive advantage. For example, the increasing intelligence of test instrumentation has enabled increased functionality in the area of data handling. By providing database-like functions in the instrument itself, entire layers in the customer's information storage and handling chain can be eliminated with little additional development cost and essentially no added manufacturing cost. This can be very disruptive to suppliers at the next level in the chain.

Finally, substitutions occur when a radical technology replacement is made in the same or similar environment. This can be, for example, a material or

[44]Porter, M.E. *Competitive Advantage* (New York: Free Press, 1985), pp. 48–52.

component performing the same function with different technology, and is not unlike the concept of "marketing myopia" as described by Levitt[45] or the threat of substitution as described by Porter.[46] For example, the substitution of optical data links for electrical wires or cables in communications systems is a simple example of the concept of substitution.

The challenge of implementing any methodology such as this is to cast the net broadly enough to identify as many realistic competitive opportunities as possible while not being ridiculous in the scope of analysis. One way to implement this is to first identify the bill of materials for the subsystem under consideration (i.e., the company's product) as well as for the entire super-system that it operates within. Then each of the methodology steps can, in turn, be considered for not only the subsystem under consideration, but also for the various elements that comprise this subsystem. The job of the design engineer, then, is to systematically analyze the subsystem and super-system bills of materials applying the five perspectives of the SAILS methodology:

1. *Standards.* The process begins with the designer seeking to understand what the trends are for industry standardization at various levels of the value-added chain and how they impact product performance characteristics. Participation in the standards process is an excellent way to accomplish this. Off-line conversations and proposals can provide significant insight.
2. *Architecture.* The designer next moves to brainstorming various architecture options available at each value-added level within the super-system. These first two steps set the stage for the rest of the analysis.
3. *Integration.* The burden on the designer here is to develop options for forward integration, backward integration, and lateral integration into the rest of the super-system. It also involves putting oneself in the position of the designer of other portions of the super-system and determining to what extent your product (or some portion of the function of your product) could be a target of their attack. This part of the analysis must be repeated for each standard and architecture option under consideration. Also, various sequences and combinations of disintegration and reintegration must necessarily be considered. Often, a blank paper approach to meeting the system or subsystem requirements is helpful.

[45]Levitt, T. "Marketing Myopia," *Harvard Business Review*, November–December 1965.

[46]Porter, pp. 273–314.

4. *Linkages.* Perhaps the most difficult (and most rewarding) task is the identification of linkages between the functional performance of all portions of the product and the performance of all other elements of the super-system. This part of the analysis also must be repeated for each standard and architecture option under consideration.
5. *Substitutions.* This step is challenging in that it requires the designer to seek out what he or she may currently not be aware of, competitive threats to a component of your product or some portion of the product that may radically replace that element. As much as with the other elements of the methodology, this requires a proactive scanning of the technical literature to know what is out there, as well as to evaluate the level of threat or opportunity it provides. The net must be cast very widely, as the most disruptive substitutions can occur quickly through the adoption of a component or subsystem that has already been developed for a very different application.

Examples

Three examples of the application of the SAILS methodology applied to subsystem-level situations are presented below. Aspects of these examples are historically descriptive, as well as predictive, or forecasting, in nature. They are intended to represent the wide range of disruptive opportunities and threats that have been and can be identified during road-mapping activities by using the components of this methodology.

Example 1: Frequency Generation Subsystems in Wireless Communication Super-Systems

Temperature-compensated crystal oscillators (TCXOs) provide the precise frequencies, stable over time and under temperature variation, which enable communication over multiple frequency bands or the synchronized behavior of a computer. While the TCXO industry has generally progressed along the lines of smaller, faster, cheaper products, some significant disruptive technologies have arisen to challenge industry participants.

A simple bill of materials for a conventional TCXO is shown schematically in Exhibit 8.3. The impedance of the crystal and varactor in the feedback loop define the resonant frequency of the subsystem. Temperature variations are compensated for through the use of a temperature sensor. A temperature-

EXHIBIT 8.3 Temperature-Compensated Crystal Oscillator (TCXO)

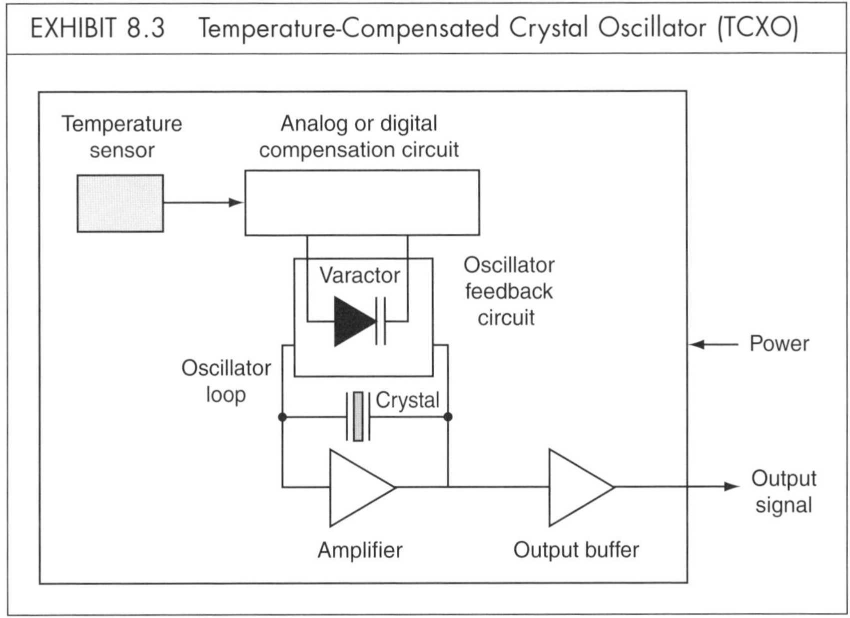

dependent bias applied to the varactor is used to modify the impedance of the feedback loop and, thus, maintain precise control of the oscillator frequency, which is a prime objective of this subsystem.

The bill of materials for a part of the super-system, in this case the cellular handset system of a wireless communication super-system, is shown schematically in Exhibit 8.4. In addition to the frequency control capabilities of the TCXOs, filters are used to control the frequency selectivity of the cellular handset. In practice, the base station would also be modeled, as well as consideration given to the land-based wire-line system and switching equipment that, in total, describes the entire communication super-system.

- *Standards.* At the super-system level, there are many standards that drive trends in product definition, including: Code Division Multiple Access (CDMA), Time Division Multiple Access (TDMA), Global System for Mobile Communications (GSM), and Personal Communications Services (PCS). Each of these standards impacts TCXO product definition in several ways, including the accuracy of defining the frequency of operation, temperature stability, and noise performance. Thus, changes in the standard of choice have the potential for inducing disruptive changes in product performance requirements and, thus, the technologies that support the TCXO industry.

EXHIBIT 8.4 Handset System of a Wireless Communication Super-System

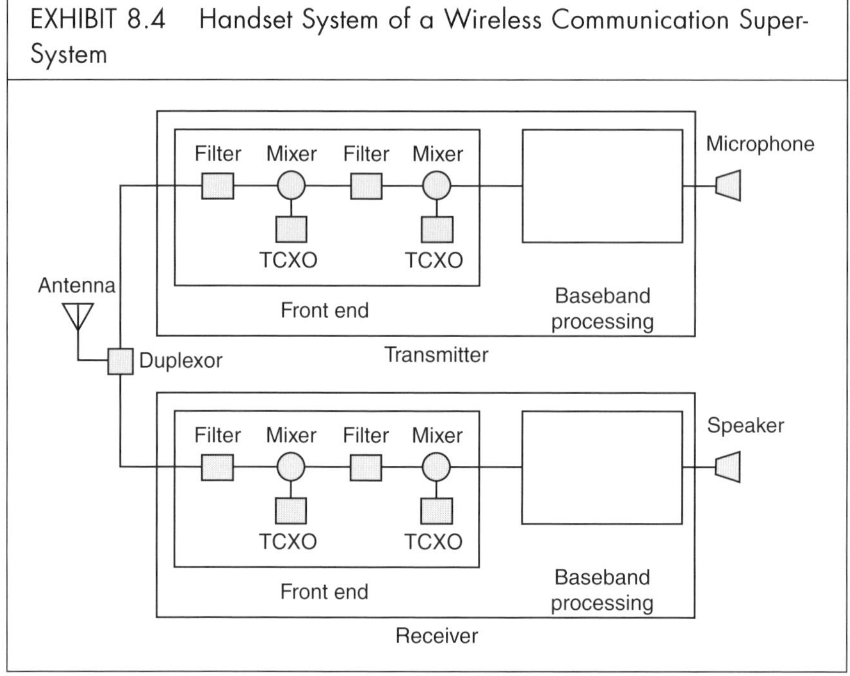

- *Architectures.* At the super-system level, there are architecture alternatives, many of which are related to the super-system standards. Additionally, different architectures are also possible within the TCXO. For example, temperature compensation can be accomplished via digital or analog circuitry, two extreme architectural options. The history of the TCXO industry reveals that the digital approach became a disruptive challenge to the analog approach.
- *Integration.* Technology-based integration can occur where common technologies are brought together on one substrate or in one package. For TCXOs, this can include integrating multiple silicon-based circuits, such as the silicon circuitry in the TCXO with silicon circuitry in other parts of the cellular handset. Further, as silicon micro-electro-mechanical devices (MEMs) become successful substitutes for quartz devices in certain applications (see discussion on substitution later in this section), integration with the oscillator circuitry is predicted.
    - An example of functional-based integration would be integrating multiple frequency control elements, such as TCXOs with ceramic filters, by the manufacturers of the filters, to form part of the radio front-end circuitry. This form of disruption, which is currently being experienced in the industry, can also be viewed as a form of lateral integration.

- Forward integration by the TCXO producer could occur if it integrates the entire front end of the radio, thus threatening the cellular handset producer. Conversely, TCXO producers are threatened by cellular handset manufacturers as they backward integrate into the frequency control function of the TCXO.
- TCXO disintegration can form an opportunity for a disruptive technical threat when the cellular handset manufacturer purchases TCXO components and builds a discrete TCXO circuit on the radio printed circuit board, a disruptive threat that has been observed in both pager and cellular handset systems. This approach allows the radio designer to control the entire design and, thus, take the value-added profit margin back into the cellular handset. Note that this form of disintegration could also be classified as backward integration by the cellular handset system producer.
- Finally, the threat or opportunity for reintegration of a TCXO exists when the disintegration of a TCXO occurs simultaneously with the reintegration of its component parts. As an example, the silicon circuitry of a disintegrated TCXO can be reintegrated with the microprocessor in a cellular handset, not unlike the technology-based integration identified earlier.

- *Linkages.* One example of a linkage opportunity occurs when an improvement in the frequency stability of a TCXO leads to reduced performance requirements of the cellular handset baseband circuitry. Also, an improvement in the frequency stability of a TCXO in the cellular handset can be traded off with frequency stability of the oven-controlled crystal oscillator in the base station.
- *Substitutions.* As technology improvements occur, the TCXO crystal resonator is expected to be substituted by silicon MEMs or nano-electromechanical devices (NEMs) in certain applications. More exotic substitution threats also exist, such as quartz MEMs and carbon nanotubes. While none of these approaches has yet led to a commercially competitive disruption in the industry, they should be anticipated and included in TCXO road maps as a potential technical threat.

Example 2: Optical Multiplexing Subsystems in Optical Communication Super-Systems

A typical optical communication system multiplexes large numbers of voice and data streams into a high-speed optical channel, transmits the information, and breaks it back out into its constituent streams at the receiving end, demultiplexing. The introduction of dense wavelength division multiplexing (DWDM) is a good example of the introduction of a disruptive technology at the systems level in this industry. To understand why this technology was disruptive, we first look at an optical system prior to the introduction of DWDM (Exhibit 8.5). In this system, information is multiplexed, concentrated, at the central office and possibly at intermediate points in the system. Each set of multiplexed signals is converted to light in a transmitter and propagated through an optical fiber to the receiving central office where it is converted back into an electrical signal, demultiplexed, and sent to the intended receiver.

The introduction of two technological advances enabled major changes in the system. The first was the fiber amplifier. Alone, it is disruptive as it replaces repeaters and extends the distance a signal can be transmitted without reconstitution. More importantly, it is broadband, enabling the use of the second advance, narrow-line-width lasers. These devices use less than 1% of the optical spectrum that a standard laser uses. In early systems, additional capacity

EXHIBIT 8.5 Optical Communication System Schematics (Dense Wavelength Division Multiplexing—DWDM)

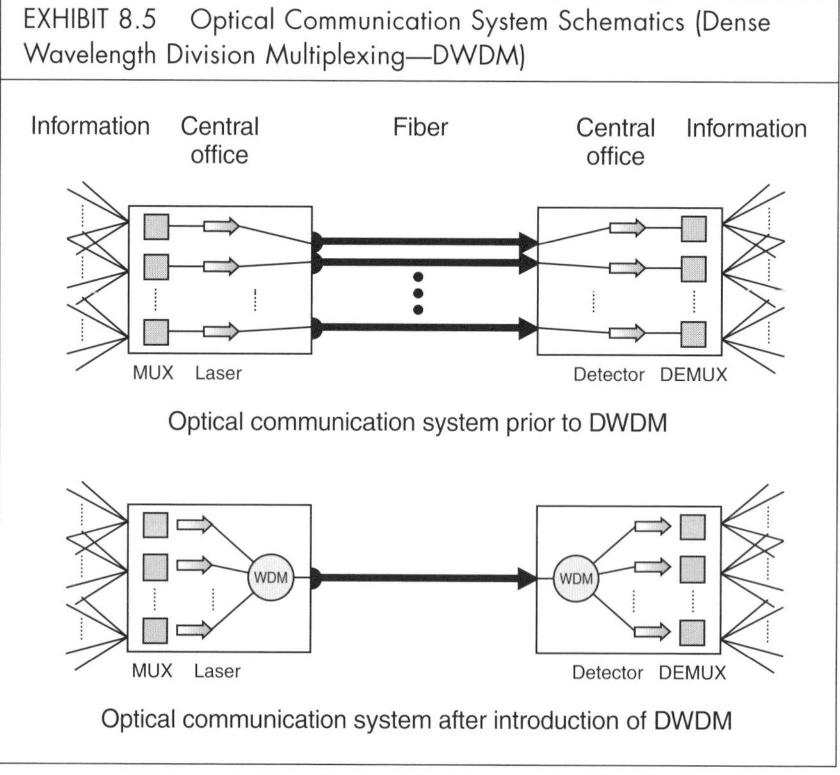

EXHIBIT 8.6 Absorption Spectrum of Optical Fiber and Emission Spectra of Conventional Laser

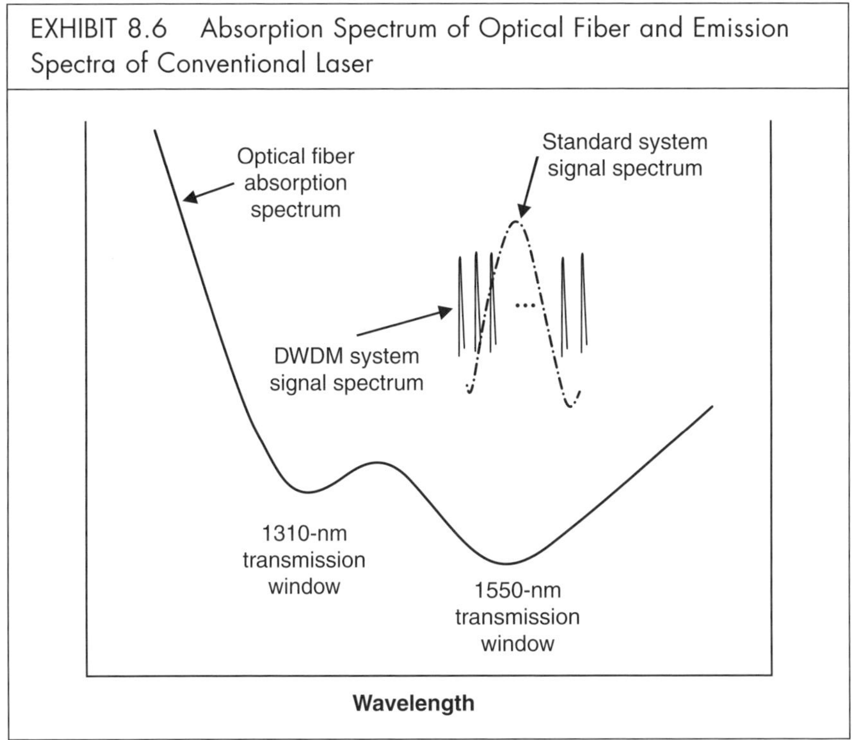

was gained by using both of the transmission windows centered around 1,310 nm and 1,550 nm in the optical fiber (Exhibit 8.6). The introduction of both of these technologies allowed many independent optical signals to be sent over a single fiber. The fact that the amplifier is practical in only the 1,550-nm window meant that the 1,310-nm window would only be used for short links, if at all, as system capacities were increased. An additional impact is that with DWDM far fewer fibers are needed for the same total bandwidth.

- *Standards.* The primary standards organizations include: Electronics Industry Association/Telecommunications Industry Association (EIA/TIA), Telcordia (formerly Bellcore), International Telecommunication Union (ITU), and the American National Standards Institute (ANSI).
  - Each of these organizations plays an essential role in creating a framework within which innovation can occur. The first uses of DWDM were within captive systems where the interfaces can be used within well-defined boundaries. Once feasibility was shown, there was a period of intense standards activity, centered on interoperability, to

enable the widespread deployment of the technology into the field. Agreements on wavelengths, wavelength spacing, power levels, and device characteristics needed to be in place before this technology could cross operational boundaries. As improvements in the technology occur, standards are modified to take advantage of them. Careful monitoring of proposed changes can provide insight into the direction of the technology. For example, the proposal to set the wavelength spacing to 100 GHz indicated that advocates of this portion of the standard were investing significant resources in this area and were preparing to commercialize this technology. The exact wavelengths to be used are important because they determine characteristics of the components that can be expensive to change. Arrayed waveguide gratings, for example, must be manufactured very precisely to a known set of wavelengths. The cost of changing wavelengths involves not only design effort, but also fabrication of new masks and re-qualification of the device. Thus, proposals for standards changes can indicate an attempt to disrupt, at least to the extent of forcing a redesign.

- *Architectures.* The rapid introduction of both technologies opened up an array of architectural choices. DWDM technology also allowed new expressions of existing architectures. For example, multiple independent rings can be implemented in a single fiber by using multiple wavelengths. This can result in significant traffic management advantages at the expense of increasing the consequences of a physical layer failure. New switching and routing approaches based on wavelength have become possible as well. These approaches are often very sensitive to the wavelength standards discussed above, and small changes can rule out entire classes of technology.
- *Integration.* The integration of switching at the optical level, which is now possible, eliminates the need in the switch for multiple optical-electrical-optical conversions and the associated hardware. This should be expected to occur and have a substantial impact on present switching systems.
    - Initial implementations involved the replacement of an entire transmission system with an integrated multiple channel DWDM system. This involved tremendous capital cost and the installation of bandwidth capability in excess of the immediate requirements, though consistent with future needs. By breaking out the individual fibers in the transmission system (disintegration) and providing for the modular introduction of DWDM technology at a pace consistent with current bandwidth needs, the initial investment could be reduced and bandwidth added, and paid for, on an as-needed basis. This change dis-

rupted the then two largest vendors of DWDM equipment and provided the initial business for the company that introduced the new architecture, Ciena.

- As DWDM systems mature, many additional opportunities for combinations of functions (reintegration) are occurring. For example, transmitters and receivers are being integrated into add-drop multiplexers.

- *Linkages.* The substantial increase in the bandwidth utilization in a fiber has delayed or eliminated the need for laying additional fibers, while at the same time placing different, more stringent requirements on the properties of the fibers. The ability to switch according to wavelength is presently resulting in changes in the way that the network itself is configured.
- *Substitutions.* DWDM technology has, in essence, replaced, or substituted for, the entire long-reach telecommunications infrastructure and is in substantial use in medium-reach systems. The advent of dynamically tunable lasers will, we believe, ultimately replace fixed wavelength lasers and, at the same time, enable new architectures in switched systems. These lasers are presently under development and in very limited use. The advantages, ranging from reduced spare parts inventory to enabling of wavelength-agile networks, assure their ultimate success. These lasers require technology that is often not part of the technology competencies of current suppliers and, at least in the short term, will be disruptive.

Example 3: High-Voltage Electrical Subsystems in Automotive Super-systems

Automotive electrical systems started using 12V as the standard voltage in the late 1950s. Twelve-volt systems have undergone substantial development. Many optimizations have occurred, and continue to occur, not only in the electrical systems, but also in the surrounding areas of the automobile. Substantial infrastructure for designing, manufacturing, and testing 12V systems is now in place. Recently, a proposal to use 42V has been put forward and is generating interest. A move to this new voltage would impact essentially every aspect of automotive electronics and a number of other automotive systems. Exhibit 8.7 depicts the layers of the automotive electrical system and potentially impacted subsystems.

- *Standards.* Those standards particular to the 42V initiative include: Society of Automotive Engineering (SAE), MIT/Industry Consortium on Advanced Automotive Electrical/Electronic Components and Systems,

EXHIBIT 8.7 Conceptual Schematic of an Automotive Electrical System

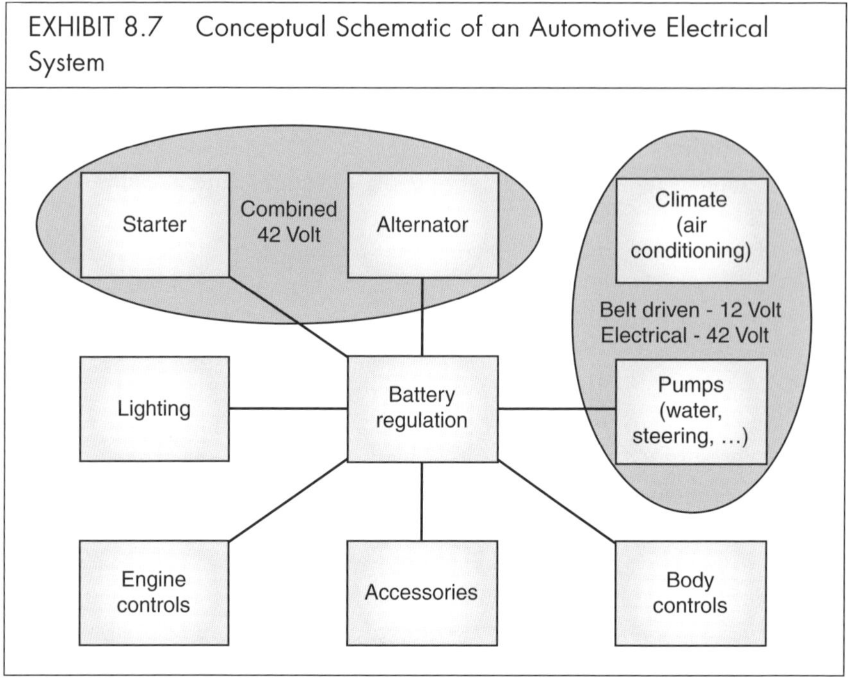

Forum Bordnetzarchitektur (Forum Vehicle Electrical Systems Architecture), and International Standards Organization (ISO).

- This area is sufficiently new that, in addition to standards organizations, industry consortia still play a large role. Ultimately, their activities will translate into standards. This is another area that can bear fruit if monitored. One proposal that could have been disruptive to the traditional automotive switch manufacturers has already been proposed. At the present 12V level, contact arcing and the associated damage is nonexistent. Switches operating at 42V, on the other hand, exhibit significant arcing. This is a well-known problem, and there has been much effort to mitigate this at higher voltages. The existence of arcing led two major automotive electronics suppliers to propose that all switching be accomplished electronically. The electronic approach blocks traditional mechanical switch manufacturers and, if adopted as part of the standard, would prevent them from selling into this market. Close monitoring of the standards proposals led one of the participants, Eaton Vehicle Switch in conjunction with Eaton's Innovation Center, to find a mechanism that allowed mechanical switches to operate in this regime at an extremely low added cost, significantly lower than electronic switches. In this case, careful monitoring of the activities surrounding the standards allowed a timely response to a potentially very disruptive development.

- *Architectures.* The increase in voltage will require new architectures for power distribution and control. While the higher voltage provides many advantages for a number of functions, there are others, such as lighting, that are more effectively done at lower voltages. Architectures involving dual voltages or multiple voltages are under development. Control systems for the electrical system will also need to be redesigned and will almost certainly be very different in logic and technology than current 12V systems.
- *Integration.* The higher voltage allows integration of the starter motor and the alternator into a single unit. At a still higher level, there is potential for even this future development to be disrupted. The relatively rapid emergence of hybrid and all-electric vehicles may eliminate the need for this part entirely.
- *Linkages.* Lower current requirements at the same power, due to the higher voltage, enable a significant reduction in the size and weight of the wiring harness while at the same time requiring new types of switches, discussed above. An additional linkage is the expectation that there will be an improvement in vehicle efficiency leading to better gas mileage and easier compliance with emissions requirements.
- *Substitutions.* The higher voltage allows the use of electric motors in places where belts or hydraulics are presently used, such as water pumps and steering assists. The potential elimination of vacuum and belt-driven accessories will be very disruptive to the present suppliers as the technologies are profoundly different.
    - Based on this analysis, we expect 42V systems, either as the primary electrical system in a conventional automobile or as the primary distribution system in a hybrid or all-electric vehicle, will be utilized. The advantages in weight, efficiency, and performance are sufficient to make the approach attractive, despite the cost of such a change.

Concluding Observations

Prediction of disruption for the purposes of technology road-mapping is intrinsically difficult. There is no single methodology that will provide certain results. The SAILS methodology is a systematic approach to the problem that guides investigation to areas that are likely to provide insight into the existence of, or potential for, disruption. We believe that the use of this methodology can benefit the expert in that it can assist in broadening the range of possibilities considered beyond the ordinary. Further, we believe it also can help the junior engineer in that it points the way to some fertile areas for identifying potential disruptions.

Acknowledgments

The authors wish to acknowledge helpful discussions with Dennis Marvin (Motorola, retired) during the preparation of the analysis of frequency generation subsystems.

PART 4

PARTNERED TECHNOLOGY AND BUSINESS DEVELOPMENT

9

Open for Business: The Air Products and Chemicals Story

John Tao and Vincent Magnotta

Background on Open Innovation at Air Products and Chemicals, Inc.

Air Products and Chemicals, Inc. (NYSE: APD) is the world's only combined gases and chemicals company, headquartered in Allentown, Pennsylvania (www.airproducts.com). It is rated approximately 300 in the *Fortune* 500 rankings. In 2004, sales were about $7.4 billion, with $604 million in net profit. The company operates in over 30 countries, serving customers in the technology, energy, health care, and industrial markets. More than half of the company's sales come from outside the United States. With about 20,000 employees worldwide, the company is known for its innovative culture and operational excellence.

Gases range from cryogenic air separation products to specialty gases for the electronics industry. Our chemicals business is focused on intermediates such as epoxy additives and surfactants. Our home care business serves the in-home market for services such as respiratory therapy.

Prior to 1995, external technology partnering was conducted by each business area and the supporting research and development (R&D) group, without any coordination of efforts between business areas and R&D groups—it was a "silo" mentality. There was no coordination of work processes or central repository of the related contracts. In 1995, Corporate Technology Partnerships was formed to centralize our external technology efforts and to develop and implement best practices across the company. This was the beginning of our open innovation effort. Open innovation is a technology management practice in which external resources are used to supplement a company's internal R&D and commercialization effort. The practice is the subject of a recent book entitled *Open Innovation: The New Imperative for Creating and Profiting from Technology* by Henry Chesbrough.[1]

Why is there a trend to move toward an open innovation model? There are many driving forces; some of the more notable are:

- Increased pressure for faster, improved, and lower-cost R&D.
- The realization that no company has more than 1% of global R&D capacity.[2]
- Reduced inflow of scientific talent to the United States.[3]
- The rest of the world has surpassed the United States in science education as evidenced by annual doctorate degrees granted.[4]

In this chapter, we will describe some key elements of the Air Products process for open innovation, "Identify and Accelerate." Specifically, we will review the process of identifying corporate technical needs and the role of external partnering in accelerating the innovation process. The external partnering strategies reviewed are university R&D alliances, global R&D insourcing, external providers, partnering with the government, licensing-in, and joint development. Finally, we will discuss measuring external R&D programs and also review recognition programs for external technologists or partners.

Process for Needs Identification

It's imperative to quantify the top needs/problems to focus the open innovation efforts. We have initiated a process corporate-wide to quantify and prioritize the top technical needs:

- Solicit top needs from business, marketing, and technology management using a common problem format.
- Rank order needs that make the first cut by a specific set of criteria based on economics, risk, strategy alignment, etc.
- Review and approve top needs list by senior business and technology management.

---

[1]Chesbrough, Henry. *Open Innovation: The New Imperative for Creating and Profiting from Technology* (Boston: Harvard Business School Press, 2005).

[2]Carroll, D. "Beyond the Lab: Innomediation and Global R&D," AICHE Management Conference, 2003.

[3]Brez, C., and Castro, C. "Putting the 'Global' in Global R&D," IRI External Technology Directors Network meeting, February 16, 2005.

[4]Ibid.

EXHIBIT 9.1 Screen Shot of a Needs Tracker Database

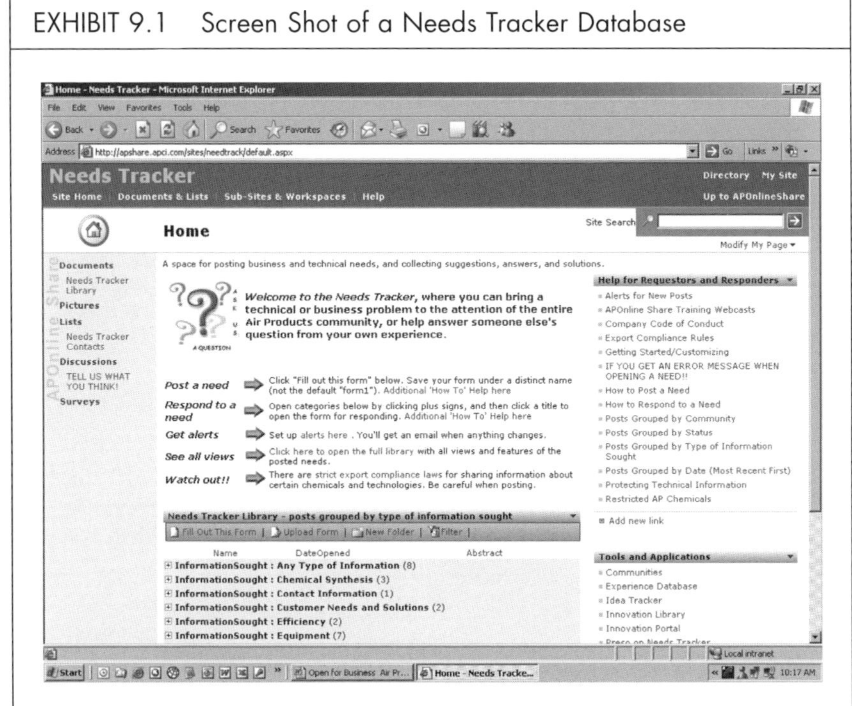

- Use top needs to broaden exposure of the needs internally and to focus the identification of external resources to meet the needs.

Technology needs are also posted on our internal corporate Web site. A new system, called Needs Tracker, has been introduced as a means to identify and log emerging internal needs. This tool is available to all employees to identify their technical needs. Employees can also propose solutions to the posted needs. A screen shot from this new information technology (IT) tool is shown in Exhibit 9.1.

Partnering Strategies

Partnering is the cornerstone of open innovation. Partnering also includes alliances with internal groups globally, but the main focus here is external groups. Partnering with other groups spans a wide spectrum of options, as indicated in Exhibit 9.2.

EXHIBIT 9.2 Partnering Options

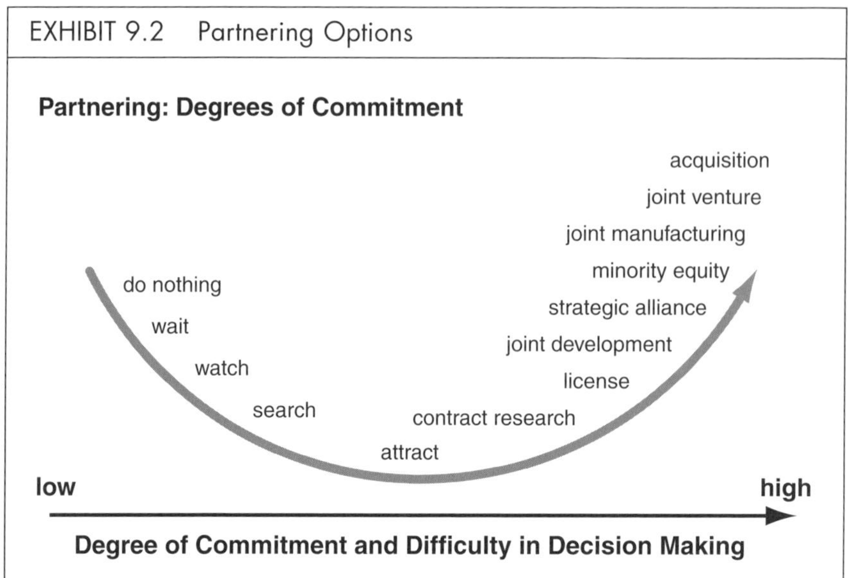

It is noteworthy that as the degree of commitment increases, so does the difficulty of decision making; more is at stake. The spectrum ranges from "do nothing" to "acquisition," with many options in between.

Where does partnering fit in the innovation pipeline? Innovations can be characterized as consisting of five stages: concept, feasibility, prototype, development, and commercialization. External partnering typically occurs during the concept and feasibility stages, but partnering can also certainly occur in the development and commercialization stages (e.g., joint venture, joint manufacturing, acquisition).

We have found some general guidelines in selecting the right partner across the spectrum of commitment:

- Identify compelling value brought by partner.
- Create clear incentive for collaboration.
- Define scope: what's included.
- Define roles: who does what.
- Contract with clear dollar amounts and schedule.
- Define process for joint decision making when issues come up.
- Build trust.

Mutual understanding of the "win-win" with well-defined responsibilities, project scope, and budget is key in creating an effective partnership. Quantifying the value brought by each partner is essential to develop a fair relationship. Building trust during the phase of alliance formation will carry through during the execution phase.

Once the partnership is formed, there are several general principles in sustaining a successful relationship. It's important to assign an alliance manager and leader on both sides with specific accountability. It's important to establish relationships at multiple levels between the organizations. Communications, including periodic meetings, teleconferences, and e-mail must be frequent and sustained. It's also important to maintain a long-term vision of the relationship while keeping an eye on the need for short-term results.

We have also found it very valuable to assemble a database of all contracts related to technology research, development, commercialization, and licensing. This searchable database, the Contract Management System, provides ready access to relevant partnership agreements. The screen shot in Exhibit 9.3 details the categories of contracts within the database.

EXHIBIT 9.3 Screen Shot of a Contract Management System Home Page

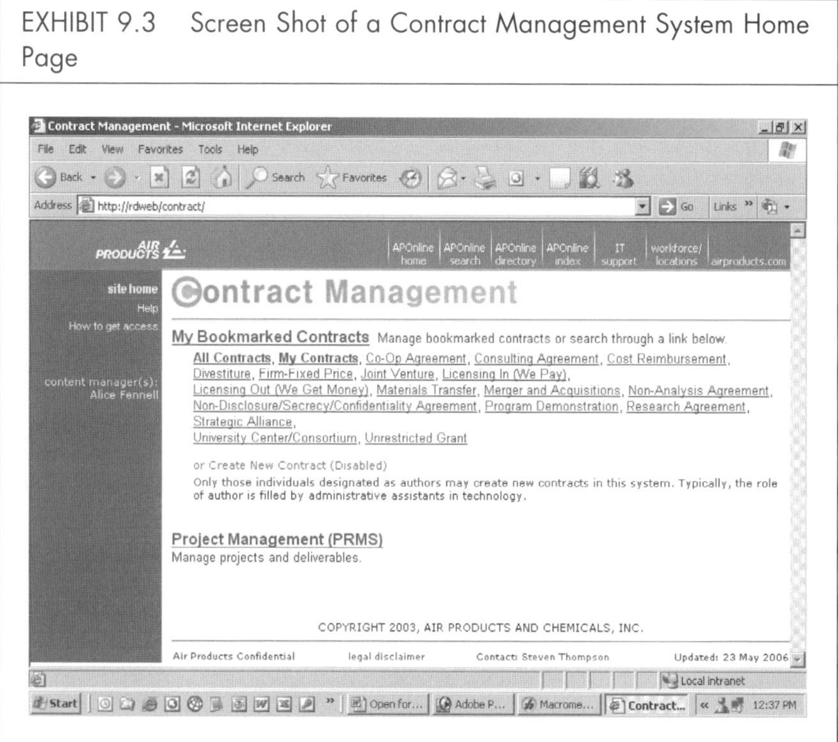

University R&D Alliances

In this section, the benefits and key elements of university-industry partnerships will be examined. The value of university-industry alliances was underscored by the National Science Foundation: "Companies can benefit from the extensive research infrastructure . . . and store of scientific knowledge . . . at universities" . . . "Universities benefit by . . . channeling academic research toward practical application."[5]

There are several dimensions to university-industry alliances. There can be a single company–single university alliance; an example is the alliance between the Pennsylvania State University and Air Products, which was formed in the late 1990s. There can also be a multicompany–single university partnership (e.g., a consortium). Also, there can be a single company–multiple university partnership as well as a multicompany–multiple university partnership (e,g, the Pennsylvania Infrastructure Technology Alliance [PITA] program, which links Lehigh University with Carnegie Mellon University and Pennsylvania companies). An advantage of multicompany alliances is that they can result in rapid knowledge building for a company with little or no prior experience in a particular technical field; a disadvantage is that the intellectual property (IP) provisions are typically nonexclusive for all member companies.

For the following discussion, we will focus on the single company–single university alliance; however, many of the comments also apply to the other forms of partnership. For the purposes of our discussion, an alliance can be an individual sponsored research project or a broader R&D relationship between the university and the company.

Benefits of Industry-University Research Projects[6]

There are many reasons why universities and industries should collaborate. Historically, industry has sought and benefited from two very important university outputs: technical human capital and research results. Likewise, universities have benefited from financial (e.g., sponsored/contracted research projects, equipment donations, student and professorial employment, corporate taxes to publicly supported institutions, philanthropy, etc.) and intellectual collabora-

[5]National Science Foundation, Science and Engineering Indicators 2000 (2000).

[6]Tao, J., et al. "Industry-University Intellectual Property," position paper. External Research Directors Network, Industrial Research Institute, National Academy of Science Workshop on Academic IP, April 17, 2001.

tions (shared knowledge from joint research projects and services, internships, advisory boards, etc.) with industry. The primary driver from industry's perspective is the ability to obtain some competitive advantage from its research initiatives, which will lead to increased profitability in the marketplace. In fact, when companies do not obtain competitive advantage, then they are no longer industrial partners, but philanthropists. It is for this reason that industry must be somewhat firm regarding ownership or rights to the intellectual property. Doing research for research's sake may be the role of government or academia, but not the role of commercial industry. Industry views university research as one of many tools it may wish to use to maintain its competitive edge. The goal is to get the best research results for the lowest possible investment. The value of the research is in the extraction of commercial value from those results. There are many contributing reasons why the industry-university relationship should be attractive and strong:

- Universities are the source, or rootstock, of the technologists who work in industry. It is in industry's best interest to have strong research opportunities available to graduate students and university professors. These opportunities help in the development of the best professors and researchers. It also better equips them to deal with the real-world problems and challenges that industries face in the commercial marketplace. This partnering also provides great general societal benefit and should be a main motivating force for universities to participate in industrial arrangements.
- Industry frequently works with universities that have the expertise and equipment available to complement their own R&D capabilities. This results in a "win-win" situation. Timing and capability are critical issues in such collaborations. If university resources supplement industry's own research progress, professors and graduate students can effectively collaborate with industrial partners in solving real problems.
- Frequently, universities have access to funds from government organizations or other organizations for basic research. This reduces the overall risks or the initial up-front money. Industry participation can be attractive in these cooperative research efforts when the work being done is fundamental in nature, with no clear vision of a commercial opportunity or application.
- Joint development work is almost always done as an extension of a good existing relationship. This is particularly true if the industrial partner actively recruits at the same university. It is beneficial to both parties to have good educational facilities and open communications so that when

recruiting opportunities occur, the school, the students, and the professors can work together for everyone's benefit.

Some key driving forces for forming alliances from a university perspective are:[7]

- "Grounding" of faculty in real industry needs
- Advance faculty academic progress and reputation
- Leverage to government funding
- Funding of graduate students
- Exposure of students to industry

Industry is not looking for university partners to do work that they can already do internally (unless it enhances the ability to do it more rapidly); nor are they looking to have their own research scientists compete against the university scientists. Furthermore, industry is not looking for an inexpensive pair of hands. Industry views university collaboration as a stepping-stone to help augment the innovative ideas of its own scientists. Basic research is probably the biggest cornerstone of the relationship; however, it is just the very first step to the many that are required in the development of a commercially viable product.

Foundations for Success

There are several foundations for success of the alliance and its individual projects. Initially, it is important for both partners to have a common definition of success as advancement of a technology toward commercialization versus collecting data to present in a published article. It is key to have senior management support for both partners. An umbrella agreement, or memorandum of understanding (MOU), is the optimal way to administer a broad relationship covering multiple projects over time. An individual needs to be committed to administer and manage the relationship. The industrial technical sponsor needs to be committed to communicating frequently with the university team to ensure that the project stays on track. It is also important for both the industrial sponsor and the university researchers to understand that the most successful R&D will result from a true team effort, having openness and trust—and that the best R&D is not an individual sport.

[7]Magnotta,V., and Pugh,T. "Anatomy of a Proven R&D Partnership: Penn State and Air Products," Pennsylvania Ceramics Forum, State College, PA, September 23, 2000.

Intellectual Property Rights[8]

Ownership and/or the rights to developing technology are probably the most contentious issues in the preparation of agreements between universities and industrial companies. When ownership and IP rights issues interfere with industry's aim to gain competitive advantage, then these issues impede open communications and collaboration. It may prevent the potential for collaboration. The starting position of industry is that if industry pays for a product or service, industry would expect to own the IP or have strong usable rights to it. Depending on the type of research and its ultimate use, the intensity of that requirement can be modified, but competitive advantage must remain the ultimate goal.

Different industries value IP differently. In most cases, IP is used to maintain product differential advantage and, hence, profitability. Profitability levels vary greatly among industries, but manufacturers, especially of commodity products, cannot afford the university business model of charging royalties on industry-funded projects. There are very few industries in which this business model is viable. The biotech and pharmaceutical industries that universities quote as common examples have very high margins that can sustain this model, but other industry sectors cannot. This is a limiting factor to the increase of the number of collaborations between industry and universities.

Looking at Exhibit 9.4, most industrial organizations evaluate IP agreements on a relative scale of expected benefit. A brief explanation of the arrangement follows:

Arrangement 1: ***The industrial partner owns the intellectual property.*** This gives the company more control for applying the IP to its business needs. Most industrial partners will enter into a contract if there is even a small advantage to the joint research. This maximizes the potential for an agreement. In addition, it embodies the concept that if the company paid for it, then the company should own it. Industry prepares the information necessary for obtaining IP rights.

Arrangement 2: ***The industrial partner owns the intellectual property, but the university retains the rights to pursue additional basic research in the technology area.*** This allows graduate students and professors to continue to develop and maintain their expertise in their field while industry retains the technology. This can be attractive to both

[8]See note 6.

EXHIBIT 9.4 IP Arrangements on a Scale of Expected Benefits

IP Arrangement	*Relevance to Business*
1. Business owns the IP generated as a result of the collaborative research.	Very high probability of collaboration. This gives the industrial partner the most freedom of action. Most likely to maximize the number of collaborations.
2. Business owns the IP but allows the university to continue with development for research purposes only.	Very high probability of collaboration. Still attractive. Allows for continuation of the research, resulting in a good outcome for professors and students.
3. University owns the IP but the business has exclusive rights.	This imposes some barriers and will decrease the number of collaborations. Not quite as flexible as the above case.
4. University owns the IP, but the business has exclusive rights in a narrow field.	This can be attractive to some industries but is limiting. Acceptable only if the business has needs entirely in the narrow field.
5. Nonexclusive, royalty free.	Limited interest in most cases, except for very basic research.

parties and foster a long-term collaborative relationship. Industry prepares the information necessary for obtaining IP rights.

Arrangement 3: ***The university owns the intellectual property but gives an exclusive license to the business (i.e., the opportunity to maintain competitive advantage).*** Exclusive rights are very important for many technology companies. However, this arrangement is more costly to administer for both parties since there are two sets of patent attorneys to satisfy. Usually, the university prepares the patent filings for U.S. patents, while foreign filings are at the cost and discretion of industry. This becomes a complex problem of administration due to the issues regarding IP costs and maintenance.

Arrangement 4: ***The university owns the IP but gives an exclusive license in a narrow field of use.*** This is appropriate when there is some singular aspect to the developing technology that industry needs and would be willing to have even if it is in a narrow area. Most industrial partners who have more than one product in a technology field of interest use IP broadly and build upon it for additional IP. A narrow field of use inhibits multiple uses of developed technology and is awkward for additional development in related fields. This is acceptable for some industries but will be a deal breaker in others.

Arrangement 5: ***Nonexclusivity is not very attractive to most industrial firms in the technology business.*** High-technology companies frequently will not accept a nonexclusive IP position. An exception might occur if the research projects were very fundamental and could serve as a platform for the building and development of a unique commercial product by industrial scientists. Most likely, the university would propose this research, which could be in the form of a consortium. This is applicable if the work is very basic science. Industry would also consider this arrangement, if necessary, to prevent being blocked in a desired technology area. There is limited opportunity for competitive advantage in consortia. Therefore, there is a low probability of coming to terms.

Most often, universities would prefer offering nonexclusive licenses so that they could work with as many industries as possible to commercialize the technology and to maximize any potential revenue for that IP. Although it sounds good, there is a fallacy in this thought process; that is, industry will preferentially avoid the nonexclusive license and this reduces the number of opportunities to collaborate.

Fortunately, many universities will accept an IP agreement with company ownership. Negotiations will determine the balance of what is important to the company and what is important to the university. Industry will weigh the need for the IP rights against the costs, the impact to business, and alternative approaches, such as doing the work in-house. Universities consider the value of a "potential" future benefit compared to the possible loss of the research grant, its impact on professors, on the students, and the university as a societal institution. There cannot be rigid rules; each aspect has to be negotiated.

Compensation[9]

Compensation to the university for technical collaboration depends on:

- The research contract
- The total costs to bring a product or technology to market
- Risk and rewards

---

[9]Ibid.

The industrial organization's IP strategy and long-term goals influence the research contract. Remember that the driving force is competitive advantage. Frequently, an industrial partner will contract for research with a university so that a product can be brought to market more effectively and more efficiently. Obviously, if industry furnishes the idea and/or direction as well as the finances, there will then be strong preference for ownership by industry to the IP that results from the work. Compensation frequently takes place through direct payments for the work done. This concept is the same as the employee-employer relationship (or, better yet, the contract employee situation) wherein the employee is paid for the work done and the employer owns the results of the work. In Europe, many of the universities will give the sponsoring company the ownership rights and accordingly charge a higher fee. This is a practice that U.S.-based universities should seriously consider doing in this ever-shrinking, competitive global research environment.

The road to commercialization is a path requiring multiple steps to achieving success. Typically, they include:

1. Idea generation and basic research
2. Development of the idea into a product/process/service concept
3. A process, technology, or manufacturing design
4. Some type of product/process/service testing
5. Marketing or test marketing of the product/process/service
6. Sale of the product/process/service
7. Start-up or initial use of the product/process/service
8. Final product/process/service acceptance

This is illustrated in Exhibit 9.5.

Each one of these steps has costs and risks associated with it. Over time, as an idea progresses toward a commercial reality, an ever-increasing application and consumption of organizational resources (e.g., time, money, and people) are brought to bear. In fact, recent research published in *Research–Technology Management* (Industrial Research Institute journal) indicates, that in general, over 3,000 raw ideas are needed at step one in order to yield one commercial success. In most collaboration, the university participates only in the very first step with little or no cost or risk. It is not attractive to an industrial partner to share a large royalty after assuming all of the risk and executing most of the work, while the university is responsible for only the basic research. The complete development of a product or process is very expensive (e.g., tens or hundreds of millions of dollars) and very time consuming. These realities need to be considered in any compensation formula as any one of the eight steps could end in

EXHIBIT 9.5 Commercialization Costs/Revenues/Risks

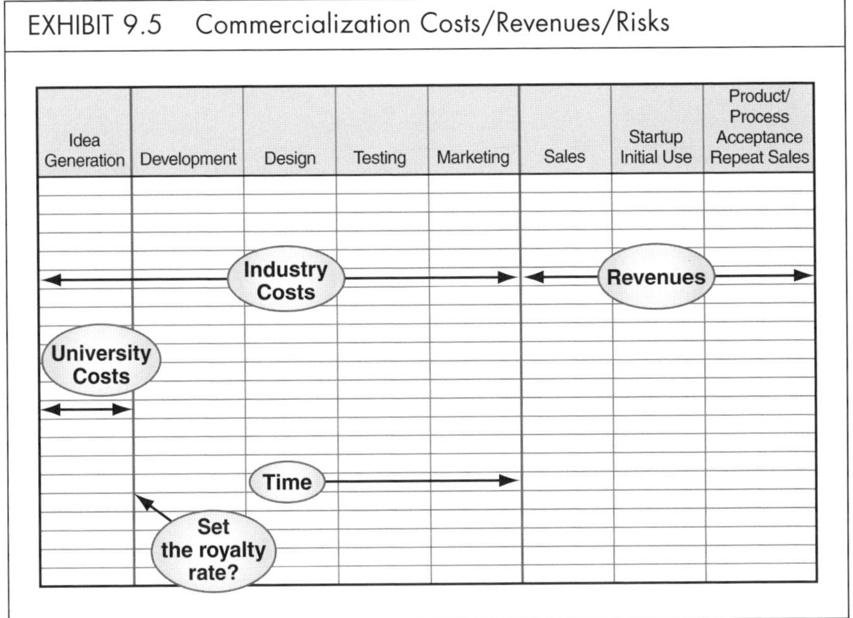

failure. The overall product could be a technical success, yet not a commercial success.

Risk and reward principles are taught at all the universities and should readily be understood and applied by the university's own technology transfer function/community. While the industrial partner is required to take on the risks through all eight steps, the university is often not willing or not allowed to assume the business and legal risks of putting a product in the marketplace. Cost and risk need to be incorporated into the compensation strategy of the universities if royalty payments are to be considered.

The amount of potential compensation to equitably reward initial research efforts can be easily misunderstood because of the focus on the successful ventures. Some very successful products in the marketplace (i.e., those that have generated significant revenues) were created by university-industry collaborations. There have also been a large number of failures. The cost of those failures will appear on company income statements, but not the universities'. At the Association of University Technology Managers (AUTM) meeting in 2000, university representatives pointed out the great value that many of the pharmaceutical industries have generated, and that royalties of 25% of earnings before interest and taxes (EBIT) were reasonable. One of the audience participants from industry brought up the issue of who pays for the failures. The reality is that successes pay for the failures. Thus, the overall success of one product should not be generalized and assumed to be an indicator of the net benefit to the industrial partner. The expenses of the failures need to be incorporated with the overall account of the successes. The universities need to consider this reasoning in their negotiation objectives.

Since the Bayh-Dole and Stevenson-Wydler Acts have been around for a long time, one would expect that there should be billions of dollars in collaborations if these acts were effective. In actuality, the overall return on an investment in university research by industry has been marginal. Many of these investments have been made to maintain relationships with research universities in order to either ensure a supply of future industrial researchers and /or for philanthropic reasons. Also, patents, outside of the biotech sector, have generally cost the universities more than they have returned.

Determining Fair Royalty Rates for University-Developed Technology Since the Bayh-Dole Act and the creation of university technology transfer departments, obtaining fair royalty rates for industrial R&D sponsors has become an important component in developing an alliance agreement. Using a literature review and including learning for our corporate experiences, a proposal is developed for determining fair royalty rates if industry IP ownership is not a viable option. This process can be used to determine fair royalty rates for other early stage technology licensing opportunities (refer to Appendix 9A).

Publication and Secrecy[10]

One of the essentials of university research is the right to publish by researchers and professors. No industrial organization would like or want to usurp this right. However, this need must be addressed in a logical manner that protects the rights of both parties. Industry is more than willing to protect the rights of the graduate students to publish their doctoral theses and technical articles. With the same consideration, the industrial partner needs to be assured that such publications will not compromise any current or future IP issues and patents. Most research documents within universities require 30 to 60 days to review prior to their publication. In most organizations, including universities, the requirement to review such works in 30 to 60 days is difficult, particularly if many IP issues either have been poorly defined by the researchers or are still pending. Patent applications may not have been filed, and it is critical that this

[10]Ibid.

be completed before publication, if patent protection is desired. Publication puts the subject matter in the public domain and can readily compromise the potential commercial benefits and foreign patent filing rights.

Industry is certainly not trying to prohibit such publication, but it is important to place proprietary and IP considerations in the forefront as they affect profitability for industry. Universities should observe industry's needs for IP protection with the same eagerness as the right to publish.

Other Issues[11]

There are several generic issues that cause conflict between universities and companies. Today, many universities seek to be more entrepreneurial and to generate wealth. The focus has shifted from the desire to conduct "blue sky," fundamental research and to educate students toward making money. While industry could view that as competition, in reality—philosophically—it is a conflict of interest for nonprofit organizations to generate profits.

Another area that causes adversarial negotiations is patent costs and maintenance fees. This is especially true of a university that wants to retain ownership of the IP, yet seeks to have industry pay for the processing of the patents, and particularly for foreign filings and maintenance. Additionally, universities are reluctant to cover the necessary legal costs for litigation in the case of infringement. In fact, they even find it difficult to enforce their patents, as they have little or no market insight as to who might be infringing. Industry routinely pays for the prosecution of its patents, but has no desire to pay for patenting the rights of others.

The documentation supplied by universities on which to make a judgment of the potential value of a patent is frequently limited. Often, a university asks a company to decide (during a limited time period) on the value of the patent based on a memorandum of invention, or an abstract of the patent filing, and to make some decisions on exclusivity for a fixed royalty. That is akin to asking someone to buy an item without knowing its full use and value. It is too early to make decisions at this time—another reason that the concept of paying for the development and owning the rights is simple and attractive.

A third issue is background rights, especially if the university has been working in the technology for some time. Generally, background rights will be required for an industrial partner to diligently participate in the value of the IP generated. Lack of background rights may, in fact, cause the value of the overall IP to be much lower than originally anticipated. This places a burden on the

[11]Ibid.

university patent lawyers to provide such information to the industry that needs to know that such background patents exist. The importance of this cannot be overestimated. The value of the potential IP may be linked to the value of the background rights.

Finally, the value of consortia needs to be appropriately recognized. In a consortium, the university frequently owns the developed technology and the consortium's industrial partners obtain a royalty-free nonexclusive license for the use of that technology and the IP developed by the consortium. This violates two of the basic issues that have been discussed in this chapter:

1. The ability to obtain competitive advantage in these situations is limited since many of the consortium members may be competitors.
2. Background rights are not clearly defined at the start of the consortium.

In addition, sometimes the university retains the right to add new consortium members for a fee, thereby gaining the university additional revenues and, at the same time, diluting the rights of the original consortium members. These new members can obtain the benefits without experiencing the initial risks.

Global R&D Insourcing

Global insourcing of R&D and technology encompasses partnering with global suppliers of R&D and also partnering between geographies within a single multinational company. The key global suppliers of R&D that we have experience with are western Europe, Russia, and China. India is also emerging as a global supplier.

Experience in Russia

Air Products began conducting research in Russia in 1992. The rationale for going to Russia included fresh perspectives on problems, lower cost, faster speed, and favorable IP rights relative to U.S. universities. This rationale has been tested and proven over the years and is still valid today. For example, for a typical project, an annual cost of about $50,000 can engage five to six full-time technical staff (more than 50% PhD level); at this same resource level, the cost for conducting this same project is over $1 million if conducted by U.S. industry (assuming a cost of $200,000 to $250,000 per professional per year).

Our initial experience in Russia involved working with an institute in Siberia. This relationship has continued each year to the present year, and we engage 57 scientists and technicians on 16 projects at the Siberian institute. In 2000, we strategically extended our reach to the over 400 technical institutes in Russia based on our success in Siberia. To date, we have partnered with eight institutes throughout Russia. The projects have covered diverse technical fields such as fuel cells, distillation, organometallic compounds, concrete additives, specialty gas synthesis, and surfactant application development.

We have used two main approaches to contract with a Russian institute: direct contracting with the institute or working through a portal group. The benefit of direct contracting is that it's simpler and faster than the portals. The benefit of some portal groups is that they will do matchmaking (linking technical needs with Russian resources), and some provide funding. There are three main portal groups to consider: the United States Industry Coalition (USIC), the U.S. Civilian Research and Development Foundation (CDRF), and the International Science and Technology Center (ISTC).

The USIC (www.usic.net) is a nonprofit association of U.S. companies engaged in Initiatives for Proliferation Prevention (IPP), a program sponsored by the U.S. Department of Energy's National Nuclear Security Administration. IPP links U.S. industry and Department of Energy (DOE) national laboratories together with former Soviet weapons of mass destruction institutes, with the goal of providing meaningful, sustainable nonweapons work through commercially viable market opportunities. USIC members help develop new technologies and services, thereby creating civilian businesses and jobs in former Soviet nations as well in the United States. Two-year funding for IPP projects typically ranges from $500,000 to $1.5 million. U.S. industry partners are required to match IPP funding with cash or in-kind contributions. Seventy percent of the funding for each IPP project supports the former Soviet partner, and 30% covers technical oversight, collaborative work, and project management by the DOE laboratory.

The CRDF (www.crdf.org) is another portal into Russia. Launched as the CRDF's first initiative in 1995, the Cooperative Grants Program (CGP) is the flagship of the Foundation's activities in Eurasia. The CGP provides up to two years of support to joint U.S. and former Soviet Union research teams in all science disciplines. The program offers an avenue into new research directions and collaborative opportunities for both U.S. and Eurasian scientists and engineers through $60,000 grants, which are awarded on a competitive basis. The CRDF gives special consideration to proposals that include the full-time participation of former weapons researchers.

The CRDF's Next Steps to Market (NSTM) program offers U.S. for-profit companies the opportunity to engage Eurasian researchers in commercial R&D projects. The CRDF will match dollar-for-dollar the U.S. company's cash contribution, up to $50,000—greatly reducing the risks and costs of international

R&D. The CRDF's Grant Assistance Program (GAP) extends its own mechanisms, tax benefits, service network, and financial and project management expertise to other organizations seeking to support R&D in Eurasia.

The ISTC (www.istc.ru) is an intergovernmental organization based in Moscow, Russia. The ISTC has a partner program that offers R&D matchmaking with former weapons of mass destruction scientists across Russia and the Commonwealth of Independent States, and can provide full project administration services. In this program, the U.S. partner (company) provides 100% of the funds for the R&D project, which includes an ISTC administration fee of 5% of the total project cost. We have found the ISTC to be excellent at matchmaking.

In addition to the portals, we have found it advantageous to have "on the ground" bilingual technical support staff in Russia to assist in matchmaking, to manage existing projects, to assist in communications with the institutes, and to assist in planning and executing visits of Air Products sponsors to Russia.

We have learned the following from our work in Russia:

- Frequent communication is vital:
  - E-mail, e-mail, e-mail
  - Face-to-face meetings in their laboratories
- Work process development is key:
  - Ideas to projects
  - Template project agreements
- Personal relationships are vital:
  - Time to nurture trust and openness

Experience in China

As with many of our peer companies, we are starting a technology center in China. Our business is over $1 billion in the region. We operate out of nine countries, and we have very strong positions. We have mostly first, second, and third market positions, and we have over 4,000 employees in Asia—the highest growth region in the world.

Just to set the stage in terms of the challenges and the benefits of working with the Chinese, let's look at the competition with the Japanese in the 1980s and with China right now. Look at the dimension differences. Aside from 1.3 billion people versus a couple of hundred million, there are world-class technologists right now who are trained elsewhere, and they are doing significant amount of technology development. There are challenges that are all related to IP.

There are many world-class universities. Faculty members that we've met very recently have either received their doctorate in the United States, the United Kingdom, Germany, or Japan, working with top-notch scientists and engineers, or they have done a postdoctorate. One top chemical engineering department at Tanjing we visited early this year had 400 PhD students in addition to another 1,200 master's students. The national academy labs are doing a lot of fundamental research, and since the year 2000 the government has poured large amounts of money into infrastructure.

Intellectual property issues that we always think about include infringement of patents, invalidation of your patent by someone else when you file there, infringement of copyright trademark, or stolen trade secrets basically leading to unfair competition. This is obviously the biggest complaint with people doing business and developing technology in China right now.

The Chinese patent administrative agencies are at different levels. There's the state patent office and the provision office, and the municipal level has its own patent bureaus. There are three patent types, but first let's discuss the difference between inventions and the utility model. Inventions are no different than any other patents we have elsewhere. Utility models are what we typically call paper patents; they don't really have the data that somebody has invented and reduced to practice. The test for inventiveness is a lot lower; typically, you can get those much more easily and quickly. The third type is a design patent. When one gets an invention patent, it is granted for 20 years, and the other two have just 10-year terms. One may have the strategy to first put a utility model patent in place and follow up with a true invention patent, and then just abandon the first one.

If you run into an invalidation, or if you try to prove that someone else's patent is invalid, you must first make the request, then go to the board for reexamination, and then finally proceed to court. But all this can occur within three months. It is possible to get that invalidation done fairly quickly. Once the board has made a decision, the invalidation will happen, but you can still appeal it on a yearly basis.

In terms of patent enforcement, well, that's the bad news. It's going to be difficult right now. However, we have to remember that in the United States our patent laws have existed for over 200 years. In China, they are relatively new, only slightly over 20 years—an order of magnitude difference. There's a lot more room for improvement, and a lot of good things are happening.

In the area of trademarks and copyrights, there is a great deal of piracy going on. Oakley, the watch and glasses manufacturer, wanted to shut down fake watch manufacturing and the like. The head of the enforcement department put up a picture of two identical watches and no one in the room could tell the difference. He commented, "When I shut that manufacturing site down, I want to hire their designer because he's that good."

The court systems in China are basically at three levels—the supreme court at the national level, and the provisional and municipal levels. But remember whenever you sue someone over infringement, it's at the bottom level—the municipal level. If you win that case, the infringer can move to another location outside of that jurisdiction. You have to start the whole process over again in the next municipality. This leads to many challenges for enforcement. The Chinese prefer arbitration and mediation, so it might be easier to settle your differences through licensing or joint manufacturing, or even outright acquisition.

The current enforcement laws and regulations need to be a lot more Westernized. The investigation and sanction, as well as the actual seizure and putting the injunctions in place are all moving the right direction. However, right now in China everything is about relationship. Toyota spent millions of dollars in a trademark lawsuit. It was the very first one that was filed in China, and they lost.

Everyone complains about the piracy of software and music in China. Regarding Microsoft's approach to this issue, Bill Gates said, "We're not going to stop them from copying three million Windows XP every year, because if you stop them, they are going to come up with something different, and you may not be able to get them to use Windows later."

Finally, with regard to trade secrets, you can almost forget about it. We suggest putting in some good processes to prevent theft. Obviously, you have the traditional noncompete clause in your employment agreement with your employees. A good approach is to educate your employees about confidentiality, trade secrets, and know-how protection, but limit their specific access to a need-to-know basis.

There is also inventor compensation law in place in China following the blue light-emitting diode (LED) lawsuit in Japan. It's approximately 2% of after-tax profits for inventions or 0.2% for design patents, which you might have to pay the inventor if that invention is made in China.

The number of patents being filed in China is increasing exponentially because they're getting better and better in developing technology. The IP problem will go away in the not-too-distant future. We had this problem with the Japanese back in the 1960s; we had the problem with Taiwan and Korea in the 1970s. It's a natural evolution process as countries move to more and more of their own inventions. The Chinese officials and business executives will learn the importance of IP systems and the value of preserving intellectual capital for the benefit of their people.

External Providers

A new tool for open innovation emerged with the emergence of external providers. These providers work closely with industrial sponsors to identify technology globally that meets the sponsor's needs. The advantage of these tools is that there is low risk if a solution is not found. Another big advantage is the breadth of diverse thinking that is accessed through the global networks. Two of the major providers are InnoCentive and NineSigma.

InnoCentive (www.innocentive.com) has a unique business model. Seeker companies post a problem ("challenge") on their Web site. They also post the "bounty" for receiving a solution that meets their criteria. Solvers propose solutions through the Web site. Seekers receive IP ownership in paid solutions.

InnoCentive's Web site indicates that scientists from over 170 countries around the world are registered as solvers. InnoCentive started with expertise in organic chemistry problems but have since branched out into the fields of biology and material science. According to a recent article, seeker companies turned to InnoCentive largely for assistance with organic synthesis problems because they were easy to define in terms of cost, yield, purity, scalability, and material supply. One client with 12 discrete chemistry challenges reported a very high return on the investment in InnoCentive's services.[12] NineSigma (www.ninesigma.com) also has a unique business model for open innovation. They are building targeted global innovation networks that identify and connect the talents and capabilities of today's most prepared minds in order to create the next generation of products and opportunities of interest to their clients. NineSigma works with clients to prepare a clear and concise request for proposal (RFP) for projects along the entire product development life cycle, including upstream technology, design, manufacturing, and applications. They then distribute this RFP to an open global network of solution providers. Solution providers prepare proposals, which are provided to the client. The client then makes an independent decision to fund a proposal and negotiate a business arrangement appropriate to the situation. There is an up-front fee for developing the RFP and presenting the solution provider proposals, and another fee if a proposal is funded by the client.

Partnering with the Government

Partnering with the government at Air Products has three dimensions: funding R&D at federal laboratories, contracting to perform R&D for the government, and acting as a consultant to third-party companies in accessing government funding opportunities.

The national laboratories contain deep expertise in many technical areas. Some of the prominent national labs we have worked with include Sandia National Laboratories, Argonne, and Los Alamos. These laboratories have a

[12]Raynor, M., and Panetta, J. "A Better Way to R&D?" *Strategy and Innovation Newsletter*, Harvard Business School Publishing, article reprint S0503E, March–April 2005.

mission to commercialize technology through collaboration with industry. Also, their technologies are often more mature than those of universities. One excellent vehicle is a cooperative research and development agreement (CRADA); it is a written agreement between a private company and a government agency to work together on a project. Created as a result of the Stevenson-Wydler Technology Innovation Act of 1980, as amended by the Federal Technology Transfer Act of 1986, a CRADA allows the federal government and non-federal partners to optimize their resources, share technical expertise in a protected environment, share IP emerging from the effort, and speed the commercialization of federally developed technology. A CRADA is an excellent technology transfer tool. It can:

- Provide incentives that help speed the commercialization of federally developed technology.
- Protect any proprietary information brought to the CRADA effort by the partner.
- Allow all parties to the CRADA to keep research results emerging from the CRADA confidential and free from disclosure through the Freedom of Information Act for up to five years.
- Allow the government and the partner to share patents and patent licenses.
- Permit one partner to retain exclusive rights to a patent or patent license.

Additionally, companies can leverage their own R&D investment by conducting R&D for the government. For more than 60 years, Air Products has considered the government an important customer and technology partner. Air Products' commitment to serving federal customer needs led to the formation of Government Systems, an integrated organization dedicated to working closely with the government to provide high-quality products, systems, and services and to cooperatively develop new technologies for the nation's benefit. Comprising engineers, scientists, technicians, financial managers, and sales and marketing professionals, the Government Systems team interfaces with associates from all business segments within Air Products to provide a gateway for government customers.

Through this integrated approach, we have successfully supplied government-specified products, developed specialized systems and services, and completed research programs that meet the technology goals of both government and private industry. Our ability to solve technical, commercial, cost, and energy and environmental challenges has been demonstrated through the years by the development of many new applications, products, and technologies.

We work with the Department of Energy, Department of Commerce, Department of Defense, the Environmental Protection Agency, and the National Aeronautics and Space Administration, as well as government prime contractors and state and local agencies.

Our Government Systems department offers third-party R&D and consulting services. Government R&D marketing consulting services includes marketing for funded opportunities, opportunity development and capture strategies, solicitation/request for proposal analysis, proposal development, and proposal evaluation and selection. Contract administration services are also provided, including negotiation of the agreement, project management, contract accounting, invoicing, reporting, and so on.

Licensing-In

Licensing-in can be a way to accelerate new-product development and commercialization. If a technology has already been developed externally to a certain stage, licensing-in can be an excellent strategy versus beginning an internal project to invent around the technology; this can save time and money. Licenses can be exclusive or nonexclusive; exclusive licenses give the licensee the complete rights to a technology. For nonexclusive licenses, the licensor is free to license the technology to others. Other key provisions of licensing agreements include the royalty rate, field of use, term, and geographic territory.

For exclusive licenses, payments can include an initial fee upon signing, annual minimum payments, and annual royalty payments once the technology is commercialized. For nonexclusive licenses, it is common for payment terms to be annual royalties once the technology is commercialized.

Joint Development

In earlier sections of this chapter discussing university alliances and working with the government, the IP issues are different than those for working with another organization in a joint development mode. Often, for-profit organizations will sign a joint development agreement (JDA) and work jointly on a project and program. In this section, we will discuss the treatment of IP from these JDAs. Typically, each party comes into the relationship owning certain background IP rights; obviously, they continue to own those rights and may grant those rights as part of the terms of how the background would be treated if they need to grant each other rights. In those instances, they can be negotiated and treated according to the value of each party's background IP. The rights, however, of the foreground IP need to be carefully thought through strategically and negotiated accordingly. First, the "field" needs to be carefully defined. This sets the boundary for the statement of work and any foreground IP that arises. The parties should also agree on whether they are exclusive with each other in this field or nonexclusive and could collaborate with others. Second, the ownership of foreground IP rights (including foreground information) should be agreed to. Typically, there are two models: one in which whoever develops it owns it, and another that defines it by assignment to one party according to "field of use" no matter who developed the foreground IP. This is especially important for inventions where the inventors come from both organizations. Depending on whether the IP is filed in the United States or elsewhere in the world, jointly owned IP may present some challenges because the parties don't have to account to each other in the United States. The best case is one in which one party owns everything if that party provided all the financial resources; the worst case is one in which one party paid for everything but ended up owning nothing and having to receive rights through a royalty-bearing license from the other party. Of course, independent of the ownership of the foreground IP, the rights may be licensed to the other party by agreeing to terms such as exclusiveness or nonexclusiveness, territories, royalty bearing or free, term (length of time) of the license, and, of course, whether sublicensing rights are included. In addition, the parties must also define in the JDA who pays for what and whether money will change hands.

Often, in the JDA, the parties also may agree on the exploitation of the results, whether a joint venture is contemplated, and how the profits and losses, as well as liabilities, will be shared.

Of course, there are many other terms in what we typically call "boilerplate"; they are by no means any less important, but for the purpose of focusing on IP, we will not discuss the other terms in this section.

Measuring External R&D Programs

Measuring the value of external R&D programs can be challenging, especially those in the early stages of development. Air Products developed a rating tool to categorize and quantify the benefits of external R&D.[13] This tool rates ten attributes of each R&D program, using a numerical rating system. An overview of the project tool is given in Exhibit 9.6.

---

[13]Tao, J., and Brenner, M. "You Can Measure External Research Programs," *Research–Technology Management*, May–June 2001, pp. 14–17.

EXHIBIT 9.6 Overview of the Project Tool

	Attributes										
Project	*New Idea*	*New Expertise, Skills, Capabilities*	*Time Saved*	*New R&D $ Saved*	*Background IP Access*	*IP Generation*	*Long-Term Access to Capabilities*	*Program Emphasis*	*Commercial Impact*	*Technical Leverage*	*Total*
Project 1	3	3	3	3	3	3	3	3	5	5	34
Project 2	2	2	3	3	3	2	2	3	5	3	28
Project 3	2	2	3	2	3	3	2	1	3	3	24
Project 4	1	2	3	2	3	2	1	2	2	2	20

The first eight attributes from "New Idea" to "Program Emphasis" are rated on a scale of one to three. The final two attributes, "Commercial Impact "and "Technical Leverage" are rated on a scale of one to five. Specific rating criteria are established for each attribute. The maximum rating for a given project is 34 points.

In addition to allowing an overall ranking of projects by total score, the tool allows grouping of projects based on any attribute. For example, the projects can be grouped by ranking in each attribute area (e.g., a grouping can be made of projects from highest to lowest commercial impact).

The tool was used to rate 42 external projects during a fiscal year. Most of these external projects were university based in the United States. Key findings included:

- Our average project saved hundreds of thousands of dollars in net R&D cost.
- An average of two years is saved with each external project.

Recognizing External Technologists or Partners

As open innovation becomes part of the fabric of corporate technology, it becomes essential to recognize and reward our external partners who either have delivered value to the company or are uniquely positioned to deliver future value.

Air Products' Corporate Technology Partnerships department created the External Collaboration Innovation Award to recognize and reward the results of external partner collaborative research so as to:

- Demonstrate commitment of relationship building to external partners.
- Stimulate IP development with external partners.
- Strengthen collaboration of sponsors and external scientists on projects.
- Focus external R&D on growth initiatives.

Since 2002, three awards have been presented: one to a Russian institute, one to the Department of Energy, and one to Ceramatec (a private U.S. firm).

Another award was instituted in 2005: the Faculty Excellence Award. This award was initiated to recognize outstanding emerging faculty in technology areas strategic to the company's long-term growth. The two winners, Dr. Judy Hoyt of the Massachusetts Institute of Technology and Dr. Jinbo Hu of the Shanghai Institute of Organic Chemistry, Chinese Academy of Sciences, received a $30,000 unrestricted gift for their institutions to further their research—Dr. Hoyt for semiconductor processing and Dr. Hu for organofluorine chemistry and advanced materials.

Appendix 9A

Determining Fair Royalty Rates for University-Developed Technology Exclusive License Option

For this example, it is assumed that the university has no patented background in the field of R&D of interest to the industrial sponsor and that the industrial sponsor funds the foreground R&D 100%—the typical case. The example also assumes the company is in the chemical industry; the methodology can be extended to other industries. The situation that maximizes the probability for an R&D agreement between a university and a company is one in which the industrial sponsor owns the foreground IP in a program that was 100% funded by the sponsor. If this is not possible, an exclusive license is the next best option.

A literature review on the profitability of chemical industry companies, the costs and success probabilities of industrial R&D, and actual royalty rates is presented. Two approaches are developed to determine fair royalty rates for an exclusive license. The appendix concludes with a moving-forward proposal for fair running royalty rates.

Profitability of Air Products (APD) and Companies in Our Chemicals Market Segment

Using annual report data, we have estimated average profitability of several comparable companies. The summary is shown in Exhibit 9A.1.

Air Products is a gas and chemical supplier. Our industrial gas competitors (Air Liquide, BOC, Praxair) are pure gas suppliers. Rohm and Haas represents a pure industrial/specialty chemical company.

EXHIBIT 9.A.1 Average Profitability of Several Companies		
	Profit before Tax	
Company	*EBT (% of Sales)*	*FY*
Air Products	9.0	2003
Air Liquide	13.1	2002
Praxair	14.0	2003
BOC	10.6	2003
Rohm & Haas	6.5	2003
Average	**10.6**	

Additionally, a recent study[14] of 126 chemical companies concluded the weighted average long-term profit margin (EBT) to be 11.1% over the period 1990–2000.

The conclusion from these studies is that APD makes, on average, 10% to 11% profit before taxes on all of our products. Some products are old and have low margins. Some products are new and have high margins; however, some new products have low or negative margins because there have been unanticipated costs. Therefore, for discussion purposes, a round number of 10% EBT will be used.

One may argue that we will commercialize only alliance-bred products with projected margins higher than 10%. There will be products in which the projected margin at the time of making the commercialization decision is more than 10 %. However, actual margins are often lower than the projected margins, and profit margins for all products decline over their life cycle.

University and Corporate Costs of Product R&D and Commercialization

The university's investment in an R&D project will be the "lost opportunity" cost of not working on an alternative, potentially more "licensable" technology with another funding sponsor (typically, either industry or government). An additional implied assumption in this "opportunity cost" is that the university's principal investigators are fully funded through the summer and are turning down projects due to lack of time.

[14]Goldscheider, R., et al. "Use of the 25% Rule in Valuing IP," les Nouvelles, December 2002, p. 123.

The overall costs to commercialize technology from the idea stage can be staggering. For the pharmaceutical industry, a recent study pegs the average cost to commercialize a new drug at $897 million.[15] Although less, the costs to commercialize technology in the chemical sector can also be substantial. A recent study was conducted for the chemical industry in which the R&D costs required to produce a patent were estimated for 11 representative companies.[16] The results indicate an average cost of $3.2 million per patent in 1997. Since any given technology typically has more than one patent associated with it, it's easy to envision a total R&D cost of at least $10 million per technology. To account for the costs downstream of the R&D expenditure, an estimate was recently made based on data from the United States, Canada, and Israel.[17] The results of this study indicate these downstream costs (scale-up, commercial development, marketing, plant investment) can account for 40% to 60% of the overall costs to commercialize technology. An additional cost not accounted for in this analysis is the cost of funding all of the technologies that failed at some point in the commercialization pipeline.

From the preceding analysis, it is concluded that the total costs to commercialize a chemical technology from the idea stage is in the tens of millions of dollars—and can approach hundreds of millions.

Additionally, it is typical that the industrial sponsor would bear the patent estate cost of university IP; overall costs over the lifetime of a single patent are in the range of $200,000 to $300,000, depending on foreign country coverage. Additionally, the industrial sponsor would pay all of the subsequent development and commercialization costs, which, as we have seen from the above, are at least $10 million to $50 million for one commercial success.

Commercialization of a new product within industry typically requires an investment in plant and equipment. If the university royalty rate is too high, the investment may not be made. Specifically, the internal rate of return (IRR) for the capital investment could easily drop below the minimum required hurdle rate required by the responsible business area to justify the capital investment required to make the new product.

If we can't justify the investment, the new product is never made, and then both the university and the industrial sponsor lose. Actually, the industrial sponsor loses more because they would have already invested significant cash to get

---

[15]Rotman, David. "Can Pfizer Deliver?" *Technology Review*, February 2004, pp. 58–65

[16]Bigwood, M. "Applying Cost of Innovation to Technology Planning," *Research–Technology Management*, May–June 2000, p. 39

[17]Pavitt, K. "Costing Innovation: Vain Search for Benchmarks," *Research–Technology Management*, 44(1) (2001), p. 16.

EXHIBIT 9.A.2 Financial Resource Sources for New Products

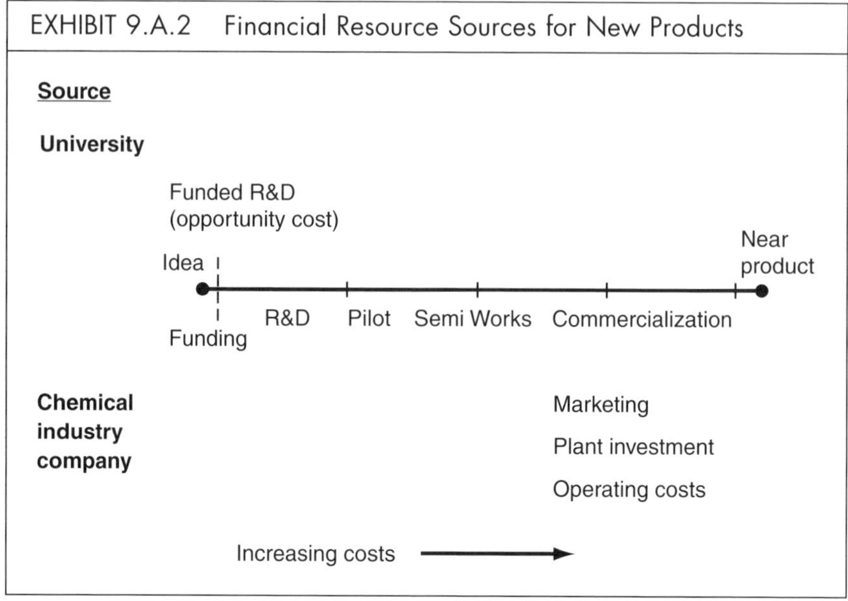

to the investment decision point. Remember, the university's only "lost" cost is the lost opportunity cost discussed above. So industry bears the lion's share of the risk due to the large costs of development and commercialization. These findings are summarized in Exhibit 9A.2.

Two approaches will be used below to develop a fair royalty rate: one based on new-product sales and one based on new-product profitability.

Approach 1: Royalty Rate as Function of Sales for Early-Stage Technology

A royalty rate range of 2% to 5 % of sales for an exclusive license is the average reported in a survey of 428 Licensing Executives Society (LES) member companies (25% nonprofits) for nonpharmaceutical technologies that are a major to minor improvement.[18] Also, a recent analysis of 72 chemical-sector license agreements found the median royalty rate to be 3.6%.[19] It must be noted that

[18]Cole, Stephen R., Davidson, A. Scott, and Stack, Alexander J. "Reasonable Royalty Rates," *CA Magazine*, May 1999, pp. 30–32

[19]See note 14.

these published survey rates reflect and incorporate "background value" to the licensee obtained from the licensor's:

- Prior R&D investments
- Know-how
- Investments in marketing/commercial development
- Commercialization of the licensed products in a good fraction of the cases.
- Bearing the costs of the patent estate legal and maintenance fees

Additionally, the licensors typically provide "future value" to their licensees by:

- Continuing R&D in the field and passing on these improvements to the licensee
- Bearing the costs of legal protection (enforcement) re the licensed IP to the licensee

Obtaining these additional values and exclusive terms results in commercial royalty agreements on the higher end of the published range.

The "background value" being provided by the university will usually be confined to the very front end of the innovation pipeline and typically consists of the principal investigator's (PI's) expertise and lab capabilities in a field of technology. In most cases, the IP to be licensed will not have been reduced to practice by the university prior to a funded project; most likely, reduction to practice will occur in the subsequent 100% industry-funded project. In fact, if the university has patented relevant background, it would typically desire to negotiate a separate license agreement for this IP.

What does the literature say about reasonable royalty rates for early-stage technologies? The published LES survey of 428 LES member companies[20] indicates royalty rates for technologies in the "Lab Phase" are historically discounted by 50% versus that for a fully developed technology (those having essentially no technical or commercial risk); it is important to note that "Lab Phase" is defined in this survey as a stage in which the concept of the invention has already been reduced to practice by, and at the expense of, the licensor—but engineering design has not yet begun. These facts indicate that the discount on royalty rate for a university alliance should be greater than the 50% cited earlier. An additional survey of 250 companies over the last three years by a licensing consulting firm, MEDIUS, specializing in pharmaceutical technology is posted on their Web site.[21] On an absolute scale, pharmaceutical technologies command higher

[20]See note 18.

[21]Johnson, H. "Establishing Royalty Rates in Licensing Agreements," *CMA Management*, March 2001, pp. 16–19.

royalty rates as a percentage of sales relative to the chemical industry in which we reside; however, this article indicates early-stage technology (preclinical to Phase I) royalties are to be discounted 50% to 95% relative to a fully developed technology. Another consultant in pharmaceutical licensing, Novelint, discusses the importance of stage of product development on royalty rate;[22] a discount of 90% is proposed for the case comparing expected royalty rates for a patent-pending versus a fully developed and commercialized technology.

Clearly, the literature indicates very early-stage technology is discounted significantly, reflecting the significant risks the licensee incurs. Based on this literature, a discount range of 75% to 90% is assumed. Using an average commercial royalty rate of 2% to 5%[23] results in a proposed exclusive running royalty rate of 0.2% to 1.25% of sales.

Approach 2: Royalty Rates Based on Earnings for Early-Stage Technology

There are many references in the literature to the "25% rule" being a good starting point in licensing negotiations.[24] That is, 25% of the EBT on a product is a reasonable licensing fee provided *certain conditions* are met. In fact, a recent survey incorporating actual chemical industry profitability and royalty rates concluded the average to be 25.9% during the period 1990–2000.[25] Therefore, using the "Rule," a reasonable royalty rate for chemical industry technology would be 25% of 10% (per Section 1) = 2.5% of sales. The *certain conditions* required include the "background" and "future" value streams provided by the licensor discussed earlier. An additional discussion on the normally required value provided by the licensor to command a 25% royalty as a percentage of profits is provided in an excerpt by Cole:[26]

> "As Goldscheider states in The negotiations of royalties and other sources of incomes from licensing" (*IDEA: The Journal of Law and Technology* 36(1) (1995), a

---

[22]See http://novelint.com/royaltyrates.html.

[23]See note 18.

[24]See note 14.

[25]Ibid.

[26]See note 18.

baseline allocation of 25% assumes the licensor is offering a strong technology bundle that includes:

- Relevant, assumable, and enforceable patents
- Trade secrets and know-how that are related to the specific technology, including marketing insights and contacts
- One or more established product trademarks or logos that could contribute credibility and goodwill to the licensee
- Software programs, advertising support, and other expressions of creative work
- An active, well-financed, and historically productive R&D facility that could reinforce the licensed technology regularly
- A pattern of successful licenses between the licensor and similar or current licensees
- A reputation for diligence in pursuing infringements of its rights
- Protecting its licensees from independent actions initiated by third parties

These conditions also assume the licensor is maintaining the patents and is also providing a ready-to-market (or nearly ready) technology. Johnson[27] also states this "25% rule" should apply when the licensor provides the licensee "significant value." An excerpt is below:

> Significant value generally implies all of the following:
>
> 1. Products with a long-term competitive advantage;
> 2. License terms that are favourable to the licensee;
> 3. The licensor has critical mass and strongly supports its products and the licensee; and
> 4. The licensee does not provide any non-cash value to the licensor.
>
> If some or all of these criteria are not met, an appropriate royalty rate based on operating profit is usually reduced.

Based on the requirements above, discounts to the "25% royalty rule" should be made for early-stage university IP licensing. Assuming a discount of 50% to 75% based on the preceding factors, and assuming a reasonable royalty rate for chemical industry technology to be 2.5% of sales (per discussion above), an expected royalty rate of $(0.25 - 0.50) \times 2.5\% = 0.6$ to 1.25% for early-stage technology resulting from a university alliance with a chemical industry partner.

---

[27]See note 21.

EXHIBIT 9.A.3 Proposed Running Royalty Rates

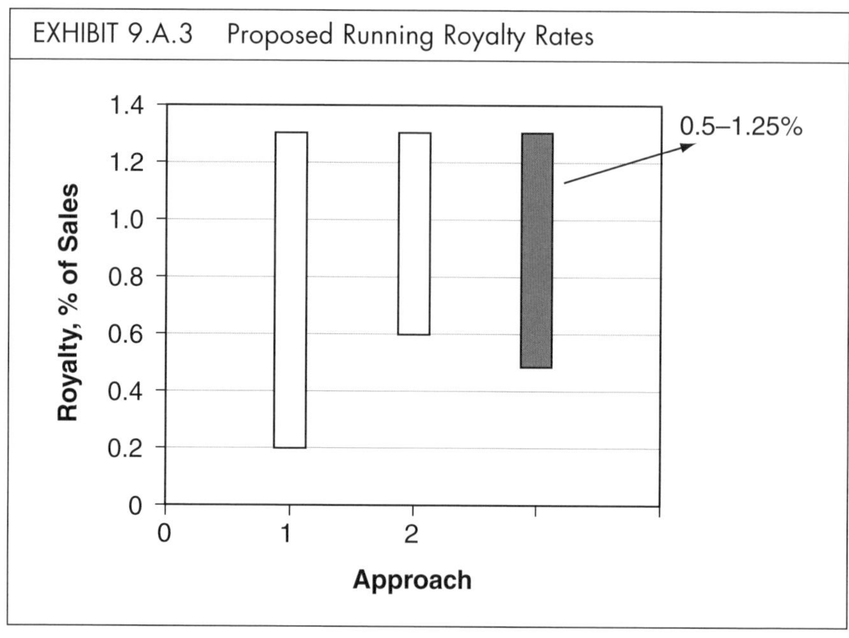

Conclusion

Reviewing the range of estimates of both approaches above, the literature study supports a royalty rate of 0.2% to 1.25% of sales for early-stage technology resulting from a university alliance with a chemical industry partner, assuming the partner pays 100% of the sponsored R&D cost and patent filing, prosecution, and maintenance costs.

Since the royalty being estimated is for an exclusive license, fair royalty rates in the range of 0.5% to 1.25% are proposed. Additionally, a cap on the running royalty should be set to reflect the relative investment made by each party.

10

Growth Strategies Using Intellectual Assets and Strategic Alliances

Dennis W. McCullough

Two of the most important dynamic business growth components for the future are intellectual assets (IAs) and strategic alliances (SAs). Both of these components offer key profitability leveraging opportunities for new growth and company renewal. This chapter discusses the interlinkage of IAs and SAs in the synergistic development of growth strategies based on their combination.

The Importance of Business Growth

John Seeley Brown, director emeritus of the Xerox Palo Alto Research Center, observed, "It is not technology *per se* that matters, but rather technology in use. That, and its role in driving business growth, is what is so hard to predict.[1] For example, here are a few infamous predictions about future product markets:

- "There is no reason for an individual to have a computer in his home." This quote, made by in 1977 by Kenneth Olsen, cofounder and chief executive officer (CEO) of Digital Equipment Corporation, looks ridiculous in light of today's reality, where 70% of U.S. households have one or more computers.
- Equally incongruent in hindsight is a 1992 quote from a friend of mine, a French chemical engineer: "Why would anyone want to buy water in a bottle?" This question pales in light of today's $22 billion annual worldwide market in bottled water.

[1]Brown, John Seeley. Foreword, in Chesbrough, Henry. *Open Innovation: The New Imperative for Creating and Profiting from Technology* (Boston: Harvard Business School Press, 2005).

- Some say the most amazing quote is attributed to Charles H. Duell, the U.S. Patent Office Commissioner in 1899: "Everything that can be invented has already been invented." With over six million U.S. patents granted since the beginning of the twentieth century and new inventions being filed at a rate of 450,000 per year, a more erroneous prediction is hard to imagine.

Looking at the issue from a higher level, the ultimate value of a technology asset is its usefulness as a foundation for business growth. Why is growth important? There are several fundamental derived benefits to growth: Value is created for everyone with a stake; customers and potential partners are attracted to growth; employees see a personal future; and momentum and confidence are built. The end result is "value growth," which is defined as sustainable value with acceptable levels of capital investment.[2]

Consider that 90% of all publicly traded companies have proven unable to sustain above-average growth beyond a few years. That is, roughly one company in ten has created above-average shareholder returns over an extended period.

We will consider strategies linking IAs and SAs with business model issues that affect business growth. Specifically, we will discuss why small business units (SBU) should be considered as a way to grow, how a small technology-based business can be a growth engine, and how strategic alliances can help grow your SBUs. (*Note:* There is a common reference of SBU to "strategic business unit" in the literature, but, for the purposes of this chapter, SBU will continue to refer to "small business unit" throughout.)

SBUs as a Growth Vehicle

Large companies mostly go after "big bets," primarily making major investments and acquisitions. They pursue these moves with the belief that only large-scale initiatives can make a difference in their bottom line. This may be true in a short-term sense; however, they often fail to recognize that they can make both large- and small-scale investments and, consequently, they fail to seek a balance in their portfolio. Small-scale initiatives are most likely to build sustainable value without the high risk of wasted capital inherent in large projects and major acquisitions.[3] They are more likely to stimulate entrepreneurial entry

---

[2]Christensen, Clayton M., and Raynor, Michael E. *The Innovator's Solution: Creating and Sustaining Successful Growth* (Boston: Harvard Business School Press, 2003), p. 23.

[3]Shulman, Joel M. *Getting Bigger by Growing Smaller: A New Growth Model for Corporate America* (Upper Saddle River, NJ: Financial Times Prentice Hall, 2004), p. xvii.

into high-growth new markets. Most new markets, in fact, begin small, where a business can be built without huge capital and competitive barriers. As Keith Hammond says, ". . . bigger doesn't make a company better at serving customers. Bigger isn't more rewarding to work for. Bigger doesn't innovate. Bigger, *per se*, isn't better. Better is better."[4]

Look at what has happened to U.S. research and development (R&D) spending over the past 20 years. There has been a dramatic shift in U.S. industrial R&D funding away from large companies toward small and intermediate-sized entities (see Exhibit 10.1). The R&D share percent was multiplied by five for entities less than 1,000, doubled for mid-sized entities, and dropped by over half for large companies. Most of this shift occurred in the last decade.[5]

The reasons for this shift in R&D spending patterns are partly due to a trend toward diffusion of knowledge, so that large companies no longer hold a "knowledge monopoly."[6] There also has been a massive shift in the United States to value creation by SBUs, which in turn attracts R&D investments even from larger-entity partners and investors.

Tale of an SBU: Three Guys in a Garage

How can all companies have access to and participate in this dynamic trend? To illustrate a possible path forward, consider the tale of a real SBU, beginning with three guys in a garage (see Exhibit 10.2). These three inventors formed a small company named Chemical Research & Licensing, and worked for seven years trying to create a viable product. They created a technology used in the manufacture of low-emissions gasoline. Along the way, they made a key move and added a patent attorney to the mix. The technology development graduated from the humble beginnings in the utility room to larger pilot plants. In the early 1980s, they licensed it to the likes of Exxon, Amoco, Elf, and others, which gave them a great degree of credibility. The innovation was called "catalytic distillation."

Catalytic distillation is the combination, in one step, of chemical reaction (formation of products and by-products) and the purification of primary

[4]Hammond, Keith. "Size Is Not a Strategy," *Fast Company*, September 2002.

[5]National Science Foundation. Science Resource Studies, "Research and Development in Industry," 1999.

[6]Chesbrough, Henry M. *Open Innovation: The New Imperative for Creating and Profiting from Technology* (Boston: Harvard Business School Press, 2005).

EXHIBIT 10.1 The Shift in R&D Spending by Company Size

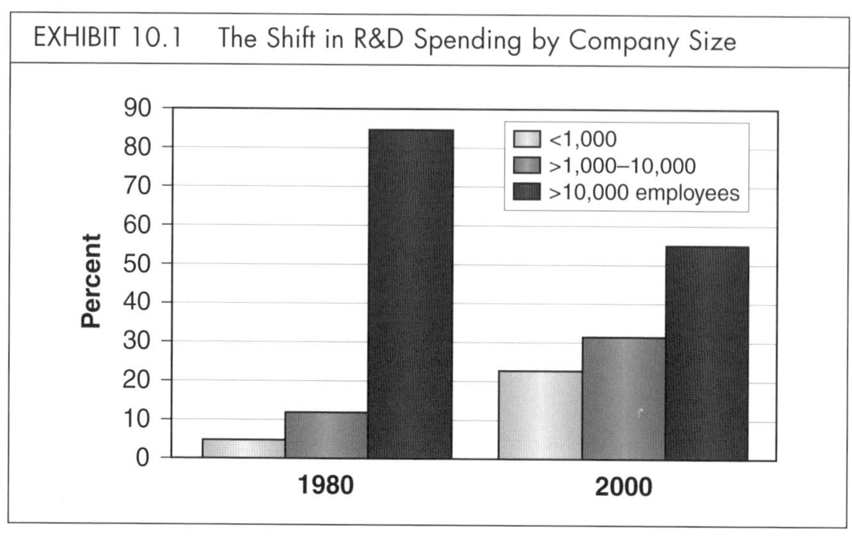

EXHIBIT 10.2 The Real Garage Where It All Began in 1977 in Pasadena, Texas

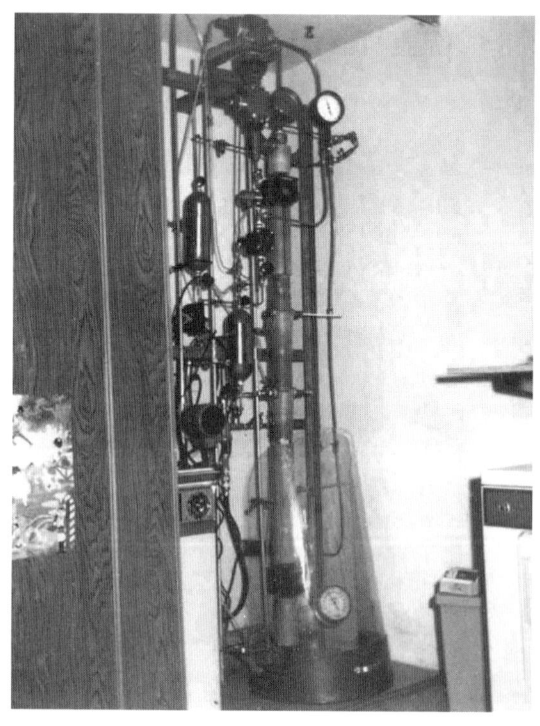

products (see Exhibit 10.3). The actual original embodiment involved wire mesh bales wrapped around with catalyst-filled sewn fiberglass pockets. These bales, nicknamed "Texas tea bags," which are stacked inside a distillation vessel, were originally fabricated using "cottage industry" techniques. This resulted in a process with lower capital and operating costs, and higher-purity products with fewer by-product contaminants.

This little company, CR&L, needed partners to realize its vision. Polysar, a Canadian petrochemical producer, acquired CR&L and joined with Lummus in 1988 to form a small technology-based licensing business called CDTECH to enhance the wider licensing of this new gasoline-producing technology and to expand the application of catalytic distillation into additional processes.

CDTECH today is a technology-based SBU. The partnership (now ABB Lummus Global and CR&L, a Shell subsidiary) has been in existence for 18 years and is a major licensor to the hydrocarbon processing industry (HPI). CDTECH has over 300 patents and more than 150 licenses, a world-class R&D center dedicated to the joint venture research, and approximately 120 people from the two partners engaged in the business (see Exhibit 10.4). By all meas-

EXHIBIT 10.3 The Components of Catalytic Distillation

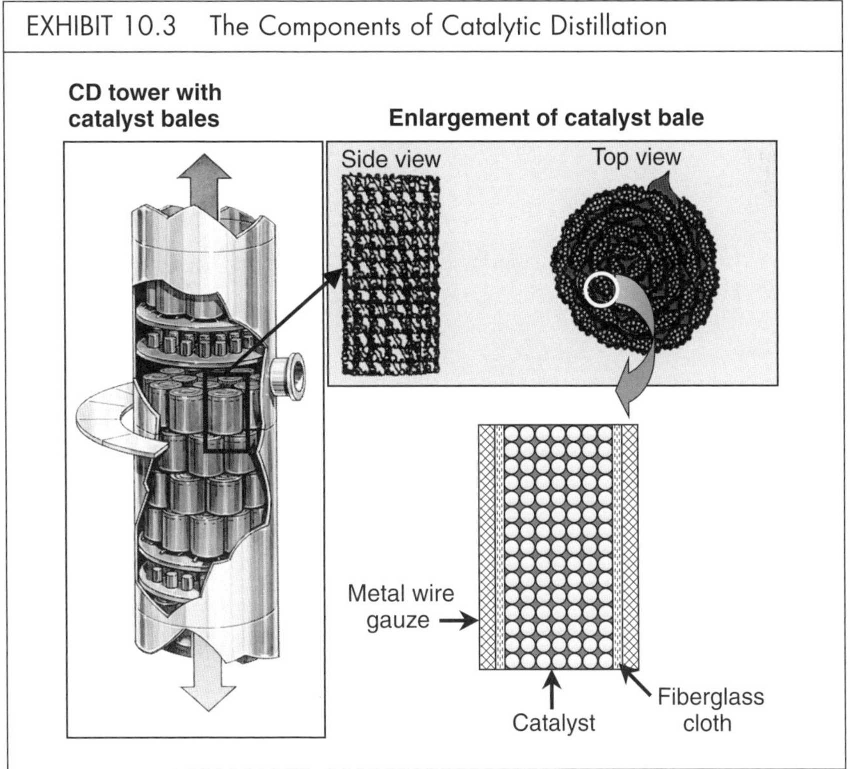

EXHIBIT 10.4 The CDTECH R&D Facilities Outside Houston, TX

ures, CDTECH has been a success, and, as alliances go, 18 years is an unusually enduring partnership, especially considering the changes in both parent companies.

Lummus Process Technology

ABB Lummus Global, historically, had been viewed primarily as an engineering contracting company that happened to have a good ethylene process technology. That all changed in 1987 when a decision was made to dedicate a part of the company to developing a process technology business. The seeds of Lummus Process Technology (LPT) were planted.

LPT's business is the development and licensing of process technology to the HPI, which includes gas processing, petroleum refining, and petrochemical and polymer production.

Its parent corporation, ABB, is a leading power and automation technology company with approximately 103,000 employees in 100 countries and 2005 annual revenues in excess of $22 billion. LPT has approximately 600 people dedicated to the development and licensing of technology for the HPI. It is a profit center with four research and development facilities in the United States, three of these in alliances. Of its roughly 30 alliances, 10 are major contributors to the business. Thus, LPT is itself a technology-based SBU.

LPT's Strategy for Growth

Think of the iceberg analogy. The annual market size in the HPI for the licensing business is approximately $5 billion; however, we estimate that the associated market, which includes catalysts, proprietary equipment, and technical services, is around $22 billion annually. The strategy: Capture the iceberg! Or as much of it as possible. Through offerings of value-added products and services, LPT tries to extend vertical growth to extract the maximum benefits that can be derived from selling the technology license itself.

Why did CDTECH fit with LPT's business strategy? LPT's strategy is to build its licensing businesses around multiple product lines based on its set of skills and technologies. Catalytic distillation is a "generic" technology with many potential applications. The result is that CDTECH has entered multiple licensing markets based on the catalytic distillation invention, including MTBE (methyl tertiary butyl ether) for gasoline, desulfurization of fuels, alkylation for producing styrene, and hydrogenation for petrochemicals.

How Can a Small Technology-Based Business Be a Growth Engine?

There are a number of advantages to technology-based businesses. There is considerable flexibility for alternative uses of the base assets, and, as mentioned earlier, one can extract the maximum from associated product markets. Alternative avenues of exploitation are through partner-owned manufacturing operations, and through manufacturing joint ventures in which the technology is contributed as the base equity asset. Of course, intellectual assets, development resources, and technology delivery capability are the "value creation" engine. This model has been a growth engine for LPT, and the growth has been sustained for over 19 years.

LPT History

It is interesting to review the growth steps taken that have allowed LPT to reach its present position. In retrospect, it is easy to see how far LPT has come since its inception in 1987, and that it has stayed more or less on course with the initial vision for its future. The challenge, then, is finding strategies to elevate LPT to the next level of vision, or even a changed vision from where it is today. Any strategy must consider that the world has changed significantly since 1987 and that the market dynamics are dramatically different.

The following is a historical perspective of a company growing into its vision. It is conveniently broken down into three phases: the early days, the growth phase, and the future.

The Early Days From a modest beginning, with only eight processes marketed for licensing and limited capital available, LPT focused on two main objectives:

1. Establish the charter/viability of the profit center LPT organization.
2. Focus on market share and results from existing technologies.

We carefully developed a two-year business plan to serve as our guiding vision document. It addressed our business charter, provided a comprehensive analysis of our target markets and our technology assets, established our base business strategy, and projected what we wanted to be in the future. With a clearer vision of where we were heading, LPT met its expectations during this period, helped considerably by a coincident upturn in the petrochemicals business. The early business plan was an accurate predictor of our first few years of existence.

Addressing our second objective, one key move during this period was improving our established ethylene technology with a step-change improvement in our ethylene furnace design. With the new SRT (short residence time) ethylene furnace, and a task force specifically set up to target projects, we increased our share of revamp contracts and new plant awards, which placed us as the overall market-share leader in the booming ethylene market. During this period, LPT also introduced, with dramatic success, its new ALMA maleic anhydride (MA) technology, which had been codeveloped with Alusuisse Italia (now Lonza SpA) and was a first-of-a-kind process for manufacture of MA from butane feedstocks. In addition to commercially demonstrating new processes and improving several of our other existing processes, this was also the period that the CDTECH partnership was formed with Polysar-owned CR&L.

It was evident very early on that growth was essential for stability, to balance the swings in the HPI economic cycles. For LPT, growth meant expanding the number and types of technologies in its process portfolio. With the time line for internal development long and expensive (as discussed later in this chapter), it was imperative to find ways to shorten the time to market. Capital limitations were also an issue. Exploring options, it was clear that there were opportunities in pursuing the underutilized assets of others. So the next phase of growth focused on partnership strategies.

The Growth Phase: Technology Expansion via Partnering, Acquisition, and Development The objectives during this period were to:

1. Acquire technology positions via formation of partnerships with established companies.
2. Selectively purchase technology assets/companies.
3. Acquire/develop process chains.
4. Expand internal developmental initiatives and resources.

LPT more or less continued to follow its original business plan during the first few years, but began to tweak it. In particular, LPT went to a product-line organization and integrated technology and market focus into its business plan. It was during this period that LPT decided to take major initiatives in expanding its refining technology business. A task force was formed to evaluate the various technology options and markets, and then subgroups were formed to go out and get it done through key partnerships. This resulted in technology alliances with Chevron (hydrocracking) and Texaco (fluid catalytic cracking).

Having delivered on the more obvious targets, LPT was faced with some stagnation. However, we had established credibility and were confident in our model, and therefore embarked on a more aggressive strategy. We evaluated our existing process portfolio to determine how to best leverage our expertise to acquire complementary processes that either immediately precede or closely follow in sequence a process currently offered by LPT for license. This would allow us to provide linkage of technology products to the customers' advantage.

One significant product area of interest was propylene, which is used mainly for polypropylene (PP) production. Most of the world's propylene (90% to 95%) is produced as a by-product of steam cracking (where the main product is ethylene) and fluid catalytic cracking (FCC; used in a refinery for gasoline production). LPT has technology positions in both steam cracking and FCC; however, both have limited flexibility to increase propylene production independent of its coproduct ethylene or of gasoline production, respectively. In anticipation of increasing PP demand, and hence propylene demand, it was evident that technologies for the on-purpose production of propylene would be of value. LPT acquired the rights to a process now called olefins conversion technology (OCT) that converts low-value butenes and ethylene to propylene. After acquisition, LPT made its own significant process and catalyst improvements to the OCT process, which led to its rapid market acceptance and successful broad licensing. Interestingly enough, this process was originally developed for the opposite reaction, converting propylene to ethylene and butene-2, at a time when propylene value was low.

LPT also formed an alliance with United Catalysts, a U.S. subsidiary of Sud Chemie, the German-based catalyst manufacturer, to acquire and license another multipurpose technology called the CATOFIN dehydrogenation process. This technology was originally developed to make butadiene from butylene and was a significant contributor to the success of the World War II effort to produce feedstocks for synthetic rubber. It was later adapted to convert butanes to butylenes as feed to MTBE plants, which were being built to fulfill the clean air–driven mandate for oxygenates for clean-burning fuels. Subsequently, the CATOFIN process has experienced a new emergence for making on-purpose propylene by dehydrogenating propane. The CATOFIN process is an example of a mature technology that keeps renewing via continuing catalyst development and application development.

The OCT and CATOFIN processes are dramatic illustrations of how a modest amount of capital can be utilized to acquire somewhat dormant technology assets and to interject new life with new adaptations in the market. Very few of these moves occurred by happenstance or luck, but resulted from conscious planning by the LPT management to implement, over time, a proactive growth strategy.

LPT consolidated other technology elements of its business as well (i.e., Lummus Heat Transfer, a division that designs and builds heat transfer equipment) to give it a greater aggregate impact on financial results. Since LHT's products (heaters and heat exchangers) were closely linked with LPT's licensed processes, this consolidation was more a true measure of LPT's technology impact and again reflected the vision of management to include associated products.

LPT also began to see the results of its own important internal R&D efforts. This included an increase in its catalysis expertise with development initiatives resulting in improved catalysts for use in its processes as well as several breakthrough catalyst innovations that are now reaching commercial implementation.

The latter part of this growth period saw the addition of complete businesses, as opposed to discrete single technologies, to LPT's technology portfolio. LPT added the Novolen polypropylene licensing business by acquisition of the technology assets and technology staff from Targor (a BASF subsidiary). It solidified and expanded the Chevron Lummus Global hydroprocessing technology joint venture and created a gas-processing technology business by moving its sister company, Randall Gas Technologies, into LPT. In all these cases, LPT maintained a common perspective: to look for businesses where it could technically or commercially improve the offering, share the risk with its expert partner, and expand market participation beyond the original sale.

LPT considered building the business through acquiring complete firms, but considered this a higher-risk strategy than the purchase of technology assets alone (see Exhibit 10.5).

The Future LPT's growth has been significantly leveraged through its partners and joint ventures. Table 10.1 summarizes the difference between LPT in 1987 and its business today. LPT has increased the number of technologies in its portfolio by a factor of nine, its alliances by a factor of eight, and its research facilities by a factor of four, while only tripling the size of its organization. Its financial growth has been equally dramatic despite the cyclic nature of its served markets.

TABLE 10.1 LPT Growth from 1987 to 2005

	1987	*2005*
Processes	8	70+
Employees	180	600
Alliances	4	30+
R&D centers	1	4

EXHIBIT 10.5 LPT Growth History 1987–2006

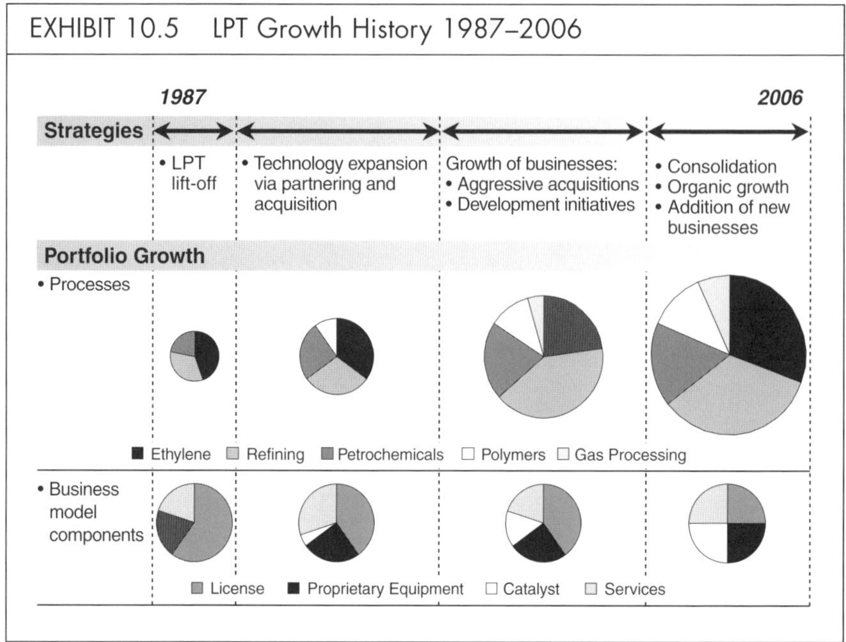

A fear of most businesses is that there is not a clear view of how to rise to the next level of promise. What will be the focus of LPT in the future that will propel its growth to the next level? Its marketing prowess will continue to distinguish it from others, but it will be even more important in the future for LPT to have technology components that others need in order to attract partners. It is anticipated that, even as it continues to grow in its stand-alone strength and competence, LPT also will continue to heavily rely on partnering as a key strategy to achieve its growth objectives.

There likely will be a balanced approach between organic growth of its existing businesses with the addition of new businesses. Organic growth begins with LPT's core belief in investing in R&D through its multiple, business-driven R&D centers. Research and development capabilities—access to R&D, control of R&D, and ability to collaborate in R&D—will be the main requirement for creating and sustaining growth where technology is the core product. LPT has four major R&D centers, three of which are embedded in alliances where partner resources are leveraged for benefit of the partnership (see Exhibit 10.6).

In addition to the R&D performed in its alliances, LPT also has built its own significant R&D resources based in New Jersey. This group has utilized its basic

EXHIBIT 10.6 Four R&D Centers in the United States, Three Embedded in Alliances

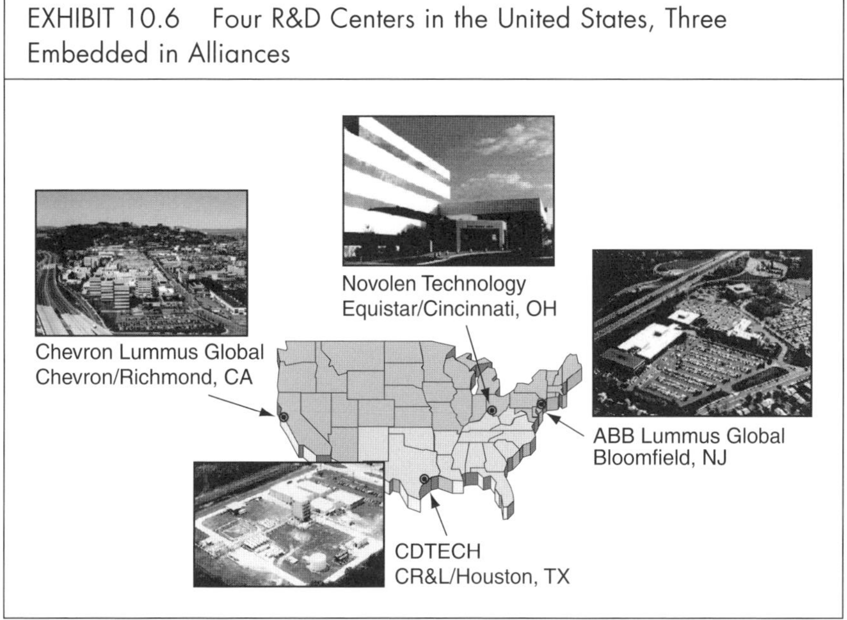

research capabilities in reaction systems and catalysis to create advanced innovations that serve as platforms for multiple process markets. These include unique structured catalysts, catalyst manufacturing techniques, and advanced reactor concepts.

Although basic research will continue, LPT's greatest strength is in the developmental step of scale-up and process design. LPT also will seek to create more applications for its existing technical strengths, such as in catalysis, that can be applied across all its technology businesses. There will be much greater linkage among all LPT technology businesses, with a significant effort to capture derivative earnings from all elements of the proprietary value chain. There will be a shift toward increasing the balance of technical competence and innovation as differentiating skills to complement LPT's highly valued marketing expertise, which will position LPT to attract new partners. It will be very critical to LPT's continued growth that it be able to attract new partners.

There will be the emergence in LPT of its plant life cycle services business as a key growth element, and all of this will be impacted significantly by the expanded e-enabled commerce. All of these elements linked together are expected to form the foundation of a growth strategy to ensure LPT's continued outstanding performance as a technology organization.

STRATEGIC ALLIANCES FOR SMALL BUSINESS UNIT GROWTH

Having discussed LPT's past, present, and future as an example of a small business unit (SBU) built on IP assets in combination with strategic alliances, what lessons can be learned to help grow your SBU utilizing strategic alliances?

As preparation for developing a plan to utilize technology alliances as SBU growth vehicles, consider the alternative approaches to the role technology licensing plays in the overall growth of a firm. Although there is a range of possible technology licensing strategies that are available to a full scope entity with its own manufacturing facilities, two basic approaches are:

1. *Tactical licensing:* Licensing that is undertaken without impacting the firm's manufacturing function. In this approach, the licensing group usually has little say in the R&D direction and very little ability to self-fund initiatives, and the technology licensed is usually not the core basis for its manufacturing units.
2. *Strategic licensing:* Licensing approach that creates an SBU that behaves as a proactive business unit. The licensing group is involved in the technology decisions of the corporation and even funds some of its own R&D. It has a profit and loss, and is judged on income rather than licensing revenues alone.[7]

The flexibility inherent in the strategic licensing approach to utilizing technology in a variety of alliance-leveraged ventures is a powerful tool for SBU growth. Here, the technology is considered a strategic asset but is not always monetized by its initial or even primary utilization through owned manufacturing operations. Instead, the strategy would be one in which the technology/IP/know-how sits at the center of a set of decision options on how to best maximize financial return. External opportunities for creating a financial return for the company from the technology are not simply considered a last resort when the owned manufacturing route has run its course or when a firm's new technology replaces the old and the obsolete IP is then licensed. All options are on the table, including collaboration under a variety of scenarios and with different timing relationships. Thus, strategic licensing becomes one of several central considerations in development of an optimum approach to creating results-driven technology alliances.

Along the spectrum of technology alliance models, there is an increasing degree of integration and commitment as shown in Exhibit 10.7. The least inte-

[7]Hastbacka, Mildred A. "Technology Licensing: A Strategy for Creating Value," A.D. Little, 1997.

EXHIBIT 10.7 Technology Alliances Vary in Their Degree of Integration and Commitment

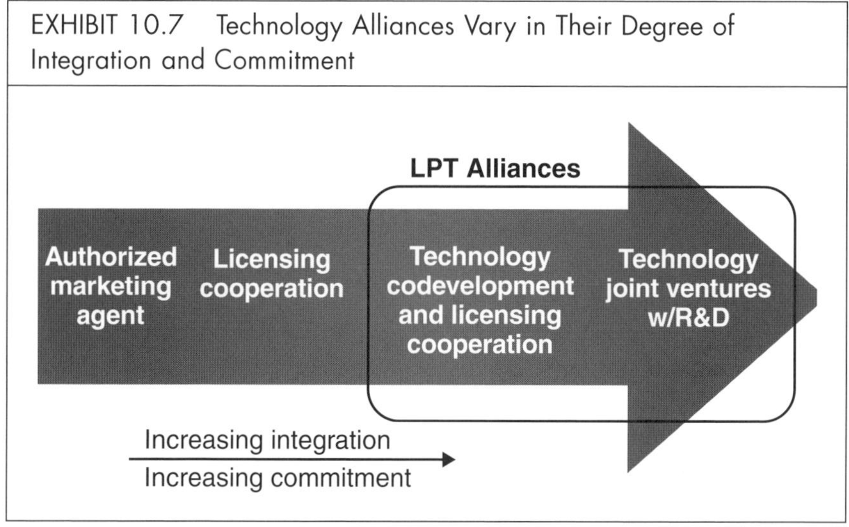

grated (and committed) is one in which one party is simply an authorized marketing agent of the owner of the technology, often on a nonexclusive basis. A step up from that is a licensing cooperation entailing some degree of exclusivity, and some collaborative standing by each party as to the source of the technology product offered for license. The next level adds technology codevelopment, where both parties commit to working to create and improve the process in addition to cooperation in bringing the technology product to the market via licensing. And the highest level, the model that requires the most integration and commitment, is technology joint ventures that include a commitment of resources and R&D by both parties through creation of a formal entity for generating results. LPT has increasingly relied on the latter two models to grow its business. Within this context, to LPT, a strategic alliance is simply one that is both core to its business and long term in its intended duration.

LPT's technology business model, shown in Exhibit 10.8, is based on the creation of an SBU formed as an alliance. The structure is normally 50–50 in control and ownership, in order to give balance and prevent dominance by either partner. It usually is comanaged, with a dual directorship and an equally balanced board. The objective is to govern by consensus. An integrated team runs the day-to-day operations, leveraging the particular strengths of each partner—the fixed assets, background IP, business experience, market channels, and operating facilities that each partner brings to the venture. There is autonomy within a defined operation (e.g., marketing, product research), but supervised by the partners' management committee to maintain vision and direction.

EXHIBIT 10.8 LPT Technology Alliance Model

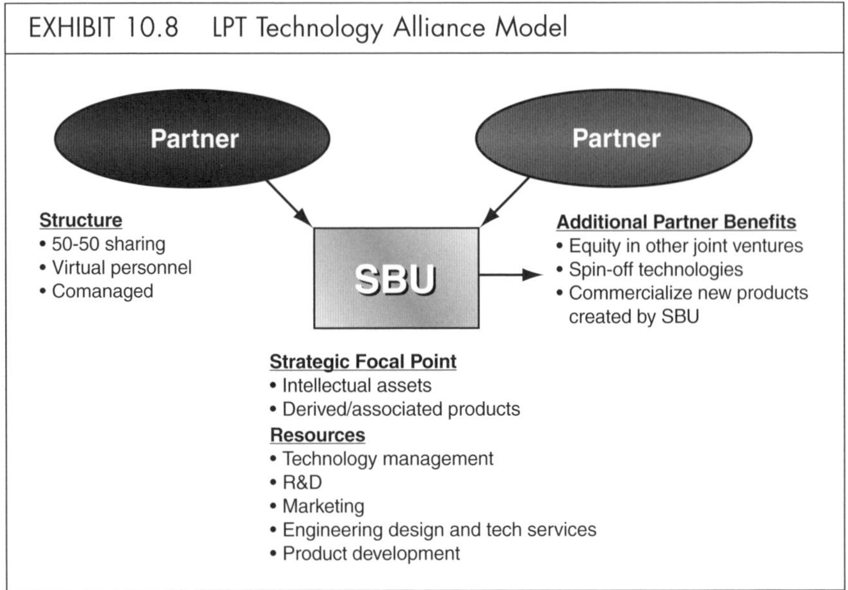

The strategic focal point for LPT's business is the technology IA and associated products. LPT also places all necessary resources inside the business, dedicated or accessible, and under its direction. In particular, the joint venture has control of R&D resources that are key to its vitality as a business. Additional partner benefits occur via having access to the joint venture's or other partner's manufacturing facilities, possible spin-offs outside of the alliance charter, and new technology commercialization options.

The strengths of such an alliance model include the synergies leading to greater competitive strength, shared costs and risks, expanded market reach, and more rapid market entry of new products. The weaknesses are that control is more complex, market results are shared, technology exclusivity is shared, and there is a greater complexity in dividing assets in the event of dissolution. On balance, we consider the benefits of alliances far exceed the negatives, and LPT has pursued alliances as the fundamental model for building its technology business.

In particular, the challenges in HPI technology development and commercialization inevitably lead to the need for a partner when attempting to develop, demonstrate, and commercialize technology advances. The technology development characteristics of the HPI are high-cost R&D pilot plants, large capital investment for a commercial plant, fairly long cycle time from development through commercialization, and significant daily losses for operating downtime should a technology fail to perform as planned. The bottom line is that the HPI technology development and commercialization cycle is a high-risk proposition. The principal technique for sharing that risk is to carry through the cycle with one or several partners.

For LPT, development of the breakthrough AlkyClean alkylation process was enabled by its alliance with partners Albemarle Catalysts and Neste Oil. This new technology produces high-octane gasoline components via an environmentally safe process that replaces hazardous hydrogen fluoride and H_2SO_4 acids with a solid acid catalyst.

The typical timeline for an HPI process development project is around eight years or longer. Of course, this varies widely, depending on whether a company is starting from basic research in a new field or leveraging off past work. Additionally, when starting from the exploratory research stage, a company must feed the pipeline with many new prospective developments to have even one make it through the entire cycle and deliver commercial results. The ratio of projects entering the funnel to those emerging at the other end is statistically about seven to one across many industries. For the HPI, it is probably higher due to the high entry barriers.

To a certain degree, the cycle can be further reduced if the development is carried out by a company that also expects to be the first to commercialize the technology and has a start-to-finish track record of continuity. However, if the technology developer has to rely on another party to be the first to commercially demonstrate the technology—as LPT must do in its technology licensing–based business—considerable skill must be used to coordinate the successful launch. LPT typically will seek a commercializing partner early on in the piloting/demo plant phase to provide hands-on experience with the technology and to build confidence at all levels in the commercializing partner's organization. Getting approvals and commitment for such a risky (and expensive) undertaking is not easy.

Selecting the commercializing partner requires careful and thorough analysis. The key is understanding that one is not yet trying to sell the technology to the broader market, but only to a single targeted user who will serve as the gateway for convincing other potential users that the technology can be utilized in a safe, reliable, and efficient manner. With so much at risk, the HPI companies are a conservative group and are more likely to wait to be the second or third or fourth user, no matter how great the benefits. The key is to identify the company that must do something, either economically or environmentally, to survive and for whom the new technology provides the survival answer. Thus, the high risk is balanced against the even higher reward. Other industries with high-cost-demonstration barriers may have similar dynamics. Others may have a low prototype or demonstration cost, but require a very high manufacturing investment to produce the product.

Another way LPT seeks to use alliances to reduce the technology time to market is to apply the concept of "other people's funnels." We maintain an active search for those technologies that have made it through the exploratory and proof-of-principle stages. Typically, this reduces the development cycle for new technologies by 20% to 30% and increases significantly the ability to pick winners. It also allows us to apply our technical staff to what it does best: the scale-up and commercialization activities (see Exhibit 10.9). Of course, results must be shared with the originator of the technology, but speed to market is all important and there is no better substitute for accelerating the development of new technologies. It is a big world and no company has a corner on good ideas. The more one is open to that external resource, the more opportunities for strategic growth.

In fact, deciding what vehicle a company wants to use for its technology entry strategy is a key decision that is likely to spell success or failure for the new-product effort. There are many options for this entry strategy: internal devel-

EXHIBIT 10.9 The Concept of "Funneling" and Reducing Time to Commercialization

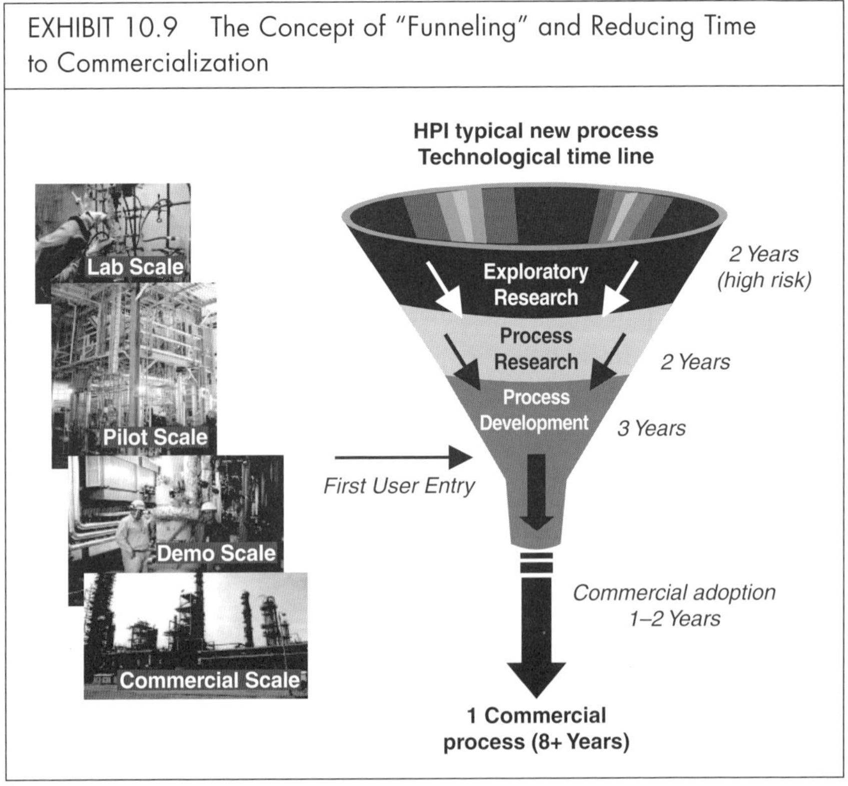

opment, acquisition, licensing-in, internal venture, joint venture, alliance, venture capital, or learning acquisitions.[8] Each has its merits and its downsides and must be chosen with care. A technology-mapping process is helpful, not only to map the market application targets, but also the initial entry path to those markets, whether by external or internal means. For the future, the successful firms are most likely to be those that selectively rely on all of these methods of technology entry and develop extensive organizational expertise in each entry channel, coupled with skill at selecting and coordinating the optimum path.

The Key Alliance Success Factors

We are aware that alliances have a bad reputation in some circles (see Exhibit 10.10). Studies across a broad range of industries have reflected a mixed record, with average success rates of only 50%. Success here is defined as meeting alliance objectives (usually financial), enhancing competitive position, and achieving certain levels of partner harmony. However, the real story is the disparity between those companies that have installed an alliance "best practices" program and those companies without such formal programs. Using best practices in forming and operating alliances more than doubles the average success rate.[9]

As a business form, alliance return on investments were significantly higher than industry-average performance and are growing dramatically as contributors of top-line revenue, estimated to be around one third of total revenues by the end of 2005. Our own business is not so formalized in codifying its alliance practices, but after 19 years and over 30 alliances, the basic culture and learned behavior of our organization is highly developed in alliance best practices. From top to bottom, we understand what it takes to be a good partner, as evidenced by the longevity and success of our alliances.

It is very important to build an alliance on a good foundation. We, as well as others,[10] have found the following six ingredients to be important factors in an alliance's success:

1. Shared objectives
2. Mutual trust
3. Long-term commitment

[8]Cooper, Robert G. *Product Leadership: Creating and Launching Superior New Products* (New York: Perseus Books, 2000), pp. 84–86.

[9]The Warren Company, 1994–2001; Booz-Allen Hamilton, 2000; BYU-Wharton Study, 2001.

[10]Lewis, Jordan D. Preface, in *Partnerships for Profit: Structuring and Managing Strategic Alliances* (New York: Free Press, 1990).

EXHIBIT 10.10 Alliances with "Best Practices" Programs Have a Much Higher Success Rate Than Those Without

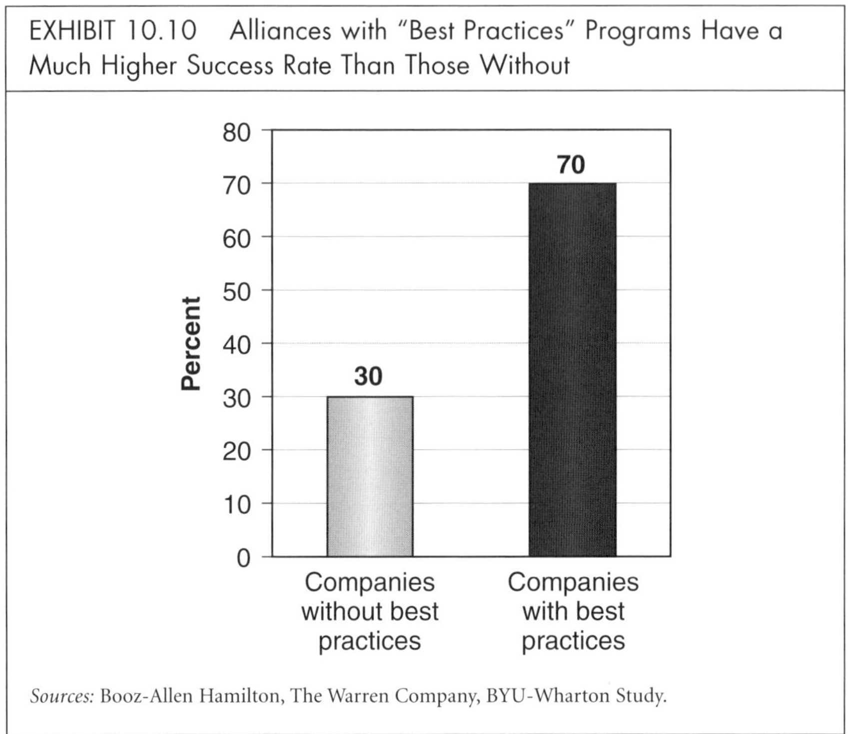

Sources: Booz-Allen Hamilton, The Warren Company, BYU-Wharton Study.

4. Defined roles and interdependence
5. Compatible culture
6. Shared risk and reward

The absence of any one of these may not mean failure, but it certainly raises the risk that performance will be less than expected.

Of course, with alliances there are always issues. Selecting the right partner is fundamental and crucial: Partnership management can be impossible if one partner wants to dominate. Conflict resolution skills need to be present throughout the organization, not just at the top. Geographic and cultural issues must be overcome, and both parties must be ready to adapt. And, even in the early stages, there must be some preparedness to determine why, when, and how a partnership should be dissolved.

We have built several concepts in our organization that reinforce our success. LPT has evolved into a small business unit that manages other small business units—a "managing SBU." It acts as an "incubator," with support to provide key resources and worldwide business contacts, linkage with other SBUs in its portfolio, culture liaison with its corporate parent, financial oversight and management coaching, and IP and legal guidance. A big-company culture just would not fit with most of LPT's alliances, which typically engage roughly 100 employees. LPT's technology business organization provides a corporate "home" to nurture the SBUs and keep pace with their evolving needs.

Another evolutionary structural advance in alliance techniques is the establishment of alliances with alliances. This is a bit complex and requires that certain fundamental conditions be met. First, the base-established alliance requires a stable alliance profile. For example, it must have its own marketplace identity, with a cohesive image, and perform as a separate entity. The alliance partners' roles should be complementary and strong in their areas of expertise. Finally, IP must be managed as an integral part of the new alliance, avoiding the "yours, mine, and ours" attitude. The payoff is a multiple leveraging effect.

CDTECH, an alliance, has successfully attracted a number of big-name strategic partners, including ExxonMobil, Snamprogetti, Lyondell, and others, to expand its portfolio of process applications. In effect, the broadening of the alliance itself to establish alliances has expanded the value of the base CDTECH asset.

In a Nutshell

Here are the guiding principles of how LPT delivers results:

- Create SBU profit centers to drive our businesses.
- Place the SBUs within a managing SBU to provide overall management and shared resources for the portfolio of SBUs.
- Diversify within businesses where we have a reputation with technology assets as our core products.
- Extract value from our IA base in creative ways.
- Leverage through partners and licensees.

I will conclude with a quote from Gary Hamel, a prominent conceptual business thinker:

> "Competitive advantage will increasingly rest on the ability to create products, services and business models that are unique and utterly compelling."

Our own positive experience with the evolving growth of the LPT technology licensing business heartily supports this view. Our business model of choice is based on utilization of strategic alliances to promote and leverage our intellectual assets through small business units. The results achieved have been rewarding and have confirmed that we are on the right track.

11

Innovation and the Biopharmaceutical Industry—Crisis or Crossroads?

Ronald Lindsay

"Success has many fathers, failure is an orphan child."

It is all but impossible to define a recipe for success in developing novel therapeutics, but harnessing the historically immiscible disciplines of chemistry and biology is very much a core ingredient. As surely as a mix of oil and water, if not constantly shaken, chemist and biologist will separate into their respective camps. Left to their own devices, scientists will doubtless produce creative and innovative research. However, it takes highly focused and disciplined preclinical research and well-managed and dedicated downstream clinical development teamwork to produce safe, effective, and commercially successful medicines. Innovation for its own sake is not enough. Lack of a clear strategy to protect and maximize the value of intellectual property (IP) is both wasteful and jeopardizes the full commercial potential of innovative products.

By nature, chemists like to build things, and biologists thrive on taking things apart; chemists fixate on analytical precision, biologists live with statistical probabilities; chemists think small molecules; biologists prefer to tinker with macromolecules and cells. Reconciling these disparate interests and skills into a productive "truce" is the art of developing drugs. At the dawn of the pharmaceutical industry, the balance of power was in the chemistry camp. As it enters its second century as the biopharmaceutical industry, we see more of a coalition between chemists and biologists and less distinction between their disciplines. Future success and shape of the industry will depend on how well such coalitions are managed and how agnostic companies are prepared to be about molecular size.

Introduction

Elucidation of the Periodic Table of elements was in no small part a driving force in the creation of the modern chemical industry and a subsequent chemistry-driven pharmaceutical industry. Similarly, elucidating the genetic code and the subsequent determination of the structure of the entire human genome has created a biotechnology industry and a biology driven biotherapeutics industry. Taken together, the branded prescription drug products from the combined *biopharmaceutical* industry and the nonbranded generics industry enjoyed 2005 worldwide sales of over $600 billion, about half of those sales in the United States.

Successful development and commercialization of therapeutic drugs requires constant innovation, creativity, endurance, and strong patent protection (IP). It also requires sound management, deep pockets, and an uncanny element of plain old-fashioned luck in the many steps from bench to bedside. Unlike few other industries, success or failure only becomes evident eight to ten years and hundreds of millions of dollars into the development process. Uniquely, the drug developer does not have the ultimate say in triggering entry of a new product to market. The final arbiter is an independent government regulatory authority that is vested with the right to give a thumbs up or a thumbs down for approval of a new chemical entity (NCE) to move forward to the marketplace. Furthermore, unlike many consumer products, there is no margin of error that allows a pharmaceutical product that has gone off the rails to simply go back to the shop for a minor redesign or makeover before getting back on track. Given the high risk and high cost of developing drugs and the relatively short period of patent-protected market life, the biopharmaceutical industry fiercely defends its innovations by seeking patent protection at every stage of the drug development process, with emphasis on building a patent estate on many fronts. Some of the key components of building an effective patent estate in the biopharmaceutical industry include filing claims for:

- Small molecules:
  - Composition of matter of the final drug substance and backup compounds
  - Composition of matter and biological properties of closely linked chemical series
  - Composition of matter and utility of the drug target (enzyme, receptor, etc.)
  - Actual and alternate methods of drug synthesis
  - In vitro and in vivo pharmacological properties of the drug
  - Composition of matter and utility of active metabolites
  - Scale-up methods for commercial scale production

  - Formulations of the drug for oral and/or nonoral routes of administration
  - Appropriate therapeutic doses of the drug
  - Methods of use and therapeutic utility of the drug in multiple indications
  - Advanced drug delivery methods using devices such as inhalers
- Biologics—most of the above, plus:
  - Composition of matter of the gene or cDNA
  - Composition of matter of the protein and bioactive fragments
  - X-ray structure
  - Methods of recombinant production in multiple host cells
  - Methods of production in transgenic animals or plants
  - Methods of purification
  - Composition of matter or post-translation modifications (glycosylation)
  - Assay methods for biological activity and detection
  - Methods of modifying half-life in humans—chemical modifications
  - Methods of modifying activity or half-life—fusion proteins
  - Antigen-binding determinants (if an antibody)
  - Composition of matter of receptor-binding partner and utility claims
  - Alternative scaffolds for achieving a similar biological effect

Current Woes of the Pharmaceutical Industry

Just as the star of the biotechnology industry has ascended in the last decade, the classical pharmaceutical industry has come under attack from many quarters, not least from investors who seen poor or no returns. These same investors used to view the industry as a safe haven, especially in a bear market. By the simplest measure of success, annual new drug approvals, there is no doubt that the industry has had a decade of really poor and worsening performance. This begs the fundamental question: Is lack of innovation driving the industry to a crisis point, or is the industry passing a crossroads from which it will emerge stronger and more capable of delivering new medicines to meet great unmet needs and growing global demand?

The Broken Pipeline

Innovation Gap The pharmaceutical industry is emerging from two tumultuous decades that have rocked the once proud and successful industry to its core. Just as the costs of adapting to new technologies and new regulations have spiraled, the industry has struggled to maintain the high profitability, research and development (R&D) momentum and balanced pipeline growth that it enjoyed in the mid-to-late twentieth century. Although still highly profitable, thanks to the unparalleled success of a score or more blockbuster drugs, the productivity of the industry as measured by new drug approvals has halved in less than ten years. This productivity gap has been widely dubbed *The Broken Pipeline* (see Exhibit 11.1).

The broken pipeline question goes far beyond being a ponderous academic issue, as any sustained fall in overall revenues within the industry does and will lead to a vicious cycle in which we see:

- Decreased investment in internal R&D budget = lower productivity
- Decreased investment in external R&D = less innovation in technology and start-ups and eventually less in-licensing opportunities
- Decreased market cap = lowers ability to acquire or fend off competitors
- Decreased venture capital = fewer early-stage companies
- Increased threat from competition at home and abroad
- Flight of talent, know-how, trade secrets, and IP

With special emphasis on the role of innovation and the protection and deployment of IP, this chapter reviews some of the challenges and forced transitions that face the pharmaceutical industry as it enters its second century. Some of these challenges are listed in Exhibit 11.2.

EXHIBIT 11.1 Annualized New Drug Approvals 1992–2003 and Corresponding Pharmaceutical R&D Budgets

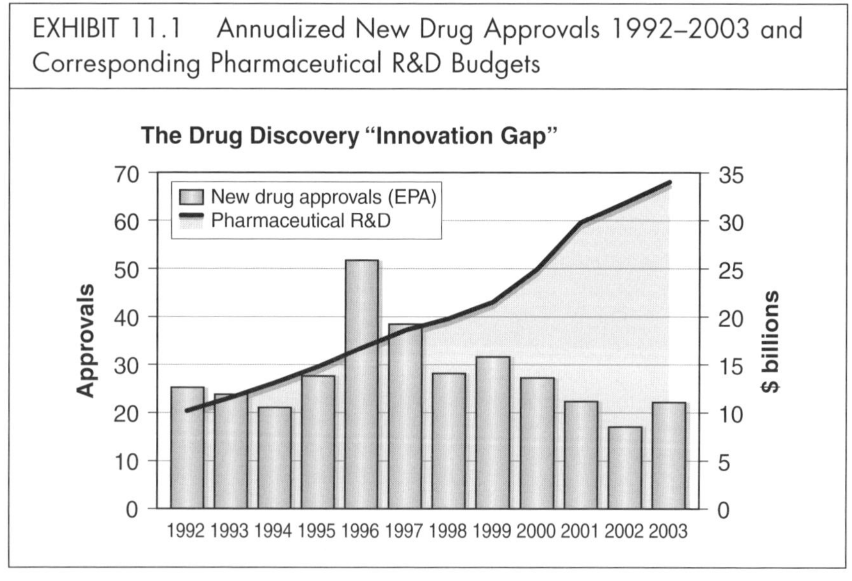

EXHIBIT 11.2 Near Term Challenges Facing Pharmaceutical R&D Innovation and Productivity

Basic Research

- Exponential information growth—*can't see the forest for the trees problem.*
- Adapting and integrating new technologies—*more is not always better.*
- Animal studies poorly predict drug efficacy in man—*need better models of disease.*
- Experience versus expertise—*greater need for downstream skills.*
- Demand for targeted therapies—*need for better diagnostic and prognostic markers.*
- Retraining scientists and clinicians—*need broader skills in translational medicine.*

Drug Development

- Staggeringly long product development cycles—*little improved in decades.*
- High failure rates—*still high late in development; especially small molecules.*

Drug Safety

- Tougher regulatory landscape—*safety, clinical end points, labeling, manufacturing.*
- Phase 4 pharmacovigilance/long-term postmarketing drug safety risk evaluation—*backlash from Fen-Phen, Vioxx, Baycol, etc.*

Reimbursement/Drug Pricing

- Pricing pressure today—*third party payers in the United States, national agencies ex–United States.*
- Specter of political interference tomorrow—*second wind for the "Hillary factor."*

Competition

- New drug classes—*biologics, RNAi.*
- Specialty pharmaceutical competition—*new IP through reformulation, novel delivery, etc.*
- Biotech competition—*market share ($) approaching 20% in 2006.*
- Generic competition—*market share of prescriptions (volume) over 50% in 2005.*
- Developing world competition—*emerging generics and biotech, especially India and China.*

Managing Change

- Industry consolidation—*mega-mergers rarely viewed as successful.*
- Managing intercompany collaborations—*short honeymoons and many divorces.*
- Loss of domain knowledge on valuable IP.

Overlaying all of these product development and marketing challenges is the vital issue of gaining and maintaining meaningful patent protection that will allow the developer to recoup the costs of the R&D behind not only the few products that make it to market, but the many that fail en route. Most recent estimates indicate that the full cost of bringing a new medicine to market is closing fast toward $1 billion.

New Competition The challenges listed above largely reflect a slowly evolving and possibly predictable change in the ground rules of the actual process of discovering, developing, and commercializing new medicines in an ever more global arena. A more ominous and near-term challenge to the profitability of classical pharmaceutical companies has been the birth and rapid growth of two completely new types of competitors—the generics industry and the biotechnology industry. Big pharmaceutical companies are now locked in battle with these new kids on the block for a share of the finite prescription drug pie.

Once dismissed by big pharmaceutical companies as niche market players, fully integrated biotechnology companies now represent fierce competition for the lucrative high ground of novel patent-protected drugs that address previously unmet needs. Furthermore, due to the high cost of production and often lifesaving potential, biotechnology products have been able to command premium pricing that are they envy of the industry. Depending on the setting of acute, short-term, or chronic care, biotechnology products price range from $10,000 to upwards of $200,000 per patient year.

On its other flank, "Big Pharma" has seen revenues from lucrative blockbusters evaporate almost overnight upon patent expiration. Expensive branded drugs rapidly disappear from pharmacy shelves to be replaced with generics. Estimates suggest that prices of branded drugs fall 40% in the first six months of the first generic hitting the market, and by up to 80% in the second six months. In little more than 20 years, biotech products have captured almost 20% of the approximately $300 billion annual sales of prescription drugs in the United States. While much lower in terms of dollar value, the magpie generics industry has in the same time period captured more than 50% of the total volume of the prescription drug market and $22 billion in sales.

Thus, in less than two decades Big Pharma has been exposed to massive pricing competition and loss of market share in the therapeutics areas where it had previously experienced its greatest innovative, public relations, and commercial successes, for example, cardiovascular disease agents and anti-infectives. On the other hand, these established players with enormous R&D budgets are being embarrassingly outflanked by high-tech innovators in therapeutic areas such as cancer and inflammatory diseases, areas where older drugs were at best partially efficacious or at worst palliative.

The common ground on which the generic companies and biotechnology companies have done battle with Big Pharma is squarely on the IP front. Generic companies make their living by finding loopholes and weaknesses in the IP estate of branded products that will allow them to be first to market with off-patent products. The biotechnology industry has used its innovative skills in new fields such as molecular biology, genomics, and proteomics to file massive IP estates on novel genes and novel proteins that have potential as either drug targets or therapeutics in their own right. In both cases, these are expensive and sometimes wasteful strategies (e.g., questionable value of massive EST DNA sequence filings in the early days of genomics). Nonetheless, they have served to make Big Pharma more mindful of the importance of managing IP portfolios at the risk of being blindsided by more nimble competitors.

Although existing alliances that big pharmaceutical companies have struck with biotech companies (e.g., Roche-Genentech; Sanofi-Aventis-Regeneron; Pfizer-Neurocrine) may prove to be a growing model that assures Big Pharma significant upside protection should biotech products (small molecules and biologics) continue to be successful and gain further market share, there is no stopping the inevitable loss of huge slices of revenue that will follow patent expiry on a slew of blockbusters in the next five years (see Exhibit 11.3).

EXHIBIT 11.3 Major Drugs Facing Generic Competition by 2011

Drug	*U.S. Patent Expiration*	*Company*	*U.S. Sales 2005*
Zocor	2006	Merck	$4.4
Pravachol	2006	Bristol-Myers Squibb	$1.7
Zoloft	2006	Pfizer	$3.1
Ambien	2006	Sanofi-Aventis	$2.1
Norvasc	2007	Pfizer	$2.6
Zyrtec	2007	UCB	$1.4
Lipitor	2011	Pfizer	$8.4

From Paragon of Virtue to Pariah in the Blink of an Eye

Just a few years ago the stocks of major pharmaceutical companies were seen as a bedrock blue-chip investment for prudent investors. No balanced retirement portfolio was seen as complete or bulletproof without representation from one or more of Merck, GlaxoSmithKline Pfizer, or Eli Lily alongside Exxon, IBM, Coca-Cola, General Electric, Procter & Gamble, and so on. Fueled by consistent double-digit growth for several decades of the latter half of the twentieth century, the pharmaceutical industry was seen as a major success story—delivery of significant new medicines for major diseases, cutting-edge research, and strong returns to investors. Companies such as Merck, Inc. were repeatedly voted by employees as among the best companies to work for in the United States, and their prestigious leaders such as Dr P. Roy Vagelos, frequently topped polls for the most admired CEOs of their era. Fast forward to 2006: We now see a bruised industry with a tarnished reputation, thin pipelines, an addiction to blockbusters and mega-mergers, disillusioned investors, litigious customers, and, at face value, a bleak near-term future.

Reduced Productivity Not Explained by Revenue Shortfall, R&D Spending, or Lagging Innovation in Basic Science

Paradoxically, this reversal of fortune has arisen at a time when revenues from several drugs or drug classes have (by an order of magnitude) quite literally blown past the quite recently established blockbuster high-water mark of $1 billion in peak annual sales. For example, as a class, the cholesterol-lowering statins such as Lipitor and Zocor had U.S. sales approximating $16 billion[1] in 2005 (Pfizer's Lipitor $8.5 billion and Merck's Zocor, $4.4 billion). Worldwide sales of Lipitor alone in 2005 are estimated at $12.2 billion and combined worldwide sales of statins in the order of $20 to $25 billion. Catching up rapidly with blockbuster small-molecule drugs, the most successful biotech biologic drug, erythropoietin, saw 2005 sales approaching the $10 billion mark (combined sales from Amgen, Inc. and Johnson & Johnson: Epogen $3 billion, Procrit $3 billion, and second-generation Aranesp $2.8 billion).

Equally surprising is the fact that the number of annual new drug approvals (new chemical entities [NCEs]) has steadily declined over the last decade from

[1]All data from IMS Health, Inc.

53 new drugs approved in 1996 to 27 in 2003, 24 in 2004 and only 20 in 2005.[2] These numbers would appear to fly in the face of spectacular and quantal leaps in innovation in many areas of biology, chemistry, research tools, and automation. During this decade there were major advances in fundamental human biology, novel chemical synthesis technologies, laboratory automation and data collection, molecular biology of disease, the pinpointing of candidate genes for mono- and polygenic diseases and information technology as a whole. A more detailed list of these major advances is shown in Exhibit 11.4, grouped around the typical steps involved in the discovery, preclinical development, and clinical development of a novel therapeutic.

No Decline in Overall R&D Spending in the Combined Biopharmaceutical Industry

Although mega-mergers over the last two decades may have reduced the total number of Big Pharma companies, on average R&D budgets have increased from 12% to 14% of total sales 20 to 30 years ago to 15% to 20% in 2005. In addition, any reduction in R&D spending through consolidation among the giants has been more than offset by huge cash investment ($350 billion, 1985–2005)[3] and explosive growth in the number of small biotech companies in United States and Europe, many with extensive programs in drug hunting and drug development.

Thus, the apparent productivity of the industry, as measured by new drug approvals and candidate drug pipelines, would seem to have stagnated or indeed declined despite ample revenues to bolster the R&D pipeline. This has occurred just at a time when a wave of innovation, new technologies, and patents should have increased productivity, decreased development times, decreased failure rates, and lowered costs.

What's the Problem—Is There a Solution and Is There a Bright Future?

In the following pages, I will attempt to outline some of the historical events and nearer-term circumstances that have created an industry that is definitely at low ebb in the eyes of the public, regulators, customers, and investors. While several more lean years lie ahead, the thrust of my argument would suggest that the

---

[2]Ibid.

[3]Data from Burrill & Company.

EXHIBIT 11.4 Pivotal Discoveries and Technical Innovations Anticipated to Bridge the Innovation and Productivity Gap

Target Discovery and Target Selection

- Completion of the human genome project—determination of the sequence of the 20,000+ genes or three billion building blocks that constitute the human genetic code.
- Concomitant filing of broad IP on genes, proteins, DNA regulatory regions.
- Advances in human genetics—identification of many candidate disease genes, via positional cloning, single nucleotide polymorphism mapping (SNPs), and most recently haplotype mapping.
- RNAi—discovery of an important regulatory mechanism that regulates the level of gene expression in cells; potentially a wholly new class of therapeutics.
- Advances in biological computing: Bioinformatic tools and LIMS (laboratory information management systems)—integrated computational tools that allow the compilation, rationalization, analysis, interrogation and simplified desktop presentation of enormous biological, chemical, preclinical, and clinical databases.

Target Validation

- Molecular biology tools and reagents that allow rapid cloning and expression of any human gene in a format suitable for functional validation, assay development, and/or drug candidate screening.
- Robust cell culture technologies that allow many normal and aberrant (i.e., cancer) human or animal cells to be studied in isolation—useful for biochemistry, gene function determination, drug screening.
- RNAi—methods that allow gene function determination in isolated cells through a "knock-down" approach.
- Gene transfer technologies that aid in the determination of the function of novel genes in animals, via the creation of "transgenic" or "knock-out" animal models.

Chemical Library Diversity and Automated Drug Screening

- Novel high throughput chemical synthesis technologies—combinatorial chemistry that permits construction of chemical libraries of hugely increased diversity and size.
- Automation—robotic, ultra-high-throughput drug-screening platforms.

Laboratory Instruments and Reagents

- DNA and protein sequencers—new or lower-cost and higher-throughput instruments.
- High resolution nuclear magnetic resonance—fast determination of three-dimensional structures.

EXHIBIT 11.4 (*Continued*)

Laboratory Instruments and Reagents (*cont.*)

- BioCore—real time tool for measuring protein-protein interactions; protein discovery tool, therapeutic antibody selection tool.
- Gene array chips—large-scale microarrays of most of the human genes on a single chip that allows measurement of comparative levels of expression of thousands of genes in normal versus diseased human tissues.

Drug Substance Production—Biologics

- Human monoclonal antibodies—HuMAb and Xenomouse technologies.
- Gene transfer technologies that allow production of important new biologic drugs (proteins and antibodies) in cells, plants, or domestic animals.

Clinical Trial End Points and Companion Diagnostics

- Non-invasive imaging technologies—new or improved computerized axial tomography (CAT), positron emission tomography (PET), magnetic resonance imaging (MRI), functional magnetic resonance imaging (fMRI) etc., that are used for surrogate end points in clinical trials (e.g., MRI used to measure reduction of lesion size in multiple sclerosis patients).
- Pharmacogenomic markers—molecular diagnostics that allow selection of high-probability versus low probability responders (e.g., immunoassay or fluorescence in situ hybridization [FISH] assay for elevated Her-2 for breast cancer responders to Herceptin, epidermal growth factor receptor [EGF-R] mutation for lung cancer responders to Iressa).

now more appropriately named *biopharmaceutical* industry is not in an era of overall decline in innovation and productivity. Rather, this industry is entering a more rational, pragmatic, and impassioned phase following a harrowing 10 to 15 year cycle of dramatic and confusing change. Specifically, I believe that we are emerging from an era that saw an unprecedented rate of discovery of the basic building blocks of life, genes (and thus the proteins they encode), without a concomitant increase in the rate at which we are able to clearly and unambiguously elucidate the function of these genes at the cellular, tissue, and whole-organism level. In the absence of a thorough understanding of their normal function and role in disease, one has to seriously question the rationale for spending billions of dollars developing drug candidates that are directed toward these admittedly novel but poorly validated drug targets.

For much of the twentieth century, the pharmaceutical industry and academic researchers worked on a simple and successful guiding principle: "function begets structure" (i.e., understanding and being able to measure a biochemical process will allow you to isolate and determine the structure of the underlying macromolecular protein players). While the ability to determine the fine molecular structure of proteins has unquestionably greatly refined the drug-hunting and drug-development processes, we should not forget that many of today's drugs were brought successfully through development before structure-determining tools were available. The genomics revolution, however, has stood the "function begets structure" principle on its head by enabling the primary structure of most of the tens of thousand of proteins of the human genome to be determined in a few years and quite independently of any clue to function.

The golden goose of genomics rapidly and exponentially increased our bank of known protein structures from a few hundred in the early 1990s to tens of thousands a decade later. However, the gene hunter's tool kit was pretty much a dead duck at speeding our ability to unambiguously determine or catalog the function of this seemingly endless spigot of innovation. With inevitable hindsight, the rush to exploit structure without understanding function may yet prove to have been the biggest and most costly mistake in pharmaceutical R&D and a root cause of today's thin or broken pipeline.

Caught in the Headlights

The veritable tsunami of genomic and genetic information that emerged in a five-year period in the late twentieth/early twenty-first century, was at once dazzling, seductive, addictive, and, finally, intoxicating to the industry. Much like the tale of the emperor's new clothes, R&D executives saw genomics as a panacea or quick fix for mediocre innovation in their own in-house R&D. The allure of a multitude of new drug targets fueled huge collaborations between Big Pharma and a handful of genomic companies. I would argue that this flood of new information and allied technologies completely overwhelmed the pharmaceutical industry. First, it derailed traditional dogged low-tech, low-throughput approaches and drug-hunting strategies (which had served the industry quite well) in favor of flavor-of-the-month high-tech target discovery methods, ultra-super-high-throughput screening platforms and the like. These new technologies were hyped to the nth degree, despite being unproven and untested as to their likely contribution to the overall drug-development process. Second, experience was forced take a real backseat to new expertise—molecular biologists and bioinformatic whiz kids displaced chemists and pharmacologists as masters of the pharmaceutical universe.

Although the preceding argument may seem rather Luddite, it makes the important point that innovation and adoption of new technologies are not in and of themselves guarantors of successful new products. Rather, careful selection, deployment, integration, and ruthless management of innovation and new technologies within existing process is the key to adding short-term value while building sustainable increases in future productivity.

A major driver of hyperactivity and hyperbole surrounding the human genome project was the fear that there was a rapid and finite IP land grab in process. In the heat of the moment, billions of dollars were diverted from traditional R&D projects and processes to secure a foothold in the new craze of genomics and the huge IP race that accompanied it. Companies that made spectacular bets in genomics include Bayer (collaboration with Millennium Pharmaceutical, Inc.), SmithKlineBeecham (investment in Human Genome Science). It may be too early to judge, but as yet less than a handful of products in clinical development can trace their start in life to large-scale genomics projects.

Bright Future? Unmet Need and Increased Global Demand Will Reshape the Industry

While today's declining balance sheets and perceptions of the pharmaceutical industry are what they are, the combined pharmaceutical industry has enormous cash reserves, extraordinary free cash flow, highly productive research, and ever sharper tools to discover, develop, and commercialize groundbreaking new medicines. The IP race for a piece of the genome is essentially over, although brush fires around the IP residing in the more extensive human proteome are likely to flare up as tools to decipher the proteome come of age.

A more orderly and pragmatic analysis of the spoils of the human genome projects will eventually deliver breakthrough medicines, but much sifting has still to be done to separate the wheat from the chaff. Once the gems are found, it is likely that they will have multiple owners who claim IP. Sorting out who really owns what may be one of the next great challenges to the industry. Overall, there will be much greater emphasis on targeted and/or personalized medicines. Significantly driven by the Food and Drug Administration (FDA), this will demand the parallel development of biomarkers for diagnosis and prognosis of disease. There will also be a push to develop objective surrogate biomarkers in order to identify responders in clinical development and possibly in postmarketing phase IV studies.

Even within existing markets there is huge unmet need and opportunity to find better medicines for degenerative diseases that become more prevalent in the elderly, even as historical killer diseases such as heart disease and cancer are tamed or abated. At the other end of the spectrum, the prevalence of poorly treated metabolic diseases such as diabetes and obesity is increasing at alarming proportions, especially in the young. Left untreated, these diseases dramatically increase the risk of cardiovascular disease, cancer, and so on, as well as the overall quality of life and life expectancy of affected individuals. Taken together, these needs will continue to spur innovation in and beyond traditional pills or biologics. New areas such RNA interference and stem cells remain in the distance, but are likely to enter clinical development and possibly the market within five to ten years.

Origins of the Industry Reveal Some Insights into the Broken Pipeline Problem

Blossoming of Synthetic Organic Chemistry Creates the Pharmaceutical Industry

The ethical drug industry as we know it today can trace many of its roots to two major fields of innovative research in chemistry and biology that emerged in the late nineteenth and early part of the twentieth century:

- Synthetic organic chemistry—a field built around a realization of the immense diversity of distinct small molecules that can be synthesized in a laboratory by exploiting the chemical flexibility of the humble carbon atom as a core building block
- Biochemistry—a field that led to the discovery of enzymes (specific class of proteins) as the key catalysts of biochemical process that underlie many biological functions, normal and abnormal

The pharmaceutical industry of the early and mid twentieth century, especially in Europe—(e.g., Bayer, CIBA, Geigy, Sandoz, Merck AG) arose partly as an offshoot of the fine chemicals industry, where emerging drug companies initially matched their innovative and proprietary skills in synthetic medicinal chemistry with rapid advances in the biological and medical sciences; advances that were largely a product of academic research. Although biology, physiology, and pharmacology were acknowledged as important contributing disciplines, this was an industry in which chemistry and chemists were definitely "king."

Low-Hanging Fruit and Limited Competition

Facing an uncluttered product landscape, little global competition, a modestly onerous regulatory environment, and revenues from their core chemicals business to underwrite early forays into pharmaceuticals, the industry flourished first at a regional level and later at international and global levels. The pace of new research information was such that a diligent scientist could well keep up with advances not only in his own field but also in the broader fields of chemistry and biology. In many cases the structure of drug targets was unknown, and thus the proprietary nature and patent protection of early products was fairly circumscribed around the chemical composition of the new drug itself. State-of-the-art medicinal chemistry did not permit easy synthesis of large numbers of closely related chemical series, thus IP estates were relatively confined.

The more regional nature of the pharmaceutical industry of the mid twentieth century and the limited IP estate constructed around marketed products made it possible for rather closely related chemical compounds from different companies to successfully coexist on the market. This was an era in which even the third or fourth "me too" drug to get to market could garnish a major share of the regional if not the international market. Two other factors that contributed to the sustained profitability of the big pharmaceutical companies of that period were (1) patent protection was for 17 years *after* the key patent issued (now 20 years from date of filing), and (2) prior to the early 1980s, there was no significant generic industry nipping at the heels of the drug hunter/initial developer companies.

Peaks Scaled but Still in the Foothills

Antibiotics, vaccines and exceptionally effective medicines for cardiovascular disease (angiotensin-converting enzyme [ACE] inhibitors, beta-blockers, statins) are among the great success stories of the twentieth-century pharmaceutical industry. Nonetheless, there remains an enormous unmet need for medicines for many diseases such as cancer, neurodegenerative diseases and stroke, psychiatric disorders, metabolic disorders such as diabetes and obesity, autoimmune/inflammatory disease, and degenerative disease of bone and other tissues. Furthermore, only a small fraction of the world's population has access to the most effective medicines of today, far less the broader pharmacopeia and the newly emerging but very costly biologics, such as the proteins Epogen, Neupogen, and Rebif, and the antibodies Reopro, Rituxan, Herceptin, and the like. Thus, without doubt, unmet clinical need and a growing world marketplace will remain as very positive drivers for the twenty-first-century biopharmaceutical industry.

Taken together, one can argue that the pharmaceutical industry faces a very different and much tougher landscape today than it did two to three decades ago. The bar has been significantly raised in many of the parameters that encompass the discovery, development, approval, safety profile, expected efficacy, patent protection, and global marketing of a new pharmaceutical product. Despite these new and onerous complexities, and others such as pricing and potential product liability, there are many reasons to believe that the industry as a whole is not in decline but is indeed at an exciting crossroads.

Passing this crossroads successfully, however, will reshape the industry away from its addiction to blockbusters and mega-mergers. Biopharmaceutical companies of the future will have narrower therapeutic focus and will put more concentrated effort into being master of a smaller universe, as opposed to having aspirations to be a jack-of-all-trades.

Failure to Invest in Preventative Maintenance and Competitive Insurance

Managing any large organization that employees ten of thousands of employees is a daunting task. Nonetheless, big pharmaceutical companies have especially poor reputations in the deployment of modern management techniques as compared to other industry behemoths such as General Electric or IBM. Delivery of double-digit growth for much of the second-half of the twentieth century was probably sufficient to keep critics at bay. This growth was initially achieved by plucking low-hanging fruit in fields where no drugs existed and later by using mountains of cash to bring about the mergers that created today's behemoths. Such growth may ultimately be unsustainable, but failing to innovate and grasp new trends is undoubtedly one of the causes of the current broken-pipeline perception.

In the many consumer products industries, failing to produce products that have receptive markets shows up very rapidly on the company's balance sheet. Thus, such companies are constantly aware that they must innovate or perish. With unusually long product development times and very high technical and financial barriers to entry, a few blockbuster products can carry a pharmaceutical company for many years. This kind of success often breeds complacency, loss of vision, and a "what can't be done today will be done tomorrow" attitude.

Flushed with success in the latter half of the twentieth century, big pharmaceutical companies developed well-deserved reputations for being hierarchical, top heavy, slow to make decision, slow to embrace new technologies, and slow to accept and realize the scope of new competitors. Several of the most successful companies, such as Merck, were also imbued with a very strong "not invented here" syndrome, shunning the possibility of in-licensing golden opportunities from smaller companies that lacked the muscle to take products to market.

Taken together, lack of internal preventative maintenance and complacency toward competitive threats (discussed later) have been major factors in the broken-pipeline syndrome.

Winds of Change: New Technologies, New Innovators, and a New Product Class

In the closing decades of the twentieth century, the previously chemistry-driven industry began to be turned on its head as upstart "biotechnology" companies entered the fray, using new innovations and proprietary techniques in the new fields of molecular biology—gene splicing, genomics, genetics, and so on—that allowed the manufacture of very complex macromolecules (e.g., insulin, growth hormone, blood-clotting factors) that had previously been known as important therapeutics but were obtainable only through isolation from human cadavers of other mammalian tissues (e.g., pig insulin).

While the bulk of the approximate $300 billion gross revenues of today's biopharmaceutical industry are still derived from the sales of orally active "pills," the sales of injectable biologics (proteins, antibodies, etc.) now account for 15% to 20% of these sales and are growing rapidly. In addition, and almost incomprehensible to many, two of these biotech upstarts, Amgen, Inc. and Genentech, Inc. are now firmly in the top ten companies of the industry based on market capitalization, having left Merck, once the darling of the industry, in their collective wake.

Elements of a "Perfect Storm"

- Paradigm shift in drug target discovery
- Irrational exuberance around genomics
- Mega-mergers
- Massive product liability settlements
- Birth of new competitors—generics and biotech companies

Innovation at Breakneck Speed Creates Confusion and Fear of Missing the IP Boat

To understand the recent ups and downs of the pharmaceutical industry, one needs to look not only at the pace of innovation in biomedical science as a whole, the raw material that drives innovation in the industry, but also how these advances sometimes emerge in reasonable synchrony in multiple fields and at other times advances are made at a noticeably greater pace in one field as compared to others.

Rarely do significant advances in drug development arise from a single "Eureka" discovery. Rather, they mostly emerge only after painstakingly piecing together a multitude of small innovative increments in a wide array of fields. These scientific fields include human biology, human pathology and pathophysiology, pharmacology, biochemistry, genetics, genomics, chemistry, manufacturing, diagnostics, drug formulation, drug delivery devices, laboratory automation, and information technologies. The process is very analogous to piecing together many parts of a complex multidimensional jigsaw puzzle, where the picture is often quite obscure until the last piece is firmly in place.

Many chronic diseases initiate from small and innocuous imbalances in biochemical process. Over time, these small imbalances chip away at the body's self-correcting mechanisms and eventually manifest as recognizable symptoms such as pain, shortness of breath, headaches, dizziness, fatigue, and so on. A tried-and-true principle of the classical drug hunter was to identify the culprit protein or gene that initiates and drives the biochemical imbalance and then to find a small molecule that would interact with the culprit to either "apply the brakes" or hit the "accelerator" to restore normal balance. During much of the twentieth century, identifying the culprits was a slow process, but declaration of guilt was declared only when there was a high degree of certainty around the biochemical, cellular, tissue, and whole animal and human "evidence." During this era, the rate of advances in synthetic organic chemistry and advances in identifying novel drug targets were certainly not identical, but for the most part over several decades were well matched.

As a direct result of the human genome project, we have been able to corral most if not all of the *possible* disease-inducing "suspects" in a way that allows them to be interrogated for clues of disease involvement. The recent development of highly automated small-molecule diversity synthesis (combinatorial chemistry) and ultra-high-throughput assays/screens and the like has greatly reduced the time it takes to go from "target" identification to a drug candidate lead. Whereas these major advances have greatly expanded the palette of the drug hunters, they have also led to data overload and confusion as to what are the reliable criteria of a well-*validated* drug target. While the bench scientist's view of a valid drug target is probably compelling molecular biology data showing a gain or loss of function in disease, the CEO's view is more likely to be one with over $1 billion in sales!

Gusher for Patent Attorneys—Who Owns What and Can I Get a Piece of It?

Just as completion of the human genome project has given the scientist an exciting and unprecedented new tool kit to aid fundamental research into basic biology and medicine, it has brought daunting new challenges, rich pickings, and much uncertainty to the world of intellectual property.

In the absence of any precedent, the gusher of gene patents that was likely to arise from early genomics companies was a magnet that attracted enormous capital investment. Corporate and venture capitalists literally fell over themselves to fund these companies. In some cases, Big Pharma shelled out tens of millions of dollars in database subscriptions to either Incyte Genomics or Celera Genomics for access to raw genomic data and the potential patent rights to the underlying discoveries. In other cases, Big Pharma embarked on mega-dollar collaborative deals with biotechnology companies, paying up to $500 million for the privilege (Bayer-Millennium Pharmaceuticals). The fairly simple and obvious rationale for paying these huge sums was that decoding the human genome was indeed a one-time event in the history of science and a fierce race for glory, not only between companies but also between academia and industry. If indeed novel genes were patentable, the human genome land grab would prove to be a rich but short-lived Klondike. Thus, fear of losing out proved to be a major driver for inking mega deals. While spectator awe surrounding the era has receded, fallout from the "genomics dust-cloud" has not entirely settled, especially in the area of IP.

As yet it remains to be tested in the courts just exactly what is patentable and what is not patentable of the many discoveries that emerged from the human genome project. It is clear that the cost of filing and prosecuting gene patents (composition, utility, etc.) has run to many billions of dollars. For the handful of biotechnology companies that had major efforts in genome sequencing (i.e., Incyte, Human Genome Science, Celera, Millennium, Hyseq), patent costs ultimately became such an overwhelming budget burden that many initial filings were abandoned. Just as companies such as the Medicines Company have attempted to make a business out of "retreading" compounds from others that have failed in clinical development, there may be significant opportunities to build value around IP from genomic companies that are literally sitting on the shelf.

Irrational Exuberance—High Cost, Low Quality

Ironically, it could be argued for many companies that the only short-term outcome of the molecular biology revolution was to add very significant additional upstream costs to the earliest part of the drug discovery process, identification of potential targets. As yet, the power of genomics and genetics have made little impact on reducing costs of the more expensive downstream aspects of drug development (preclinical pharmacology, clinical trials, manufacturing, regulatory issues etc.). Implicit in the haste to jump feet first into genomics was the rather misguided expectation that many of the newly discovered genes would be associated with disease processes and thus make excellent targets for new drugs. I firmly hold that a significant cause of the decline in approval of NCEs in the past five years is a direct result of irrational exuberance on the part of R&D chiefs who jumped too far, too fast, with big checkbooks, into the genomics revolution. As applied to Big Pharma, this entailed being mightily led astray by the weak assumption that having all the human genome at your fingertips would miraculously speed the drug discovery and development process and create brimming pipelines. It is fair to say that significant direct value from genomics has already been created and some of the genes discovered in this era are emerging to be ideal drug targets. However, the much ballyhooed promise of swiftly cutting drug development times and costs in half is unlikely to materialize,

Mega-Mergers—Short-Term Fix That Derails Innovation and Productivity

The frenetic pace of new drug target discovery driven by genomics happened to coincide with one of those sporadic periods of major industry consolidation, a bout of mega-mergers that has given rise to today's big pharmaceutical companies (e.g., Glaxo + Wellcome → GW + SmithKlineBeecham → GSK and Sandoz + CIBA-Geigy → Novartis, and the most recent Sanofi + Aventis [$61 billion]).

Such mega-mergers are mostly driven from the boardroom with the laser-sharp objective of a quick fix to the bottom line while papering over the cracks in thin pipelines. This bottom-line massaging, arguably often achieved by savings on consolidated R&D costs as much as by top-line growth, may feed an external perception of a successful merger. Certainly, merging two enormous companies, particularly those with competing drugs, may result in removal of rival drugs and remove duplication of costs in R&D and sales and marketing. That makes the industry seem more efficient in the eyes of its investors, and merged companies do end up with at least a temporary increase in market share. Most analysis would indicate that mega-mergers do not increase innovation or bring prolonged improvement to the pipeline.

Regardless of the economics, you only have to live in proximity to one such mega-merger to understand the havoc and uncertainty that is created in the trenches during the inevitable management fallout and massive reorganization that follows the closing of such deals. There is no easy way to measure the loss of productivity that is created by such mergers, but it is fair to say that rebuilding, realigning, and galvanizing a new R&D team is a process measured in years rather than months.

Product Liability—Lighting Strikes That Kill the Golden Goose

Ultimately, patient safety is the most important factor in developing any pharmaceutical product, and all major countries have regulatory authorities such as the Food and Drug Administration (FDA) whose major remit is to ensure that patient safety is the paramount concern in drug testing, drug approval, and drug marketing. Nonetheless, there is no such thing as a risk- or side effect–free pharmaceutical, and approval remains very much a process of thorough evaluation of the risk-benefit profile to patients. This is nowhere more evident than in the case of certain classes of cancer therapeutics, where many of the effective drugs are essentially metabolic poisons that achieve their effect by being marginally more toxic to tumor cells than to normal cells. Given that many late-stage cancers are inevitably and often quickly fatal, the acceptable risk side of the equation is clearly much greater than with most other diseases. Furthermore, clear demonstration of efficacy in a relatively small clinical trial is usually acceptable for accelerated review and approval of new cancer drugs.

Outside of cancer, the late-stage clinical development process, Phase III pivotal trials, involves testing the drug in many hundred if not several thousand patients. Such trials have fixed goals to establish greater statistical confidence in preliminary efficacy seen in earlier smaller trials, and to show an acceptable safety profile in a broader group of subjects. Obviously, adverse events that may only occur with frequencies of 1 per 1,000 or 1 per 10,000 or greater, or occur only after continuous long-term treatment, will not show up in such trials. Many of today's blockbuster drugs end up being prescribed chronically to millions of patients. Thus, disaster may still lurk for apparently safe drugs as their use extends to larger and more diverse patient groups than could possibly be tested in a preapproval clinical trial.

Such has been the case for Bayer's statin or cholesterol-lowering drug Baycol, American Home Products' (now Wyeth) weight loss drugs, Pondimin (fenfluramine) and Redux (dexfenfluramine), and most recently Merck's COX-2 anti-inflammatory pain killer Vioxx.

Starting with Redux (one of the components of the popular Fen-Phen duo) in 1997, Baycol in 2001, and Vioxx in 2005, all three drugs were hastily pulled from the market following reports of fatal or life-threatening adverse effects. Baycol use was attributed to be the cause of more than 100 deaths and a much larger number of cases of a muscle-wasting disorder, rhabdomyolysis. Pondimin and Redux use have been closely implicated in heart valve disease, while chronic exposure to Vioxx has been purported to greatly increase patients' risk of death from heart attacks.

Due to the ongoing nature of litigation with all three of these drugs, there is no hard data on the final cost to the respective companies, but in the cases of Bayer and Wyeth, this is already counted in billions of dollars, and the thousands of Vioxx liability lawsuits pending against Merck are likely to push costs in a similar direction. Not diminishing sympathy for any real damage caused to patients, the greatest damage to each of the companies has been the immediate loss of major revenues and a very visible tarring of their image. The withdrawal of Vioxx instantly removed $2.5 billion in sales for Merck, while removal of Baycol resulted in a loss of Bayer's fastest-growing drug and much needed blockbuster.

While many predicted the demise of Bayer as result of the Baycol debacle, it has survived as a leaner, independent company and recently improved chances of further recovery through a merger with Merck AG of Germany. Ironically, while Bayer lost a veritable cash cow in Baycol, there was only the briefest downward blip in overall prescriptions of other statins in 2001. Clearly, patients and physicians continue to believe that the benefit of reducing coronary heart disease still outweighs the risk of a rare muscle disorder.

New Kids on the Block—Generics and Biotech

Once cosseted by the regional nature of their businesses, few major competitors, and relatively limitless potential in terms of market opportunity and need, the pharmaceutical industry has been increasingly buffeted since the early 1980s by two new classes of competitors: the generics industry and the biotechnology industry. The generics industry has created enormous pressure on how big pharmaceutical companies defend sales of their existing products. On the other hand, the fledgling biotechnology industry has brought innovation and cut-throat competition at every stage of the drug-hunting process and furthermore established a whole new class of drugs: recombinant biologics.

Generics—Eroding a Fair Return on Investment or a Spur to Innovation in R&D and Patent Strategies?

While born out of the U.S. government's concerns and actions to review the safety and efficacy of many "old" medicines brought to the market prior to 1962, the generics industry as we know it today came of age largely as a result of the Drug Price Competition and Patent Restoration Act of 1984—commonly referred to as the Hatch-Waxman Act.

There is still an endless debate about the pros and cons of opening up the branded pharmaceutical industry to generic manufacturers. Big Pharma would argue that the generic companies are little more than parasites or bottom feeders who invest nothing in R&D and thus have no right to benefit from the risk and time invested in the development and approval of a new drug, now approaching $1 billion and eight to ten years. With patent protection now covering 20 years from initial filing date, generic companies (as well as the public and third-party payers) would argue that ten to twelve years of market exclusivity post launch (possibly more via court-mediated extensions) is more than adequate to recoup R&D costs, especially of a blockbuster. With current U.S. sales of Lipitor around $8.4 billion (2005), it is not hard to see everybody's point of view! The generic industry thus sees or justifies itself as being essential and healthy competition that ensures (post patent expiry) that effective drugs are made available at a fraction of the branded cost to a much broader and needier public. Suffice to say that the generics industry is here to stay, with U.S. sales estimated around $20 billion in 2005.

It is hard to find numbers that adequately address the issue of whether or not the generics industry has had a meaningful impact on innovation in R&D, but it is interesting to note that Big Pharma's R&D spending, as a percentage of sales, has crept up from low teens to high teens in the last 20 years, pretty much in parallel with the emergence and growth of generics. Nonetheless, it is obvious that the generics industry has spurred the branded industry to pay much more attention to patent strategies and product life cycle management. In this vein, the pharmaceutical industry has certainly poured large numbers of R&D dollars into extending patent life of major drugs through approaches as simple as reformulation of an active drug to achieve less frequent dosing. This usually has the benefit of greater patient compliance. While once fixated on the orally active pill as the only way to deliver a medicine, Big Pharma has been forced to accept that other drug-delivery strategies, largely pioneered by small start-up companies (e.g., Alkermes, Nektar, Transform) are indeed effective and can provide significant patient benefit (e.g., lower steady-state doses giving better safety-efficacy profile) and improved or more targeted delivery strategies (patches, inhalation, depot) that proved better pharmacology than oral dosing.

Away from the lab, Big Pharma has learned how to use legal delaying tactics to extend the period of market exclusivity. By exploiting loopholes in the 1984 Hatch-Waxman legislation, the expiring patentee can initiate infringement litigation that automatically triggers a 30-month stay. For a drug such as Lipitor, this stay has a value of tens of billions of dollars to Pfizer. It has indeed been possible to get multiple 30-month patent extensions, but new legislation will close this loophole.[4]

Biotechs—The Upstarts Who Dared

The generics industry has had a huge impact on how big pharmaceutical companies develop and execute patent strategies to defend the market position and, where possible, to extend the market life of successful existing products. The biotech industry, in contrast, has emerged as a full-blown competitor in the most lucrative end of the business, novel branded drugs for largely unmet clinical need.

In the early days of biotechnology, the great philosophical divide between classical pharmaceutical companies and the newly emerging industry was all about size—molecular size. Driven by their medicinal chemistry expertise and a firm belief that patients would not tolerate drugs that are not orally active pills, Big Pharma (with the notable exception of Eli Lily) shunned the notion of developing biologics (protein- and, more recently, antibody-based therapeutics) that would require injections or infusions. That distinction has all but gone as the biotech industry has brought important new biologic medicines to the market and racked up sales that reached $70 billion in 2005. Big Pharma has scrambled in the past five years to deal with their previous lack of vision and to stem the erosion of future market share. This is especially true in diseases such as anemia, neutropenia, cancer, and inflammatory conditions such as rheumatoid arthritis where several biologics have already reached blockbuster status. Blockbuster natural proteins include Epogen, Neupogen (Amgen), Rebif

[4]Goldberg, L.A., and Farid, N. "The FDA's Generic 'Final Rule'." *Modern Drug Discovery*, January 2004.

(Serono), and Betaseron (Biogen-IDEC), and antibody or engineered protein blockbusters include Reopro (Centocor-J&J), and Herceptin (Genentech-Roche) Enbrel (Amgen).

As mentioned earlier, the biotechnology industry pioneered by Genentech arose from the first technology that allowed "gene splicing." This technology confers the ability to isolate and purify specific strands of DNA and then stitch them together to create "artificial" human genes. Further innovations allowed these isolated human gene sequences to be recombined, or inserted back into the genome of immortalized mammalian. Such cells that can be cultured indefinitely in large fermentation vats in the laboratory. Following selection, the modified cells become a mini-factory that produces large amounts of a desired protein that corresponds to the human gene introduced into the cells—hence the term *recombinant* proteins.

Armed with this new technology, the first product goal in the cross-hairs of the industry was to introduce a recombinant version of a number of well-characterized human therapeutics, such as insulin, growth hormone, and blood-clotting factors. Hitherto these biologics had been available only by isolation and purification from animal (pig for insulin) or human cadaver tissue or human blood products. Manipulating human genes was initially met with considerable resistance and public trepidation. However, other events quickly made it obvious that having methods to tightly control the production of human therapeutic proteins in contained environments with much more reliable quality control and quality assurance was greatly preferable to harvesting tissue and blood from questionable sources. The unwitting infection of many patients with HIV/AIDS in the late 1980s following treatment with proteins isolated from human donor blood plasma was a big driver to the unreserved acceptance of recombinant production of biologics. Furthermore, the cloning of human genes makes it possible to produce almost any human protein in large quantities; prior to this, all insulin for diabetic use was of porcine or bovine origin. While such animal proteins do show biologic activity in man, minor differences between the structure of animal proteins and those of man are enough to produce antibodies in man. Such antibodies can have the potential to block the desired therapeutic effect.

Following moderate commercial success by providing human versions of already known therapeutic proteins such as insulin and growth hormone, the biotech industry has greatly advanced by reaching into almost all therapeutic areas—in some cases remaining focused on entirely novel developing biologics (Amgen, Genentech, Biogen, Serono, Genzyme), in others using innovations in the biotechnology field (molecular biology, genomics, genetics, etc.) to form specialty small-molecule companies (Gilead, Vertex).

High-Stakes IP Legal Battles Sharpen the Mind

Viewed from their lofty perches today, one should not forget that Amgen and Genentech did not get there without tough IP and financial challenges even as they continued to innovate, develop special know-how, and build powerful IP estates along the way.

In a very high-stakes Texas Hold 'Em winner-takes-all scenario, Amgen's legendary patent battle with Genetics Institute (GI) over who had the rights to market erythropoietin was one of the most costly, acrimonious, and protracted lawsuits in the industry. Amgen's win resulted in billions in spoils, while GI's loss led to its eventual demise via acquisition. Facing financial collapse in its early days, however, Amgen was not quite so fortunate, as it was forced to sell certain marketing rights of its about-to-be-wonder-drug Epogen, to Johnson & Johnson for a few million dollars. Now a blockbuster under the J&J brand name Procrit, this surely was the biotech product steal of the century with a return on investment (ROI) of many thousand-fold.

Recasting the Game for an Even Bigger Win

From its earliest days, Genentech espoused a vibrant, freewheeling culture in which science would drive business. Staffed by the brightest in the emerging fields of molecular biology, the early Genentech made great contributions to basic science across many fields, including cardiovascular disease, metabolism, neuroscience, and immunology. From a commercial perspective, however, Genentech's early stable of biologics that included growth hormone, tissue plasminogen activator, and pulmozyme were only moderately successful. In what might someday be regarded as one of the boldest and highest-risk refocusing strategies in the biotech industry, Genentech underwent a major restructuring around 2000, less than 20 years into its history. This involved ditching or outlicensing its neuroscience, cardiovascular, and metabolic disease expertise to focus almost all of its efforts on developing a franchise in cancer, with a specialty in antibodies and engineered proteins.

This strategy has already yielded two major therapeutics, the already blockbuster Herceptin and the soon-to-be blockbuster Avastin. The latter not only exploits very fundamental vascular biology carried out by Genentech in the 1990s that led to the discovery of the vascular endothelial growth factor (VEGF) family of endothelial cell growth factors, but also incorporates in-house proprietary protein engineering technology (and broad patents). Thus, through sharpened disease focus, Genentech was able to recognize major therapeutic utility and a blockbuster drug by bringing together the technology, patent estates, and know-how that resulted from earlier work that was not directly related to cancer.

The preceding anecdotes serve simply as examples of how innovation combined with endurance, entrepreneurship, and determination can create a whole new industry within a couple of decades. Not bad for an industry where the downstream barriers to entry are both intellectually daunting and financially mind-boggling.

Big Pharma Fights Back (or Not): Exploiting Innovation and IP Developed by Others

While it is easy to lambaste Big Pharma for its complacency in the face of the blossoming biotechnology industry, several of the majors, especially Roche, have won handsomely, not by trying to compete as late starters to the game, but by strategic investments in the front runners. By acquiring marketing rights to sell Genentech's products in Europe and through their major stake in Genentech itself, Roche is one of the biggest beneficiaries of the recent success of antibodies as therapeutics.

Beyond strategic investment in Genentech, Roche is also poised to take on biotech at is own game. In the first real competition to Amgen's highly successful anemia drug, Epogen, Roche is in late-stage trials with the synthetic molecule CERA (continuous erythropoietin receptor activator). Epogen may also be exposed to further competition in the form of a synthetic peptide mimetic of erythropoietin, Hematide, under development by Affymax.

Failing to Exploit Technical Advantage

Failure to exploit strategic advantages also seems evident among some of the early players in the biologics field. Lily and NovoNordisk have dominated the insulin market for decades, making Lily one of the rare Big Pharmas to embrace small-molecule and big-molecule cultures. Despite the enviable downstream infrastructure to manufacture biologics, an immediate barrier to entry for many, neither company seems to have fully exploited this know-how and technical advantage to the fullest.

Although Lily has invested in in-house and external collaborations in biologics, its only biologic product beyond recombinant insulin is Xigris (activated protein C). Despite being the first drug approved for sepsis, four years after launch, worldwide sales of Xigris in 2005 were only $200 million. Through its investment and long-term control of Zymogenetics, NovoNordisk was an early mover in genomics as one of the earliest subscribers to Inycte's genomic data machine. As yet this has not yielded any significant products, nor have products been acquired by in-licensing or acquisition. With the exception of launching factor Factor VII, NovoNordisk has remained close to its roots in diabetes but has seen little organic growth of its business.

Do Recent Trends Predict Successful Stenting of the Pipeline?

Recent Cancer Success Indicates Innovation Is Alive and Well

Despite the often misguided and ill-informed external perception of a profit-before-all industry, especially when litigation opportunities appear ripe, the biopharmaceutical industry has much to be proud of in recent years. This is particularly true in areas such as cancer.

Small-molecule drugs such as Gleevec (Novartis) and Velcade (Millennium) and antibody drugs such as Herceptin (Genentech-Roche), and Erbitux (Immclone-BMS) have begun to make inroads into changing the face of cancer from a disease you used to "die of" to a disease that you "may die with." For each of these drugs there is a fascinating story surrounding the trials and tribulations of bringing these new medicines through the tortuous path from an idea on the back of napkin to the clinical and commercial reality of an effective therapeutic. Although still modest in some cases, these drugs literally save and extend patients lives. With our collective very short attention spans, it is all too easy to fail to fully appreciate that these are great feats of ingenuity and creativity. Each drug required a decade or more of development, with minefields of concept failure, technical failure and cash constraints at every turn. It goes without saying that in the absence of a strong patent estate on the composition of matter, method of treatment, method of production and manufacturing, and the like, none of these products would have seen the light of day.

These are true tales of amazing innovation reflecting the sum of unstinting commitment, driving personal ambition, effective academia-industry collaborations, and plain old blood, sweat, and tears. Gleevec represents the first drug for cancer that was precisely tailored to block a tumor-specific enzyme, BRC-ABL kinase, derived from a chromosomal aberration found commonly in patients with chronic myeloid leukemia; Velcade is the first drug to target a compartment of each living cell that functions as a "garbage disposal" unit—the proteasome—a pathway barely recognized, far less understood in the early

1990s. Herceptin and Erbitux are the first realization of the 25+-year-old dream of using antibodies as "magic bullets" to target cancer cells.

Antibodies as Drugs—If at First You Don't Succeed . . .

Often dismissed by Big Pharma "as too big to be pills, too difficult to make, too costly to develop, and unlikely to work," antibodies as therapeutics have had a rough ride. Early clinical trials using antibodies derived from mouse antibody sequences were highly disappointing failures and gave some justification to Big Pharma's skepticism. However, it was quickly understood that the antibodies as drug concept was not flawed, only that mouse derived antibodies are themselves immunogenic and thus not suitable for human treatment.

Far from throwing in the towel, these initial failures spurred remarkable innovation that resulted first in the ability to make chimeric antibodies where just tiny pieces of the "business end" of the mouse antibody is stitched into the backbone of a human antibody. This required advances in immunology, molecular biology, and protein engineering. Most of the currently approved therapeutic antibodies are such chimerics. The next generation of antibody products will soon emerge from technology that allows the direct derivation and manufacture of fully human antibodies. This major advance resulted from the ingenious creation of genetically manipulated strains of mice (Abgenix, Medarex) in which a large part of the mouse immune system genes have been replaced by the equivalent human genes.

Building IP estates around antibodies and their targets is a major growth industry for today's patent attorneys. Complex and overlapping claims to genomically discovered antibody targets is sure to be a major source of future litigation as biopharmaceutical products derived from these claims reach the market. Ironically, one of the potentially biggest winners in the antibodies-as-drugs stakes defaulted at the start gate. Although recognized very early by the scientific community in the form of a Nobel Prize, the United Kingdom's Medical Research Council with its ivory tower wisdom failed to apply for broad patent coverage on groundbreaking work of Kohler and Millstein in the field of monoclonal antibodies. This is now a classic tale of creativity and innovation in the laboratory not being matched by vision and commercial foresight in the back room.

The recent success in finally bringing antibodies to the market as effective therapeutics in cancer and inflammation has also heralded a glimpse of how the biopharmaceutical industry may evolve in the future through Big Pharma–biotech partnerships. Although achieved through quite different business structures, both Herceptin and Erbitux were finally brought to market following major investment from Big Pharma in the respective early developers—Genentech in the case of Roche and Immclone in the case of BMS.

New Cutting Edge but Lots of Room for Improvement

While not diminishing the near-term patient benefit of the new cancer drugs mentioned above, each has limitations in terms of absolute efficacy, safety margin, and cost. Together, these limitations are already driving the need for further innovation. In the case of Herceptin, Genentech is already well advanced with clinical development of second- and third-generation products that take advantage of both fully human antibody technology and protein engineering tricks that allow the development of antibodies with greater ability to kill tumor cells. In a sign of how much more proactive some big pharmaceutical companies have become toward competitive threats, Roche recently bought out Swiss start-up Glycart for $250 million. A fledgling Swiss company, Glycart was years away from entering any products into clinical development and had little cash but appeared to be the owner of what may become mission-critical IP in the area of modifying sugar residues on antibodies. This technology may prove to be a strong buttress to the commercial success of several third-generation cancer antibodies in the Roche-Genentech stable.

None of the four drugs, Gleevec, Velcade, Herceptin, and Erbitux, could be exactly described as cheap, with the two antibody drugs being priced in the typical range of biologoics (i.e., many thousands of dollars per course of treatment). The near prohibitive cost of Herceptin, for example, has recently created some high-profile patient–third-party payer battles in the United Kingdom. Several local health authorities have denied filling prescriptions for breast cancer patients, arguing on poor cost-benefit grounds.

The Future: Personalized Medicine, Integrated Innovation, and Global Health

Paraphrasing a recent quote of Steve Burrill (Burrill & Co.), the future of the biopharmaceutical industry lies in the three "P"s: *prevention*, *prediction*, and *personalization*.

If there is one thing we can be sure of in the biopharmaceutical industry, it is simply that the days of the "one-size-fits-all" drug are over. While we may be a long way from the idealized vision of personalized medicine, we are perhaps further along that path than is generally recognized. Many of the tools to make it fully possible are already in place, and a surprising number of low-tech biomarkers are already embedded in clinical decisions.

Pressure from outside the industry will be a major driver to develop better markers to diagnose disease, predict outcome to treatment, and monitor response to treatment.

Some of the obvious benefits and regulatory and market forces that will drive the introduction of targeted or patient-specific treatments are listed in Exhibit 11.5.

Whether it be termed *personalized medicine*, *pharmacogenonics* or *targeted therapeutics*, we already have some examples of reducing disease risk or selecting likely responders using simple blood tests or tissue biopsies. On the widely used scale, lipid panel diagnostics, especially low-density lipoprotein (LDL) cholesterol and LDL/HDL (high-density lipoprotein) ratios are used to

EXHIBIT 11.5 Benefits and Forces That Will Accelerate Biomarker Discovery and Implementation

Patients

- Avoid risks of exposure to drugs with no benefit.
- Increase demand (and willingness to pay) for effective medicines.
- Avoid false expectations of benefit.
- Avoid costs of drugs that will of little benefit.

FDA

- Will mandate use in trials to enrich for responders.
- Will seek use of companion diagnostic as part of new drug approvals.
- Will eventually seek use in postmarketing pharmacovigilance.
- Will up the bar for safety/efficacy risk-benefit profile for drug approvals.

Payers

- Reduce huge cost of paying for high-percentage nonresponders.
- Will seek biomarker data as rationale for reimbursement.

Companies

- Reduce cost of clinical trials by enriching for responders.
- Allow better selection primary and secondary end points in clinical trials.
- Support premium pricing.
- IP around tandem diagnostic-therapeutic products—"theranostics."

determine both therapeutic and prophylactic decisions in the prescribing of statins. In a more narrow field, and perhaps the first FDA-mandated test to be part of a drug approval, prescription of Herceptin in breast cancer is restricted to patients with a high score in the Her-2 assay.

In itself, personalized medicine is simply an objective; getting there will require major innovation not just in R&D but also in how companies operate. Just as the one-size-fits-all drug will soon be a thing of the past, it is hard to see how a one-company-does-all model will survive indefinitely. Reflecting limitations in knowledge that have hampered full exploitation of the potential bounty of the human genome project, many of the issues in Exhibit 12.6. will require focused innovation before personalized medicine will become a reality.

Global Health Issues

Widespread antibiotic resistance, the risk of pandemic diseases such as bird flu and the ever present threat of bioterrorism will also force broader public policy decisions that should positively affect the biopharmaceutical industry. Future success in these areas will not only bring new commercial opportunities, but will be a major driver in restoring the industry's tarnished image.

New Therapeutic Modalities—Soon to Be in the Spotlight

While the challenges in Exhibit 11.2 will need several years of basic research before they impact clinical trials or the practice of medicine, several recent innovations from small companies bode well for exciting new developments:

- RNAi—Alynlam & Sirna
- Designer therapeutic enzymes—Direvo, Catalys
- Allosteric modulators—Addex
- Beefed-up antibody killers—Biowa, Glycart (aquired by Roche)

There is much speculation from many quarters as to the probability of clinical success with any of these new therapeutic approaches. Two things, however, are already very obvious in the RNAi field:

1. Big Pharma is not sitting out on this dance; barely into late preclinical development, both Alynlam and Sirna are already thick as thieves with big partners, Novartis and Pfizer.
2. Building patent estates around the technology has been a bedrock preoccupation of both companies.

EXHIBIT 11.6 Future Innovations That Will Drive the Biopharmaceutical Product Pipeline

Chemistry and Drug Substance

- Greater chemical backbone diversity—combinatorial chemistry has added lots of branches and twigs but few new "trunks."
- Better computational and experimental tools to predict toxicity early in drug development.
- Better computational and experimental tools to predict oral bioavailability and to select ideal drug formulation.

Target Discovery and Target Validation

- Completion of the human proteome—the myriad of proteins coded by the genome.
- Full understanding posttranslational modification of proteins—glycobiology.
- Mapping of DNA methylation and correlation of DNA methylation with disease.
- Production of protein array chips analogous to gene chips.
- More extensive in vivo animal data and experimental human data that implicates drug target to disease.

Diagnostic Tools

- Greater academic and industry investment in diagnostics.
- Completion and integration of single-nucleotide polymorphism and haplotype mapping.
- Large-scale acquisition of metabolite data.
- Methodology innovation to make proteomics a reality.
- Large-scale acquisition of proteomic date.
- Improved and uniform assay methods to detect trace levels of DNA, proteins, and small molecules in body tissue and fluids.

Human Biology

- Integration of genomic, proteomic, and genetic data derived from large populations.
- Major advances in neuroscience for greater insight into psychiatric and mood disorders.
- Greater access to human tissue and blood samples—normal and disease.

Preclinical Research

- Derivation of animal models predictive of human disease.
- Preclinical tools that can predict potential human immunogenicity of biologics.
- Preclinical tools to predict mechanism-based toxicity.

Clinical Research

- Greater access to clinical trial data—open access.
- Implementation of biomarker strategies in all trials.

Conclusions

Bumpy Skies before Reaching Clear Air

In the early days of man's attempt to defy the laws of gravity with winged flight, the only way to test early flying machines was literally to jump of a cliff. That hard-won experience, plus advances in every aspect of aeronautical engineering, physics, material sciences, propulsion units, CAD/CAM tools, and so on, made it a fairly safe bet that Airbus's gargantuan new A380 airplane would safely take to the sky the first time out of the box in 2005. It did indeed perform flawlessly, a testament to the benefits of well-controlled innovation, tight design control processes, and thorough planning and execution. By analogy, the pharmaceutical industry is still emerging from the era of the single engine, open-cockpit, string-and-sealing-wax biplane—functional but unpredictable!

Remarkably, even with a century of experience, there is still a very high risk of drug-development projects falling over the proverbial cliff every time an investigational new drug enters clinical development. Biologics have generally fared better than small molecules, in terms of fallout rate due to safety concerns or lack of efficacy, during clinical development. This comfort zone was recently rocked when a Phase-one trial of a new immune modulator antibody went terribly wrong, with almost fatal consequences for six volunteers (Tegenero.com),

Confidence that a new aircraft will fly trouble free the first time lies in the fact that every aspect of design, construction techniques, component materials, airframe performance, and the like, can be simulated and computationally stress tested long before anyone so much as picks up a wrench. Paradoxically, in the drug-development process, we simply have too little high resolution population data to even begin to accurately simulate how a drug substance will perform in a diverse population of sick patients. Although our genomes are more than 99.9% identical, that < 0.1% difference is sufficient to make it currently impossible to simulate or predict safety or efficacy of drugs. Herein lies the greatest opportunity for innovation and improvement for the next era of the biopharmaceutical industry. Lots of room for high fliers!

In summary, the much touted innovation gap in the biopharmaceutical industry is something of a myth, despite clear evidence of a substantial decrease in new medicines reaching the market in the past five years. While there are forces that have created a break in the product pipeline, the patient is stable following drug-eluting stent insertion. There is currently a huge bolus of both biotech and pharmaceutical drugs in clinical development, especially in cancer. Even using traditional clinical trial failure rates of 60% to 80% for small molecules and less for biologics, we can expect a major increase in approvals in the next five to ten years. Pricing pressures may be even greater for existing drugs, but targeted therapeutics with tandem biomarkers should command premium prices on the grounds of greater efficacy. It is hard to predict whether or not industry behemoths will become extinct—despite flaws in integrating innovation and managing discovery research, their skills in development and marketing and sales have not been broadly challenged by biotech. As already evident, most of the big pharmaceutical companies are now fully on board with biologics and many have first products on the market or in late-stage clinical trials. Some are adding product candidates by acquisition (e.g., Pfizer-Rinat). Similarly, large-tier biotech, which has had some false starts in building small-molecule capability via organic growth, now seems be taking a more serious plunge through acquisition (e.g. Amgen-Tularik). Genentech's huge success following a restructuring that decreased therapeutic breadth but increased competitive depth in a few areas may prove to be the winning model that sustains full pipelines.

12

Building Companies on Not-So-Fertile Soil

Teri Willey

Introduction

University and corporate spinouts may be considered microcosms of intellectual property (IP) management, IP creation, innovation, and partnering. Starting and growing them is not about growing just a company but also a community and, like any partnering effort, is dependent on aligning interests of stakeholders.

Boston, Austin, and San Francisco are examples of "fertile soil" for new company creation. The comprehensive environment in these regions is the exception, not the rule. The impacts of new company creation on the economy in these regions are significant, and outside of these regions, in "not-so-fertile" areas, efforts in Boston, Austin, and San Francisco serve as a model for others.

As a result of the strong research funding base in the region, the U.S. Midwest is flush with excellent science and seeds (inventions).[1,2] The seeds in this not-so-fertile Midwest are regularly commercialized in fertile soil regions like San Francisco through new ventures and existing ventures.[3] So, assuming it is desirable to do so, what does it take to grow them closer to where they originate?

There are several notable works on community connectivity and innovation-based prosperity creation that illustrate key elements with charts for

[1]ARCH Development Partners Offering Memorandum, 2003.

[2] Association of University Technology Managers (AUTM) Annual Report, 2004.

[3]www.autm.net.

plotting the next regional economic development campaign.[4,5,6] This is not one of those works, and though my efforts during the past 20-plus years have relied on academia, I'm not technically an academician. So this is not an academic work, either. However, I will provide a practitioner's view: observations and lessons learned, for individuals and institutions who want to know (from my perspective, anyway) what might work (and what doesn't) when considering new venture creation close to home in not-so-fertile soil.

Impediments and Missing Pieces

Money changes everything,[7] but it isn't enough. Venture capital–invested/inspired university science–based ventures or corporate spinouts require more than just money. They require new-venture infrastructure, meaning a critical mass of the following five key elements:

1. *Management:* Experienced management (fund management and emerging company management)
2. *Money:* Smart money (experienced investors at a variety of stages)
3. *Providers:* Experienced service providers (new-venture experienced lawyers, accountants, property managers)
4. *Policies:* Supportive state, institutional/university, and local policies, leverage and incentives
5. *Science:* Intellectual property based on science and technology (local or not)

This list does not address the issue of culture because, regardless of cultural vectors, these five elements are of paramount importance.

Management. Start-up chief executive officers (CEOs), directors (members of the board), scientific advisory board (SAB) members, product development managers, and the like who have relevant experience are key. In not-so-fertile areas we have to grow some of our own, and in doing so, we need to make sure we have at least a few key players with experience bringing the others along. For example, a first-time start-up CEO with relevant product devel-

[4]Fuller, Mark. Presentation at the Village Ventures Fund Managers meeting in Boston, September 20, 2005.

[5]New Economy Strategies various reports, www.neweconomy.com.

[6]Florida, Richard. "The Rise of the Creative Class." www.creativeclass.org.

[7]"Money Changes Everything" (song by Cyndi Lauper).

opment experience might work well with an experienced board and investors. The following are a couple of lessons learned:

1. Set up an initial board of directors right away so the company functions like a company and not a project. This starts to align efforts toward obligations to shareholders that are about maximizing value and return on investment for all shareholders.
2. Unrecruiting management is as important as recruiting management. Be prepared to change management along the way. Set up incentives (equity against milestones, etc.) and socialize the concept that the initial CEO or other members of management may not be the right people for some future phases of the company. Doing this well can be critical to company success, and also support creation of experienced CEO pools in the community.

Another issue under the category of management is fund management. Having experienced venture fund managers in the region is not to be taken for granted, which leads us to the issue of "smart money."

Money. Funds are critical at all stages and take multiple forms. Sometimes called gap funding, dollars that allow a very early-stage idea to be developed through some proof of principle are key. Dollars of this type are usually applied at the university level to determine if an invention works as intended, conduct market research, evaluate the scope of potential IP protection, and so forth. Next, seed dollars are needed to bridge into institutional rounds of financing. Smart, experienced seed investors can be a catalyst to attract additional funding by thoughtful structure of this initial funding. Then, access to investors who invest at the series A, B, and C levels is needed. Access to these investors can come through relationships of syndicate partners (coinvestors) in the earlier rounds, as can relationships with investment bankers. In addition to access to capital at various stages of investment, it is also important to have investors that invest in the industries critical to a specific community or region. That is, many funds, angels, or corporate partners invest in specific industries, and this specificity brings with it a network relevant to the new company. Deal structure and thoughtful syndication are critical. A company can have a lot going for it, but if the deal structure is a barrier to follow-on investment or the syndicate is feuding or each investor has a different idea about the exit, it can all go away.

Providers. Corporate attorneys, IP attorneys and accountants who understand licensing, partnering, and emerging science and technology–based businesses and can assume the risk associated with these types of clients are key. Also, access to investment bankers for various levels of transactions from small mergers and acquisitions (M&A) to initial public offering (IPO) is critical as well.

Developers who understand the places companies live, grow, and thrive can make a significant difference as well. Make sure the early-stage companies have experienced legal representatives who understand this stage of company and investor structure even if you have to leave town to find them. These are not projects for training new attorneys. Cultivate relationships with investment banking firms, and get them involved early. For example, use them to help set a strategy for acquisition. A year or two before an exit, canvass your potential acquirers and ask, "What would it take for our company to be an attractive acquisition candidate or product development partner? Would you like us to keep you up to date on where we are against the milestones you just suggested?"

Policies. In not-so-fertile-soil areas, the leverage of community, university, and state programs can be a catalyst for a culture that embraces this risky business as critical to local economic health. Access to capital can be impacted through programs to encourage venture capitalist participation or angel investment. Examples of these programs include incentives for institutions in the community, university, or state to participate as limited partners in funds, or high-net-worth individuals to participate in angel pools. States can provide gap funding in the form of grants or convertible loans, support entrepreneurs, and start-up CEOs in residence or programs for mentoring and matching scientists with start-up management. Until not-so-fertile soil becomes fertile, this is where the leverage lies until market forces can line up. It's about leadership and innovation, not just in the laboratory but in policy making and understanding where a few public or private dollars can leverage a bigger effort. It's not about parochialism and forcing business inside the state only. Incentivize universities to license to companies inside the state or to invest funds inside the state, as a plan for economic development can be well intended but counterproductive. It is better to provide incentives and resources to make state and local companies attractive investments and licensees based on business principles rather than political pressures.

Science. Science and technology and the corresponding IP are critical elements and are movable. Intellectual property created in Midwest institutions is routinely commercialized by companies on fertile soil.[8] Having one or more major research institutions on your soil is nice, but their presence becomes most helpful when those institutions provide more than just IP by being a player in the leverage of new venture creation through thoughtful policies and practices in technology transfer, investment, and infrastructure. Scientists with innovations having significant commercial potential may have many options, including creation of companies on fertile soil. Accordingly, if it is of interest to grow

---

[8]See note 1.

these in your not-so-fertile-soil area, a case must be made that aligns with the interest of the founding scientist(s) as well as other stakeholders and market forces. This brings us to the issue of stakeholders and aligning interest.

Aligning the Interests of Stakeholders

When managing the expectations of multiple diverse stakeholders in a regional venture economy, one must take into account the following groups:

- Founders/scientists
- Local area participants (community, state, region)
- Universities (in the case of university spinouts)
- Corporations (in the case of corporate spinouts or partners)
- Investors (funds and individuals as well as limited partners/investors in the funds)

Recognizing stakeholders and understanding and aligning their interests are critical, as is managing their expectations. For each of the foregoing, here are a few critical elements and lessons:

Founders. This is where it starts. In not-so-fertile soil, scientific as well as many business founders will be new to starting companies. Matching them up with experienced managers and investors is critical. Helping them understand where their interests are aligned with other stakeholders, and where they are not, can compress the time to success. Taking the time to understand their objectives in starting a company is necessary for achieving this goal. Generally, scientific founders should not be CEOs or directors. Growing a company in infertile soil is hard enough without having trainee management and board members. Nevertheless, growing talent is important, so having founders as board observers and participants as active members of the SAB is key to helping more stakeholders develop skills and capabilities toward the next venture as well as the current one in which they are engaged.

Community. It's about more than jobs, and it's about prosperity. Companies founded on nonfertile soil are at a disadvantage, and smart regional, state, and community programs, including university programs, are what distinguish successful programs in these areas. In fertile-soil areas, the pieces all exist now for creation of new ventures. Where the pieces don't exist, something besides market forces must intervene. Leaders in the community may be able to leverage the arbitrage opportunity to investors—that is, lower valuations for a great company, lower cost of living, local and state grant programs. Nondilutive grant funds, which don't require selling equity for funding, skillfully applied can leverage equity investments. Some interesting experiments are under way in Kalamazoo,[9] Michigan, where the loss of jobs from large corporations over time, and more recently the impact of the consolidation of the pharmaceutical industry, inspired community leaders to support a private sector–backed economic development organization that, in a very short period of time, built incubator facilities, raised venture dollars, attracted fund managers to the community and region, and influenced the creation of state programs to leverage their efforts all to capture the talent being dumped on the market as a result of the pharmaceutical industry consolidation.[10,11] These scientists and managers, with the support of the community, have started several new ventures, and the experiment is impressive and worth watching. A critical success factor in a venture-based economy is exits (returning capital to the investors and other shareholders). One of the challenges in state and local economic development–driven initiatives is that an M&A exit, when the emerging company is acquired by an entity outside of the state, is sometimes mistakenly seen as a failure. In managing expectations, it is critical to understand that a healthy exit is a positive-economic-impact event even when the acquirer is out of state. It sends a message to investors that there are companies worth considering for investment in the state. Acquirers pay dollars back into the state through license fees, royalties, and cash for equity, all of which are distributed broadly; create wealth among investors in the state; and create the very resource that is a critical gating factor for regional new-venture creation: management that have had successful exits and want to do it again in the region, and investors who have had a positive experience and want to invest in risky start-ups again in the region. Healthy acquisitions are positive-economic-impact events.

University. A multifaceted institution. Though universities are considered institutions in the community, they warrant their own discussion, as universities are not homogenous organizations, and within their walls they have multiple stakeholders of their own: faculty, research administration, finance administration, technology transfer, state outreach, and so forth. University missions generally encompass teaching and research to enhance knowledge and outreach to the public (or economic development).[12] In general, the university is involved to see that the ideas generated during the course of teaching and

---

[9]Kalamazoo, Mich Pegs Revitalization on a Tuition Plan" the *Wall Street Journal*, March 10, 2006

[10]Broome, Barry. CEO, Southwest Michigan First (personal communication) (Broome moved to GPEC in Phoenix, AZ in February 2005).

[11]"Wish You Were Here," *The Scientist*, March 7, 2006.

[12]Macilwain, Colin. "More Than the Money—Technology Transfer Offices Learn from Their Mistakes. So Should the Academics They Serve." *Nature*. Vol. 440, April 13, 2006.

research reach the public in a meaningful way. This is primarily carried out through teaching and publishing; however, in some cases, in order for certain ideas to reach the public for benefit to the public, commercial channels need to be harnessed. Sometimes this means creating a company to carry the idea forward. Furthermore, in my view, the objective of the university, where only a very small fraction of the research is state funded and where they have an obligation under federal law, is to find the best entity in the United States (or with U.S. manufacture) to take an invention forward through commercial channels. A small local organization's making this case is optimal, and thoughtful community involvement can help them do so. Furthermore, there are plenty of nonpolitical practical business reasons to work with local entities. Pressure to provide preferred terms to local companies over a better-suited commercialization partner, though well intentioned, can be counterproductive.

Corporate Partners. A different bottom line. As corporations in the United States and around the world shift their attention away from R&D and toward product manufacture and distribution, they seek ideas for their product pipeline from universities and small companies.[13] Corporate partners are critical to emerging companies, as collaborative arrangements leverage resources—dollars, expertise, access to the market. Additionally, many corporations also have venture funds that invest for a variety of reasons but, in general, invest to provide a window on important emerging science and technology not easily observed otherwise and for strategic positioning in M&A. Corporate partnerships can be critical to the success of an emerging company, especially one in not-so-fertile soil, as it provides validation from the market, even before products, such as those involving medical innovations, might reach the market. However, it is paramount to thoughtfully structure a corporate deal that builds value without putting the young company in a position to be solely dependent on one corporate partner (potential acquirer).

Investors. They're not all created equal. For new venture-based economic development to work, investors need to make a return. Individual investors (angels), venture investors, and the investors in venture funds (limited partners) all have a goal of return on investment; however, their definition of success and timing can be very different. It's about exits, and, in general, a successful exit involves agreement on the target result among all the stakeholders and timing and instruments that maximize the enterprise's value. When syndicating an investment (pulling a group of people or institutions to invest initially or over time), understanding their objectives in the investment and aligning these investments is critical.

---

[13]Van Brunt, Jennifer. "Big Biotech Venture Forth," *Signals*, June 9, 2006.

Step by Step, Deal by Deal

Another way to look at this issue is managing for success one deal at a time. In our fund, we manage deals by constantly evaluating and balancing the various risks inherent in early stage investing.[14] These risks are inherent in the key elements above and for start-up companies, regardless of their location, include:

1. *Management risk.* Is there management in place or can you find it? What are the management risks, and how will they be addressed? Furthermore, what is the stage of board development? What are the governance risks, and how will they be addressed?
2. *Market risk.* What's the addressable market, and how do you get to it? What are the risks in getting there, and how will they be addressed?
3. *Financing risk.* How much time and how many dollars will it take to get to each financable milestone? Where will the money come from, and how will risks (not having the dollars to get to the next step up) be managed? More immediately, is there a cap table suffering from infinite weirdness that will deter financing in the first round, and, if so, how does it get fixed?
4. *Technical risk.* How far along is proof of principle? Is it a scientific, technical, or commercial proof of principle? How much time and money will it take to get to each of these? Is there or can we pull together a good SAB to help address this risk?
5. *IP risk.* What's the stage of patent protection compared to what is needed to execute the business plan? Has FTO (freedom to operate) been addressed? Are licenses complete? What's the patent strategy, and how will risks in executing this strategy be managed?
6. *Regulatory (including reimbursement) risk.* What are the regulatory hurdles, and how well do we understand them? In the case of medical opportunities, what are the reimbursement issues?
7. *Exit risk (incorporating all of the above—"the investment case").* How much time, money, and success (hitting milestones) is needed? What exit value is required to make a venture return via an M&A transaction or maybe an IPO?

[14]Willey, Teri F., and Churchwell, Thomas L. "Finding Untapped Potential," in *Life Sciences Venture Capital: Leading Venture Capitalists on How to Find, Manage, and Exit Successful Investments in Life Sciences Companies (Inside the Minds)* (Boston: Aspatore Books, 2005).

Conclusion

The experience in regional venture economics isn't particular to the United States. There are experiments going on all over the world,[15,16] whether you're in Kalamazoo or Cambridge. Whether you evaluate this from a crucial resource, stakeholder, or risk management perspective, the critical issues remain the same and can come together only when someone leads. Individuals make the difference as they step up, step out, and take risks to lead entrepreneurial efforts through example. Innovation doesn't just occur in the laboratory and entrepreneurship in new companies; it occurs in community organizations and public service, too. The takeaways, in my opinion, are what you would expect. The elements, regardless of location, are the same as those discussed herein and are provided on a continuum: good science and a means to protect it (file and manage IP); gap funding; support at the local, regional, and national levels; policies to encourage collaboration and leverage of resources; skilled company management; skilled seed and early-stage investment management; smart capital at a variety of stages; and a means to exit in a way that is interesting to investors (a way to get investments back at some positive multiple).

The important local, regional, national, and global message is this: Don't cause investment in, or cause state universities to license to, state and local companies because they are state and local companies. Invest and license to them because they are the reasonable partner from a business standpoint. Do business for business reasons, not political ones, and the economic impact will be more robust. State and local companies should be preferred investments or preferred partners despite geography. Accordingly, state and local programs should focus on bringing state and local companies up to this standard versus pushing engagement with companies that do not have the means to be successful.

Openness creates competitiveness. Closed "fortress" or "protectionist" economics creates mediocrity.[17]

---

[15]Southwest Michigan First. www.southwestmighicanfirst.com.

[16]Freeman, Roger, Tang, Kenny, and Vohora, Ajay. *Taking Research to the Market: How to Build and Invest in Successful University Spinouts* (London: Euromoney Institutional Investor, 2004).

[17]Thomas, Alan. Director UCTech, University of Chicago (personal communication, June 2, 2006).

INDEX